COMPILED FR
Great L George
National Boundary Line
Carltonville
Drummond's Isl
Middle Strait
Boundary Line
STRAITS OF
MACKINAW
Light House
Spectacle Reef
E b S ½ S. 138 miles to Grt. Manitou Passage
N.W. ¼ W. ½ W. 60 miles
N.W. by W. ¾ W. 50 miles
Hammonds Bay
Adams Pt
CHEBOYGAN
Cheboygan L
Mullet L
Burt L
PRESQUE ISLE
OTSEGO
MONTMORENCY
ALPENA
CRAWFORD
OSCODA
ALCONA

X ISLANDS, NORTH AND SOUTH

sour... th...

e possible ac... sition of North Fox Island.

...d the p...

The Fox Islands
North and South

This printing is made possible, in part,
through the generosity and confidence of

Suttons Bay Bookstore
Suttons Bay, Michigan

and

Victor International, Inc.
Southfield, Michigan

The Fox Islands
North and South

Lake Michigan Islands

Volume II

By Kathleen Craker Firestone

Lake Michigan Islands Series
Volume II

Published by
Michigan Islands Research
Northport, Michigan

Cover by
John Sullivan, Aerial Associates Photography

Endsheets: Portion of 1862 map by
John Farmer

The Fox Islands, North and South
Volume II
ISBN 0-9625631-4-5

Portions of this book were first published in 1983
under the title *They Came To South Fox Island.*

Design and production by
Charles D. Mueller

Color Separations by
Alitho Graphics

Printed in the United States of America
by BookCrafters, Inc.

PHOTO BY K. FIRESTONE
Bright skies over South Fox Island, as seen from Leelanau County shores.

Dedicated in memory of my parents,

Sterling Nickerson II
and
Bernice Weaver Nickerson

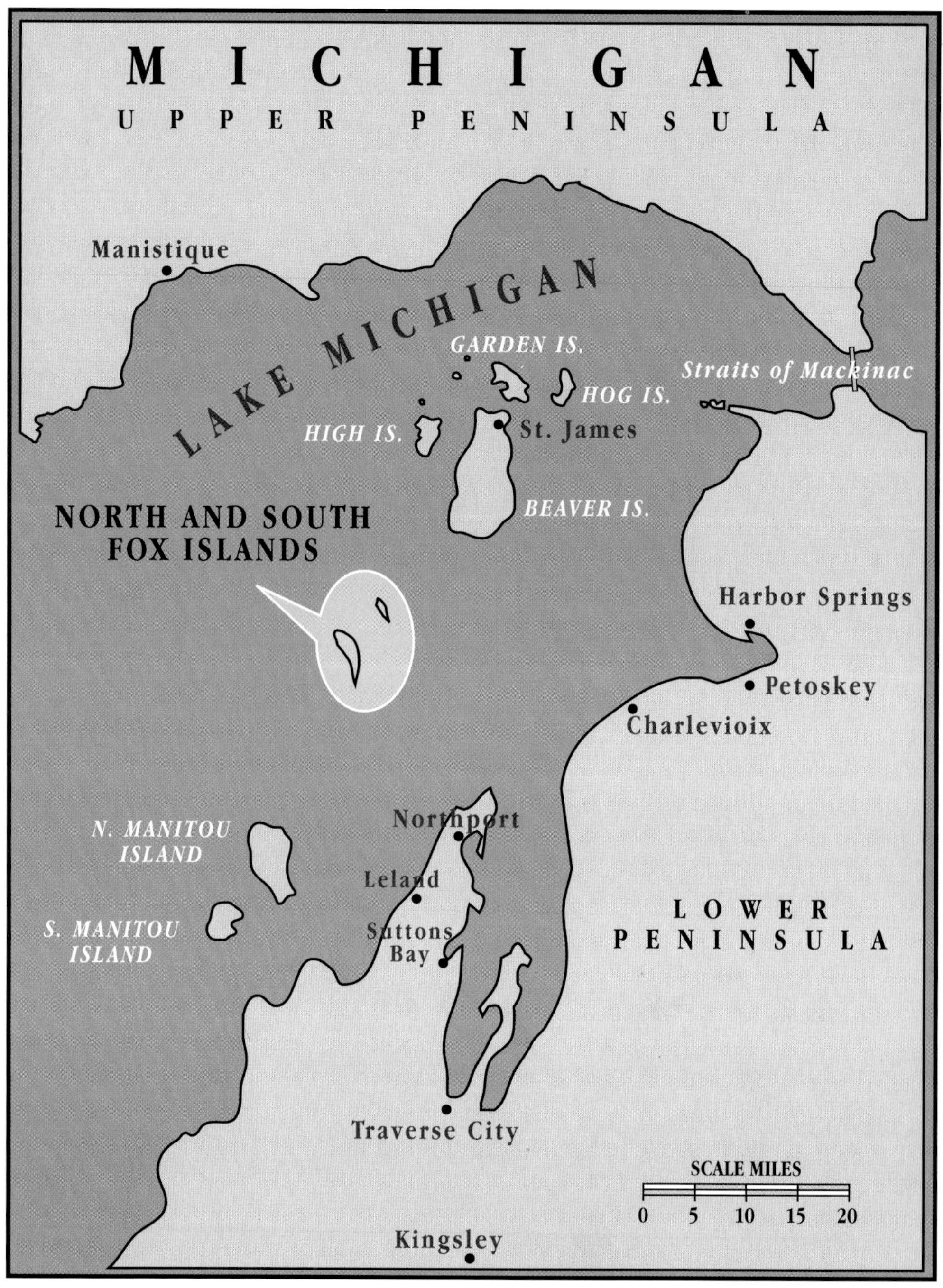

Map created by : Grace Dickinson and Charles Mueller

Table of Contents

Introduction 8

Mirada Ranch. 10

Natural Features. 20

In Search of Fur and Fish. 34

King James Jesse Strang. 48

Island Farming. 58

Native Americans. 66

Maritime Memories 76

With Ax and Saw 100

Deer Herds and Hunters 126

Crime and Punishment 144

Emergency! Fox Island Calling! 146

Children of The Fox Islands 152

Development Dreams and Dilemmas 172

Mystery, Fantasy, Poetry 188

Epilogue: Traveling Back in Time and Place 196

Appendix

- Vascular Plants of the Fox Islands 202
- Bird Sightings on the Fox Islands 210
- Employee List 212

Information Sources 214

Index 219

INTRODUCTION

North and South Fox Islands lie northwest of Michigan's Leelanau Peninsula. They are the most isolated of all Lake Michigan islands, with South Fox's closest point on the mainland being Cat Head Point at 16 1/2 miles. North Fox lies between South Fox and the Beaver Islands, separated by four miles of water to South Fox and eight miles to Beaver.

North Fox Island is about two miles long and one mile across and is surrounded by 5.5 miles of shoreline, holding 832 acres. In the 1847 survey, Orange Risdon called it "a miniature island in the size and height of its hills and ridges."[1]

GALE FAMILY PHOTO South Fox Island

South Fox Island is about four times the size of North Fox, at about 5 1/2 miles long and nearly two miles across the widest part. Its crescent shape is outlined by 11.8 miles of shoreline which enclose about 3,300 acres. On the southern tip stands the 1867 lighthouse.

Both islands are known for their beauty; with majestic dunes, broad beaches, lush forests and profuse displays of wildflowers. Migrating birds and butterflies use the islands as resting points.

On an 1839 map David H. Burr, geographer for the U. S. House of Representatives, named the bigger island *Thomas Island* and the smaller one *Pierces Island*. In the Ottawa and Chippewa language the islands were called *Wau-goosh-e-min-iss*, translated roughly as *Foxes, their island(s)*. James J. Strang, with his attempt to colonize several islands with his break-away Mormon followers, called these islands *Patmos* and *Paros*. But their official names were already *North* and *South Fox Islands*. To some, they were simply known as *Big Fox* and *Little Fox*.

The Fox Islands, like many other islands, were inhabited before much of the nearby mainland. Fur traders, fishermen, farmers, wood dealers and lighthouse keepers occupied the many islands of Lake Michigan. Those with development dreams have been on the scene since before 1900.

The written history of the Fox Islands has been limited to a sentence here and there in other historical or natural history books, and to an occasional newspaper or magazine article. *They Came To South Fox Island*, published in 1983, was the first compiled history regarding the Fox Islands. *The Fox Islands: North and South* is an updated version of that first publication and now includes both North and South Fox Islands between its covers.

In the writing of history, it is always easier to end the compilation of events before the writer gets to present tense. That is because, when writing of the status of people and place, the present soon fades into the past, and what was an up-to-date account becomes out of date. "He says..." on a printed page can no longer be true after the interviewed has departed this earth. "So-and-so is now the owner," can be past history by the time a book reaches the library shelves. The easiest way to avoid this is to end the account — say 25 or 50 or more years — before the present date.

Because I wish to bring the reader as far back in time as research will allow and as close to the present as today's newspaper, I am left with this problem of keeping the historical events current and in the correct language tense.

In writing of North and South Fox Islands, I have chosen to begin with the present, as it is in 1996, and then take the reader back in time. There are scattered pages throughout the book for the reader to add tomorrow's information, if so desired. I am always happy to hear from readers about their historical connections to and interest in Great Lakes islands. But, there you see it — when I say "I am happy," someone can say of me when I have also departed, "She was happy."

One cause of happiness for me is in knowing that the histories of North and South Fox Islands will not be lost and forgotten.

PHOTO BY K. FIRESTONE North Fox Island

Kathleen Firestone

[1] Orange Risdon in 1847 U. S. Government Survey.

PHOTO BY GORDON CHARLES
PHOTO BY CHARLES MUELLER
MIRADA RANCH PHOTO

With this printing, in 1996 the owner of both North Fox Island and all of the private lands on South Fox Island is David Victor Johnson. Although changes may be in store for North Fox, South Fox Island is expected to remain nearly in its present state for some time to come. About two-thirds of the way down South Fox's eastern shore lies Johnson's hide-away.

MIRADA RANCH

From the stables of green-grassed Kentucky to the corrals of parched-prairied Texas, one could not find a more beautiful setting for an equine ranch than on Lake Michigan's South Fox Island. A rider exercising his horse around the stable yard can enjoy the fresh air of the Big Lake, the sounds of lapping waves breaking the island's solitude and a view of the sister island, North Fox, four miles across the blue water. The sandy shore, just down the gentle bank from the stable, provides miles for rhythmic gallops, and several flower-strewn trails about the island lead the rider through the sweet smells of forests and to the shoreside bluffs. It's no wonder South Fox Island has been chosen as the perfect place for a get-away from fast-paced corporate business.

South Fox was purchased in May, 1989, by David V. Johnson, a developer based in Southfield, Michigan. Johnson had been considering looking for an island in the Caribbean but decided against it because he "didn't like salt water or bugs." When availability of the private lands on South Fox, two-thirds of the entire island, came to his attention, David Johnson and his wife Lesli inspected the island and were delighted with what they found.

Johnson's Victor International, incorporated in 1984, is the outgrowth of Maple Associates and Abbey Development Company, which had interests in acquisition, marketing and management of real estate development and income properties. Maple Associates grew and expanded for several years, after Johnson established it in 1974. In 1978 David Johnson was injured in a diving accident and was told he would probably not walk again. But he did, slowly, favoring his right side; and during that long recovery, he did a lot of thinking. Deciding that in development, "more is not better," he determined to limit his development projects, but that all developments would continue his lifelong dedication to quality. He founded Abbey Development Company in 1979, aimed at creation of luxury residential communities and unique commercial developments. One example has become "Bay Harbor" near mainland Petoskey, 46 miles due east of South Fox Island. The development, with its man-made Bay Harbor Lake, 750 building sites, and 500 planned boat slips, all set on the site of an old cement factory, has gained recognition as the largest land reclamation in the United States. In 1995 the State of Michigan awarded the Bay Harbor project the Environmental Excellence Award.

With the purchase of South Fox, at age 40, Johnson wanted a quiet place to bring his wife and small daughter, a place away from corporate life and its demands. As he investigated further, he became aware of the importance of the island's famous deer herd and management of the deer population. Although not a hunter himself, he accepted the responsibility and determined to do the best that he could for the deer herd and for South Fox Island.

Also on South Fox was a pair of horses which had roamed freely for several years. The horses occasionally came close enough for handouts or to munch on bales of hay. When one of the pair was found dead and the remaining one seemed distressed, Johnson and island manager Rod Hayward had the idea of bringing more horses to South Fox. Although Johnson had no previous experience with horses, this was the beginning of what came to be Mirada Ranch. The word *Mirada* has at least three meanings — in Spanish it's "to view;" in French it's "to reflect on," or "view from the heights," and in Latin it means "miracle." Indeed, when one *views* the beauty of South Fox Island, *thoughtful reflections* must bring the conclusion that such magnificence is truly a *miracle*.

PHOTO BY CHARLES MUELLER
In 1993 Second Pilot, Glen Worrell, (L) joined Chief Pilot, Kenneth Chio, (R) in flying Victor International's private King Air. Chio had completed 30 years of flying world wide for General Motors and began service to David Johnson in 1992, flying to South Fox and elsewhere.

By spring, 1991, Johnson saw the need for year-round residents on the island. Rod Hayward became Ranch Manager of Mirada, and Rod's wife, Ruby, added a "woman's touch" to the South Fox ranch. Hayward and Randy (Bean) Parr cleared the old island trails and forged some new ones. A clean-up of old machinery and debris was launched, and in keeping with a "safety first" effort and a goal of increased accessability, a longer, wider, 20-acre airstrip was constructed. The new airstrip formed a "V" with the older strip and sat on higher ground, out of the area of down drafts. Soon Johnson's private aircraft — a Chieftain twin engine, a Beechcraft King Air E90, and a Beechcraft King Air B200 turbo prop — were landing on the 4,200-foot, FAA-approved runway. In 1995 work was begun to expand the runway to 5,000 feet. Other improvements were made, including an underground sprinkler system installed in the airstrip and in-ground lighting designed to be activated from aircraft. A visual landing system, a 62-foot mono-pole beacon, was erected for nighttime approach.

Sometimes there is a need for transportation other than aircraft. The cigarette boat *Island Fox* waits at Bay Harbor to take the Johnson family and others to the island oasis. Although there are no docking facilities on South Fox Island, boat moorings are placed offshore of the Mirada Ranch location. Three two-ton anchors and one four-ton anchor were placed in 1990 and were professionally engineered to hold a fifty-foot boat in ten-foot waves. The Lake Michigan ice took these away, however, just as it had previously destroyed many island docks through 150 years of recent history. In 1993 another two-ton anchor was put in place to hold summer boats and challenge winter ice.

Transportation of construction materials and other supplies to South Fox has been a major undertaking, under direction of Charlie Blacker. The first barge trips embarked from Ironton, near Charlevoix, and required that supplies from various sources arrive in Ironton at about the same time. Barge transports took approximately four days to load, travel to the island, and unload. They carried a year's supply of construction materials, operating supplies and equipment. Horses and horse trailers, along with 1,000 bales of hay, were loaded and unloaded by using a crane. A Barge trip often included 17 semi-truckloads, reaching two stories high, about 40 feet wide and 110 feet long. Onlookers watched with interest in 1993 and 1994 when the cargo being loaded aboard the barge stretched 40 feet wide and 200 feet long. As the Mirada Ranch needs have become more predictable, barge trips have been established at about four per year. After Johnson's purchase of South Fox,

MIRADA RANCH PHOTO
A barge laden with supplies for Mirada Ranch arrives at South Fox about four times yearly.

Ranch Manager Rod Hayward was put in charge of the island machinery, including keeping the electrical, water and other mechanical systems operating. Along with these duties, Hayward took on management of the growing herd of horses. Property management, special building projects and accompanying work crews and supplies became the responsibility of Charles Blacker. Ten or more people worked on summer projects, as a new home, a manager's house, a bath house, generator house and corrals were built, as well as a 10,000-square-foot, 124 by 42 foot, two-story stable for the horses. A Fourth of July tradition is the building of a new cottage each year. Cottages for guests have been constructed and given the names Whitetail, Beach House, Guest House, and Lair. Even Jacuzzi whirlpool tubs have brought evidence that a distant island needn't be without comforts. Cellular and mobile telephones, a fax machine, citizens band and ship-to-shore radios have made needed communication with the outside world a near guarantee. In contrast to all the work being done at Mirada Ranch, an annual event is held, orchestrated by Jamie Gibbs, a close friend of Johnson. Sometimes a party is thrown, sometimes a search is made for a new island trail.

PHOTO BY CHARLES MUELLER
Charlie Blacker in the generator house.

MIRADA RANCH PHOTO Rod Hayward oversees arrival of horses to South Fox Island.

In 1991 the first of several Tennessee Walkers, Ebony Ann, was transported to South Fox Island. As the ranch has grown, so has the work, and in 1992 Leon Ratza was hired as an additional ranch hand, working with the horses and various maintenance projects. By the summer of 1994 there were 16 horses at Mirada Ranch, predominantly Tennessee Walkers, and including two spring foals. At times, some of the horses are removed temporarily to Mirada Ranch/Stonewood Farms in Clarkston, Michigan, for show training. In June, 1994, David Johnson rode in his first show horse competition and took a blue ribbon in Western Pleasure while riding Ebony Ann. His Tennessee Walker, President's Jackie O, won the World Champion Weaning Filly Award at the Tennessee Celebration and the Horse of the Year award in the Tennessee Walkers Owners' Association Show. Three more foals were born at the South Fox ranch the spring of 1995, perhaps three more champions. Also added to Mirada Ranch in 1995 were eight Tennessee Walkers transported to South Fox Island on the *Embarcadero*, a 56-foot military landing craft, newly purchased by Johnson. The total number of horses by summer 1995 was 24. The main stallion of Mirada Ranch, Final's Nightline, was sired by Pride's Final Edition, a nine-time world champion.

Proper care of the Mirada Ranch horses is aided by Johnson's close friend and veterinarian, Dr. Jeffrey Powers. Dr. Powers is heavily involved in the horse-breeding program and advises on medications and nutrition.

A saddled horse on South Fox Island has proven to be an advantage to David Johnson, since his earlier injury will not allow intense walking. Getting away from the motorized pick-up trucks and small four-wheelers, horseback riding makes quiet

PHOTO BY CHARLES MUELLER
Denise Vidosh riding Final's Nightline as David Johnson looks on, 1995.

explorations possible. Donald Brown had been deer hunting for twenty seasons on South Fox when Johnson bought the island, and Brown offered his knowledge in exploring and mapping horse trails. Some of the names of old logging and hunting trails have been replaced with titles given by Johnson and his ranch hands, in addition to new trails being blazed and named. Other locations on the island have also been labeled. The main road extending to the North and South of the island has become Mirada Drive. Noble Road goes from the ranch, down the eastern side of the island, to the old lighthouse. Another route to the lighthouse is called Whitetail Trail. A horseback rider taking the Trillium Trail during the month of May will see the woodland floor covered with the large, white blooms of thousands of trillium. David Johnson took his first ride on a new trail blazed to the northwest side on his 41st birthday, and the route was aptly named Birthday Trail. The northwestern dune holds

MIRADA RANCH PHOTO
In 1994 the first foals were born at Mirada Ranch.

PHOTO BY CHARLES MUELLER
David and Lesli Johnson with their daughter Samara, 1995.

Surprise Blow Hole, which Johnson first explored during a ride with his young daughter Samara Danielle and her godmother, Linda Munson. Vietnam Valley blowhole is sculpted out of the southern part of the dune. Cape Cod Cut is the wide and low dune beach area along the northeastern shore. And in the northwest part of South Fox Island stands the Valley of the Giants, a collection of old cedar trees with twenty-foot girths. Johnson's wife, Lesli, and their daughter, Samara, also have their days of enjoyment of the horses of Mirada Ranch. Samara began riding at age four, with her favorite riding horse being Shaker's Bold Bandit.

PHOTO BY K. FIRESTONE
The large stable overlooks Lake Michigan

Although the horses bring many hours of enjoyment for the Johnson family, they are not the only source of delight. Lesli Johnson is an avid hiker and enjoys the miles of beaches and woodland trails. She says the island gives her a "sense of peace and freedom," and she especially likes hiking to the northern point of South Fox, and Big John's Lookout is a favorite spot for watching sunsets, before heading back to Mirada Ranch.

Dreamers of the past have thought about creating dude ranches on South Fox Island, but Mirada has become the only fruition of such a dream. The South Fox deer herd has been the island's focal point of fame for decades, but since the Johnson ownership, the ranch has become the center of activity. The deer hunting season, although still bringing excitement to the hunters, is secondary.

MIRADA RANCH PHOTO
Jamie Gibbs and his trophy buck.

The island's small farm acreages of the past now provide space for the summer hayfields of Mirada Ranch. The sounds of wild birds have been joined by the clucking of farm chickens, and daily eggs are collected for the ranch house kitchen. The mainstay that sustained the early pioneers and Native Americans is also sometimes found on the ranch house dinner platters—small-mouth bass caught offshore of South Fox Island.

There are no free-ways, no crowds—only an occasional, deserted log cabin at the edge of the woods, the sounds of birds and chipmunks, the smell of fresh air coming across Lake Michigan and the sighting of a deer at the far side of a clearing. The modernization of the facilities has not changed the character of solitude that is often connected with islands.

PHOTO BY K. FIRESTONE
Modern homes have replaced rustic cabins of the past.

Forest management plans for South Fox Island and reforestation planting for the ranch have been initiated with the assistance of Donn Vidosh of Vidosh Landscape Centers. And the expertise and guidance of Dr. Gordon Guyer, Director of the Michigan Department of Agriculture, have aided the island management planning from the time of the island purchase. Proper planning should assist the deer and aid in reforestation. According to Vidosh, South Fox has maple trees which are "perfect in shape." Two hundred maple trees had been relocated as of 1995, as well as the introduction of 200 sycamores to South Fox. Young maples placed along the roadway behind the large stable have brought the name of Maple Lane. Donn Vidosh gives his assistance both at Mirada Ranch and at the Bay Harbor project, as does Bernie Fekete, one of the chief designers of Bay Harbor and a principal at Johnson, Johnson and Roy engineers.

Along with the many names and faces which are familiar to Mirada Ranch, Mark Hubbard often travels to and from South Fox Island with David Johnson. Hubbard, Chief Operating Officer of Victor International, contributes his knowledge and support to Johnson's business dealings, from Victor International, to Bay Harbor, to North and South Fox Islands. Cameron Piggott, Johnson's long-time friend and attorney, also visits the island holdings and provides his expertise.

In 1989, when newspapers reported that South Fox Island had been purchased by developer David Johnson, rumors began to fly that the island wilderness would soon be speckled with condominiums, golf courses and all the luxuries that accompany such development. Johnson's private and peaceful island ranch does not appear to be headed in that direction. And his 1994 purchase of all of North Fox Island is, according to him, an insurance against large-scale development of the smaller island.

Posing in front of transportation, old and new, are L-R; David Johnson, Charlie Blacker, Denise Vidosh, Mark Moore, Leon Ratza, Bill Hedges, and Samara Johnson in front.
PHOTO BY CHARLES MUELLER

It is David Johnson's intention to keep South Fox Island private. It is his "secret spot," his get-away from end-to-end meetings and obligations on a busy calendar. Although the island sometimes serves as a "brainstorming base" for projects such as Bay Harbor, it is, most of all, a place of peace and solitude. A place where Johnson can wear blue jeans and saddle a horse for a mid-day ride along one of the ranch trails. Haney's Blowhole, a rugged and beautiful northwestern site, is the destination of Johnson's favorite riding trail, and a place for personal thoughts. Reflecting on life before his diving accident and the months that followed of being strapped into a rotating bed and hung upside down to stare at the floor, Johnson is reminded of what he learned about the important things in life—the love for life itself, for God, family and friends.

Johnson believes that large developments are better situated on mainland areas than on these special islands. His world-class development of Bay Harbor is destined to become an important focal point for mariners of the Great Lakes. A yacht club of equal class and an associated world-class golf course will provide top-quality vacation and retirement opportunities on the shores of Lake Michigan. Boaters from Bay Harbor and other resort areas will be able to view the pristine beauty of South Fox as they pass by on their "island hopping" from the Beaver Islands to the Manitous. A public effort could secure public ownership and preservation of Johnson's North Fox Island, which would allow boaters to visit its shores.

Although his ownership of North Fox could be turned into financial profit, that is not David Johnson's aim, if a property trade can be made with the State of Michigan. Johnson, as well as many others, believes that a trade — transferring all of Johnson's North Fox Island to the state, and the state's one-third of South Fox going to Johnson— could benefit all. Without such a transfer, North Fox remains vulnerable to, at least, some development or change. If some people fear that South Fox will then be developed, Johnson seeks to dispel that fear. For the present, Johnson just wants South Fox Island to remain the unique island gem that it is. North Fox Island has that same potential for preservation, if private or government entities wish to make it happen.

With this glimpse of North and South Fox Islands' present, the wonders of the natural features of both islands and their separate, yet related, histories can be told.

Top, MIRADA RANCH PHOTOS: Snowy Owl; Charlie Blacker on the South Fox dune.
Bottom, PHOTO BY K. FIRESTONE: North Fox Island, east side.

NATURAL FEATURES

Let them give glory unto the Lord,
and declare his praise in the islands.
Isaiah 42:12 KJV

Islands! The word alone stirs our souls. They are special places on the Earth, whether in the South Pacific or the Great Lakes. Each island has its own character and is a world unto itself, connected by oceans and seas, rivers and lakes. Lake Michigan's Fox Islands are no exception.

Of the two islands, South Fox is the biggest at about 3,300 acres, compared to North Fox Island's 832 acres. They are separated by about four miles and are oriented with their longest dimensions in a northwest to southeast direction. North Fox is a little over two miles long and about one mile across its widest dimension. South Fox is slightly more than five miles long and about one-and-a-half miles wide.

Because of their average of 20 miles from the mainland, the climate of the Fox Islands is affected by the thermal mass of Lake Michigan. Summers are cooler and winters have less snow than on the mainland. Weather can change rapidly, as winds sweep across the lake, bringing fierce gales and torrents of rain.

In his book *Island Life in Lake Michigan,* Dr. Robert Hatt, former Director of Cranbrook Institute of Science, says the Fox Islands may have been connected by a land bridge in the distant past.[1] Other scientists concur, believing that the Beaver Islands were joined to the mainland by way of the Waugoshance Peninsula and that North Fox Island was probably connected to the Beavers. The Manitou Islands were attached to each other and to mainland Leelanau County. But, they agree it's possible that South Fox, from the time of the glacial melt, was never connected to any other island. However, it was much bigger, extending north and south to three times its present length, which would have brought it closer to the shores of North Fox, which was also bigger. Hatt says, "The water fringing the Fox Islands was then probably 200 feet lower than at present."[2] Dr. Brian T. Hazlett states in his dissertation that the Fox Islands "were always surrounded by water since their emergence from the ice sheet."[3] In any case, with the rising and receding of the waters of Lake Nippising, the islands took their approximate present form.

James Strang, in his description of South Fox, called it "exquisitely beautiful," and he described North Fox as a miniature of the bigger island.[4] With dunes and bluffs, woodlands and fields, beaches and wildlife, and glorious sunrises and sunsets, the islands offer both exhilaration brought by nature's wonders, and blessed solitude, so rare in today's world.

PHOTO BY JOHN SULLIVAN

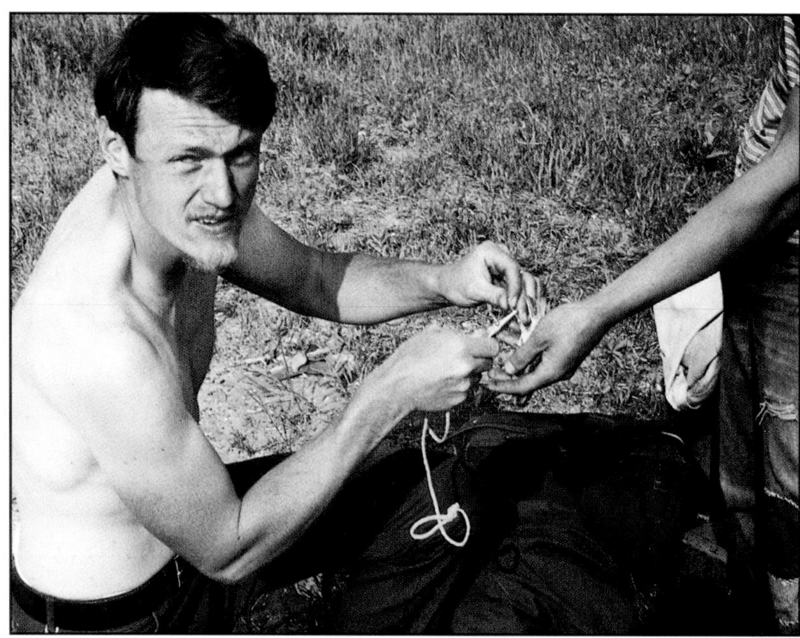

PHOTO BY KATHY HALL Dr. William Scharf banding birds on South Fox Island, 1972.

GALE FAMILY PHOTO Jason Fatseas feeding Canada geese on South Fox.

Scientists and lovers of nature are drawn to these and other islands nearby. In 1937 Dr. Hatt and a party of others visited several Lake Michigan islands and recorded their findings. Hatt studied the vegetation, wildlife, geology and glacial topography. Studies by Arthur Staebler, Josselyn Van Tyne and Leslie Case of the University of Michigan and George N. Fuller of the University of Chicago were also incorporated in Hatt's *Island Life*. In 1961 F. H. Test and E. U. Clover collected plant specimens on South Fox, as did Larry

Wolf. Test also made botanical collections on South Fox in 1962 and North Fox in 1963. Further studies were made by James R. Wells and Paul W. Thompson of the Cranbrook Institute of Science in 1973-74. Between 1971 and 1974 Dr. William Scharf of Northwestern Michigan College in Traverse City accompanied students to South Fox Island to study bird populations and published his findings in several booklets and periodicals. James R. Wells and Paul W. Thompson made further studies on North Fox in 1975, assisted by the island owner and geologist, Francis D. Shelden. Thompson and Wells returned to North Fox and also to South Fox, in 1994, along with Brian T. Hazlett and Susan P. Hendricks of the University of Michigan. Studies were also undertaken on North Fox in 1986 by ecologists Dennis A. Albert and Gary A. Reese. G. Dulin and Phyllis Higman conducted brief studies on North Fox in 1990. This is, by no means, a complete listing of scientists who have surveyed the Fox Islands.

The islands have been home to many kinds of birds, as well as stopping places for various migratory species. As they fly from the south in spring, migratory birds go "island hopping" once they reach the Sleeping Bear Dunes area of Michigan's Leelanau County. With the first island stop at South Manitou, the birds rest, feed and then continue their flight, with stops at South Fox, North Fox and on to the Beaver Islands and lands to the north. The north-south pattern of these islands and the distance between them provide a good flight-and-rest sequence for the migrating birds. In the fall the order is reversed, as the birds head for warmer territory.

The resident and migratory birds have been a source of enjoyment to human settlers and visitors on both islands. There have been several sightings of eagles, with nests being spotted on both North and South Fox Islands. A compilation of birds seen by various parties on the Fox Islands is shown in the Appendix of this book.

In the late 1930's, the men at the South Fox lighthouse built two houses for purple martins, and a large colony of the birds took up residence there. A Canada goose, decided he liked South Fox and stayed behind at the Nickerson logging camp when the rest of the flock made its fall migration to southern states. Keeping watch for the crumbs that were thrown to it, the goose became quite comfortable with humans. The Chappels, later caretakers of the logging camp, were also entertained by friendly Canada geese, just as more recent Island owners have been entertained.

Hatt and Scharf agree in their conclusions that humans have helped some types of animals to survive on the islands, especially on South Fox. During his 1937 visits, Hatt observed that the presence of man had aided in the survival of some animals by providing them shelter in buildings, sawdust piles, cleared fields and driftwood.[5] According to Scharf, the open fields on South Fox are essential to birds which nest there, such as bobolinks, field sparrows and the Savannah sparrow.

Several kinds of butterflies exist on the islands. During the 1937 modernization of the South Fox Light, George Clark Craker saw a sizable colony of migrating monarchs settle in one tree, making the tree look as though it were in bloom with a blaze of orange. Stopping for only one day, the monarchs were gone the following morning.

Foxes are not abundant on these islands, in spite of the island names, but red foxes are occasionally seen on both islands. The foxes feed on rabbits, chipmunks, mice, wild berries, and–on South Fox–dead deer. Except for humans, the foxes have no predators on these two islands. Coyotes have recently appeared on South Fox and use the same food supply as the island foxes. Coyote howls ride on the westerly breezes, coming across from the dune area in the evening.

Chipmunks are usually plentiful. Hatt and Scharf observed that the South Fox Island chipmunks are more closely related to the Wisconsin chipmunks than to those found in most of Michigan's lower peninsula. Speculation is that they reached the island either by crossing the ice or by hitchhiking on driftwood or boats.

Snowshoe hare populations fluctuate markedly. In some years, South Fox farmers chased and herded them together where the hares were clubbed to death. The farmers felt it was the only way to save their crops. In other years, scarcely a track can be found. During a plentiful year, the observer can spot the rabbits, even though their coats change from brown to white with the coming of winter. The Snowshoe hare on North Fox Island has also risen and fallen in a cyclic manner, just as on South Fox.

Aerial view of North Fox Island by PHOTAIR.

In the 1920's the establishment of a skunk ranch was attempted on North Fox, but the visitor need not worry about encountering skunks now, on either island.

Other small fauna are frogs, toads, snakes, mice, and a wide assortment of insects. The lower beaches of the northern end of North Fox, in the pools between the rushes and boulders, are good breeding grounds for frogs and toads; and driftwood along the shores of both islands supplies shelter for deermice, snakes and toads.

Because South Fox Island is known for its large deer herd, a visitor to that island might expect to see deer crossing in front of him at every path. Though the deer are abundant, they are not so easy to see, since the heavy tangles of ground cover and fallen cedars make excellent hiding places. An observer would be more likely to spot a deer by waiting patiently on an elevated mound or a comfortable stump until the animal happened by. Whitetails usually move very quietly and are alert to sounds of movement around them. A former deer herd on North Fox Island has been totally eliminated. The deer of both islands are discussed in a following chapter.

The forests of North Fox consist mainly of sugar maple, beech, birch, basswood and ash on the island plateau and, in lower areas, by fir, cedar, birch, poplar, mountain-ash and dogwood. Ecologists Dennis Albert, Gary Reese and others have observed that North Fox has three natural "habitat types;" namely, Northern Swamp, Mesic Northern Forest and Boreal Forest.[6] According to Reese, "They represent very high natural quality — the best in the state or tied for the best in the state."[7] Reese said the Boreal Forests of North Fox Island are like those in Canada, where the fog keeps the forests cool and moist.

PHOTO BY NANCY NICKERSON
Steve Craker holds a South Fox milk snake, 1983.

PHOTO BY GORDON CHARLES
Whitetail deer on South Fox Island.

The interior of South Fox is mostly covered with hard maple, beech and birch. There are a few clearings where farms were once laid out. The dunes area and shoreland add aspen, cedar, fir, ash, balsam, willow, basswood, ground hemlock, juniper and spruce. Pines, which are conspicuous on other large islands, are almost non-existent on both North and South Fox Islands. Dr. Brian Hazlett, states that (including smaller plant life), "Surprisingly, North Fox, the smallest island, has a slightly higher number of native species than South Fox."[8] The Fox Islands, being farthest from the mainland of all the Lake Michigan islands, are less likely to contain alien plants, imported from the mainland. However, South Fox has had more human intrusion than North Fox, by way of logging, farming, hunting and other activity; and, consequently, has had more alien plant introductions. North Fox has maintained its more natural vegetation.

During the Nickerson lumbering operation on South Fox in the 1950's-60's, a white cedar was cut which measured 15 feet in circumference. With 14 rings per inch, the tree was believed to be more than 400 years old. A comparison with records kept by Pearce (Pat) Stocking of Empire, Michigan, showed the South Fox Island cedar to probably be the world's largest white cedar log recorded in the world up to that date, though larger living cedars were still growing on South Manitou Island. Ted Malpass towed the South Fox log to East Jordon, Michigan, where it was put on display. It was later believed that such a legendary tree would have made a better living monument. Other large white cedar trees still grow in the South Fox western dunes area. Outdoor writer Gordon Charles writes in the *Traverse City Record-Eagle* in 1992 that these cedar trees "easily equal their more-famous rivals on South Manitou."[9]

In 1972, while surveying for boundaries for the division of hunting lands on South Fox Island, Carl Roser, John Swanson and Fred Wagenschutz, of the Department of Natural Resources Traverse City Field Office, discovered a "rare quirk of nature."[10] Two "witness trees," or bearing trees, which had been used by the 1847 surveyors, were found. Though one was only a stump, they were recognized by slashes in the trunks where the section corner numbers had been carved.

Although the numbers were no longer visible, the surveyors' distinctive notches were. What was so unusual about the discovery of these trees was their age. Birch trees in Michigan normally survive from 60 to 80 years, but these witness trees were determined to be about 200 years old. The one living tree was only 28 inches thick, small for its age. The men also found balsam trees which were retarded in growth. One was well over 100 years old but was only about four inches thick, "indicating that it was receiving just enough nourishment to survive, but was getting an insufficient amount to reach normal growth."[11] Speculation was that the low nourishment was why the witness trees were also smaller than their old age would indicate. Roser compared the island's sterile soils on the northwest slope to the rugged climate in European alpine areas, where trees sometimes grow only a few inches high in hundreds of years. The northwest corner of South Fox was "as hostile a hunk of forest" Roser had ever surveyed.

MIRADA RANCH PHOTO South Fox Island forest.

North and South Fox Islands have been used in the business interests of many woodsmen. Though John Ingwersen had been a logger both on the Manitou Islands and on South Fox, he felt some remorse for cutting down these sentinels of the past. Some of his sentiments are recorded in his poem about South Fox Island and is printed in a later chapter.

There are seasonal ponds and marshy areas on North Fox Island, most notably a fern pond where the southern dune blocks drainage. Except for a few shoreline cold springs, South Fox is a well-drained dune rising out of Lake Michigan.

GALE FAMILY PHOTO
Katie Mull, in 1986, on a boulder on the west side of South Fox Island.

GALE FAMILY PHOTO
Erwin Gale in a cave on South Fox's western side, 1988.

PHOTO BY K. FIRESTONE
Northeastern beach of South Fox Island.

One of the most unique qualities of islands are the beaches. Where else can a hiker begin walking one direction and, without turning around, eventually catch up with his or her own footprints?

Perhaps the biggest attraction of South Fox Island is the varying shoreline. Broad beaches of quartz sand on much of the eastern shore provide good barefoot walking and sitting. The beach narrows at the northeast end of the island, and in years when the water is high, the cliffs in that area seem to rise out of the water. The northern tip is blunter than the southern, but has a broad, gravely beach where Hatt says gulls were nesting during his explorations. Scharf found no evidence of nesting areas during his more recent visits to the island.

PHOTO BY NANCY NICKERSON
"Blowout" in the South Fox dune, 1983.

PHOTO BY K. FIRESTONE
The North Fox dune, looking to South Fox, 1993.

The gravel continues for a distance down the northwest side and then changes to fine sand again. Perched dunes are scattered along South Fox's western shoreline, the biggest being about two miles north of the southern tip of the island. The dunes in this area rise to about 334 feet and are probably the highest point on the island. Since the prevailing winds are from the west, the dunes are areas of erosion which are moving slowly across the island. Some of them have reached about a mile inland. An explorer on the dunes will notice skeletons of trees protruding from the sand. These were covered as the sand shifted and then exposed again as the winds blew the sand farther toward the middle of the island. At the southern tip of the island, near the lighthouse, the sand has moved completely across the island, and it is lacking in much vegetation. From the mainland, South Fox Island seems to be split where this small dune area is.

The 11.8 miles of South Fox Island shoreline is approximately double the 5.5 miles of shoreline on North Fox. On the western shore, facing its sister island, the northern beach of North Fox is a pebbly, marshy area. Broad, sandy beach appears about half way down the western side, and continues south to meet the 178-foot dune area near the southern tip of North Fox. The dune is much smaller than that of South Fox Island, but is also beautiful, with its fine, white grains swirling in the breeze. The western shore of North Fox has many boulders, but the eastern side is deep very near shore. Much of the eastern shore of North Fox Island is a wide, deep bank of heavy gravel. From this area it's easy to understand why a gravel contractor bought these western lots in 1890. Toward the northeast portion, the beach becomes a sandy, rocky combination, until it reaches the marshy areas of the northern end.

Away from the city lights, the stars above North and South Fox appear brighter. Northern lights perform their color dance.

Wildflowers bloom on the Fox Islands from early spring throughout the summer. Jack-in-the-pulpits and lady-slippers grace the woodland floors. Black-eyed Susans, daisies and buttercups cover the summer fields. The fragrance of wild roses and honeysuckle fills the air, and buzzing bees gather nectar. When strawberry blossoms disappear, the wild fruit, tiny but sweet, ripens to provide food for animals and for humans who stop to pick a handful.

Many things have brought people to the Fox Islands: the woodlands, the fish, the deer, the good farmland. It's the beauty and uniqueness that begs them to stay.

MIRADA RANCH PHOTO
South Fox Island trail.

MIRADA RANCH PHOTO
The South Fox Island dune meets the water on the island's western side.

John Ingwersen expressed it well in his description of his first days on South Fox: "... I walked into virgin hardwood. It was a hot, humid day with no wind; soon my maps and my compass were meaningless — a long dreaming day lost in that great gone forest. Those first days alone on the island—the weather was beneficent, I slept on the beach with no tent. I ate oranges and Hersey bars and the roasted legs of a big snapping turtle (it seemed the spirit of the place), offered to me as it ran out of the rocks toward the water, letting me catch it by the tail. Once I paused to take a compass bearing, and heard an unseen tree fall. Another time a goshawk and I stared at each other. I was hooked."[12]

As a visitor walks the varied beaches, listens to songbirds in the woodlands, smells the sweetness of wildflowers or sits on the western shore of North Fox Island to see the sun setting behind the South Fox dune, it's easy to be "hooked" on these beautiful islands.

[1] Robert Hatt, *Island Life in Lake Michigan* (Bloomfield Hills, Mich.: Cranbrook Institute of Science, 1948), p. 13.

[2] Ibid, p. 12.

[3] Brian T. Hazlett, *Factors Influencing Island Floras in Northern Lake Michigan*, dissertation, University of Michigan, 1988.

[4] James J. Strang, *Ancient and Modern Michilimackinac* (1854; reprint, Mackinac Island: W. Stewart Woodfill, 1959), p. 85.

[5] Hatt, p. 48.

[6] Dennis A. Albert and Gary A. Reese, *An Overview of the Plant Community Ecology and Natural Area Significance of North Fox Island, Leelanau County, Michigan*, 29 Nov. 1989, p. 3.

[7] "3 rare natural habitat types are on N. Fox," *Leelanau Enterprise* 2 Nov., 1989.

[8] Hazlett, p. 42.

[9] "Hunting on Island is Natural," in *Traverse City Record-Eagle*, 29 Nov., 1992, p. 8D.

[10] "S. Fox Survey Finds Ancient Birch Tree," in *North Woods Call*, 24 Feb., 1972.

[11] Ibid.

[12] Letter to author from John Ingwersen, Feb., 1982.

COURTESY LEELANAU HISTORICAL MUSEUM
The Mackinaw boat was the favored vessel of early fishermen.

COURTESY GRAND TRAVERSE PIONEER AND HISTORICAL SOCIETY AND MUSEUM
Although these deer were carried down Lake Michigan from the state's upper peninsula, this 45-foot vessel, the Onekama, *also carried barrels of fish caught by Fox Island fishermen, 1898.*

IN SEARCH OF FUR AND FISH

Wau-goosh-e-min-iss is the Native American word for what is now known as Fox Island(s). In the Ottawa and Chippewa language the fox is called *waugoosh*, and *miniss* means island.[1]

During the fur-trading years in America, the silver-gray fox was considered one of the most valuable furs in the Great Lakes area, along with the black fox, the cross fox and the red fox.[2] While the Fox Islands were probably never a major contributor to the fur industry, several historical writers claim that the French stopped on these islands in the early 1600's and later.

According to historian Myron Vent, by 1672, Jesuit maps showed the islands situated in "Lac de Michigami." Vent relates that La Salle gave this 1680 description: "Those (islands) in the lake of the Illinois are a hazard on account of the sandbars which lie off them."[3]

This hazardous area became known as the Manitou Passage — the water between the Manitou, Fox and Beaver Islands and the mainland. Others called it "the channel." Traders and voyagers at first traveled in canoes which were between 35 and 40 feet long and carried up to five tons of freight and crew. It is believed that the French used the Fox Islands and other islands as places of refuge on their travels up and down Lake Michigan. Native Americans and French missionaries often traveled with them.

When La Salle sailed through the Mackinac Straits in 1679, he became the first white man to do so. With the coming of his ship, the *Griffon*, movement on the Great Lakes increased, which furthered the fur trade. That same year, La Salle established a trading post at Mackinaw, and John Jacob Astor's American Fur Company on Mackinac Island soon followed, becoming one of the leaders in American fur trade.

In James Strang's *Ancient and Modern Michilimackinac*, Chippewa, or Ojibway, Indians are said to have lived on the Foxes where they farmed and fished.[4] Although Strang was a brilliant man, his historical writings are not always to be trusted. If he can be believed in this account, we find that the Fox Island Indians traded fish and corn to the fur traders in exchange for European goods such as knives and cooking utensils. Small vessels called "hookers" joined the canoe-bound traders in the 1800's.

In addition to foxes, the fur traders transported elk, deer, wild cat, wolf, marten, ermine, mink, badger, skunk, otter, wolverine, bear, raccoon and smaller skins up the lake to the trading posts at the Straits of Mackinac. The major markets for these furs were in Europe, where they were made into coats and hats for royalty and other wealthy people.

It's true that white men established the markets and have usually been given full credit for the assault on the American wildlife, but the Native Americans also played a part. In Chase and Stellanova Osborn's book, *Schoolcraft, Longfellow, Hiawatha*, they relate an account by an early fur trader, Nicholas Perrot, that the Chippewas were using both guns and bows and arrows in 1718, as well as snares. Perrot stated that 2,400 moose were taken by the Chippewas on Manitoulin Island in 1670-71, using only snares.[5] In the same book an account is given of 54 Indian hunters who killed 994 bears during the 1828 season.

This type of trapping, hunting and trading by both Native Americans and immigrants took place along the shores of Lake Michigan and up the rivers that emptied into the Big Lake. Many of these early Europeans and Native Americans passed by the Fox Islands and sometimes took refuge from the storm or stopped to rest. The French and the Indians often traveled together, and the government back in France encouraged friendship and marriage between the two groups. For the French, it was advantageous to bring the Indians into their national family. They found "encouragement given for intermarriage between the French and natives; whereby their new empire may in time be peopled, without draining France of its inhabitants."[6] The evidence of this remains with Native American families who have French surnames. Some of these French-Indians are recorded on later census records of the Fox Islands. Also, some residents of South Fox just after 1900 recalled that a clearing about two-thirds of the way down the island's eastern shore was referred to as "French Town," although the reason for this name was not known.

Though the market never disappeared, the supply of furs dwindled rapidly. As early as 1721 Charlevoix wrote, "When we discovered this vast continent it was full of wild beasts. A handful of Frenchmen has made them almost entirely disappear in less than an age, and there are some the species of which is (sic) entirely destroyed."[7]

Whether any foxes were taken from the Fox Islands, we do not know. In 1853 James Strang of Beaver Island reported that the silver-gray fox was the most valuable fur, commanding more than $50 a pelt.[8] The silver-gray was very rare at that time and remains so. Whether or not there were silver-grays on the Fox Islands is hard to determine. The only foxes living on these islands now are red foxes. Though seen occasionally, they are not reported to be very abundant.

If the islands were being named today, North and South Fox Islands would probably not be the first choice, but such is the case with many places where the names no longer seem to fit.

PHOTO BY GORDON CHARLES

With the disappearance of the fur trade in the 1830's, a new industry began. The American Fur Company changed its emphasis to commercial fishing. By this time, the population of Michigan and the surrounding areas had grown rapidly, providing a ready market. In spite of this growth, the Traverse City *Morning Record* of December 10, 1889, recorded that before 1847 "there was not a white man living in all Leelanau County, from Cat Head Point to the present boundary of Benzie County . . ..[9] There were a few Native Americans, and south of the present Leelanau County boundary, white settler Joseph Oliver lived with his Indian wife and supported his family by trapping and fishing. There were white fisherman living on the islands at that time, and the development of better lake transportation made the big-city markets more accessible.

Many Europeans, upon hearing of the fertile fishing grounds of Lake Michigan, had come to America to continue the trade they had practiced in their homelands. Those who had not been involved in fishing soon learned how to pull their nets, sometimes in freezing spray. On shore, they reeled the nets, made repairs to their equipment, and cleaned and salted the fish. In the beginning, no fresh fish were shipped, but were salted and then bartered for goods with dealers and traders.

At first, most fishermen were based at Mackinac Island, since it was the most civilized area. After ranging out in their small sailboats and getting a full catch, they returned to the island. As the men ventured further west and south, they began building shelters on the Beaver Island chain, including the Fox Islands.

In his 1847 survey notes for North Fox Island, Orange Risdon recorded "3 bark fishing shanties"[10] in Section 13, on the eastern shore. With the survey completed on both islands, they were opened for ownership, and some fishermen staked their claims. In the cusp of the northwestern side, facing South Fox, Risdon designated "White Fish Bay" and called it "a great place for taking white fish and trout."[11]

Although he didn't own property, Samuel Rice was one of the earliest known fishermen on South Fox, arriving about 1846. In *Island Stories*, Marion M. Davis gives this account.[12] In the early 1840's, Rice left Fort Wayne, Indiana, with his wife Sarah and five little daughters. They traveled by covered wagon to Prairie Ronde, Wisconsin. After much hardship, Mrs. Rice died, leaving her husband with a baby and the four other young girls to care for. At first, Rice left the children with relatives while he went to Mackinac Island, where he established a home for them. After being settled at Mackinac, they spent the next summer on South Fox while Rice fished in the area. Arriving on a large vessel called the *Twin Brothers*, they and their little fishing boat, the *Sea Gull*, were lowered to the water, and Rice rowed his family ashore.

The Rice family was not the first to arrive during this period, evidenced by the fact that Mary Snell was already there and cared for them in her home until their own little house was ready. John Snell was a "chainer," who had come from Beaver Island to work on the surveying of the island. It is not known how many other inhabitants there were at this time. When the Rice house was completed, the girls kept house for their father and a hired man. As Rice brought in his catch, the hired man cleaned and salted the fish to prepare them for pick-up by a larger boat.

About two years later, after spending more time on Mackinac Island, the Rice family moved to mainland Northport. In his diaries, Northport resident, The Rev. George Smith recorded that Rice married a woman he had met during fishing expeditions to Beaver Island. In Northport, Rice took the job of property assessor, in addition to continuing some fishing. In 1863 his daughters were students in the first school house in Traverse City.

In 1850 five Mormon families arrived from Beaver Island and took up fishing and farming on South Fox Island. Strang reported in his newspaper *Northern Islander* that the Mormon settlers on South Fox spent the winter of 1850-51 chopping wood, knitting fish nets and making cedar staves for fish barrels. The abundant supply of fish made possible the settlement of these isolated islands in Lake Michigan.[13] Local history records many confrontations between Mormons and "gentiles" (as named by the Mormons) throughout the Beaver Island chain and on the mainland, most accounts blaming the Mormons. They were accused of stealing the catches and equipment of other fishermen, and of breaking almost every law that existed. On June 23, 1852, The Rev. Smith recorded in his diary, "Near night, the 3-masted schooner *Emmlin Cleveland* anchored here loaded with flour and goods for a Mr. Cable of (South) Fox Island. He is moving here (Northport) to get away from the Mormons who are robbing him of his property. He is obliged to flee to save it."[14] Not long before that, brothers James and Alva Cable had fled their property on Beaver Island to escape the Mormon intrusion and had apparently thought life would be better on South Fox Island. Other South Fox residents left during the Mormon era, and with the assassination of the Mormon leader, James J. Strang, in 1856, the Mormons left too.

Thomas Retford (Redford) and his wife Sarah bought land in Northport in 1855 but were spending some time on South Fox Island, probably fishing between the islands. In November, 1856, when the fishing season was over, the Smith diary reported, "The *Juliana* came in about noon with Mr. Retford and family from Fox Island."[14]

With both Mormon and Gentile fishermen leaving the islands during this troubled time, South Fox was deserted for a few years. Unlike South Fox, North Fox Island did have a population in 1860. These families, most likely, fished in the warmer seasons and cut wood during the winter. The census records Robert Boyd, age 23, from Scotland; and with him a four year old boy, John Fitz, from England. The Subnow family was also on North Fox: John, age 27, and his wife Catherine and year-old daughter, Edell. Rushand and Harriet Roe, ages 48 and 38, completed the 1860 North Fox population, along with their children, Henry and Laura. Two years later J. Haines Emery owned about 150 acres, on the eastern shore to about the center of the island.

On South Fox, in 1863, Daniel Falkerson bought the property of Richard and Marriet Cooper, who, in 1850, were at Little Traverse and later involved in the building of the Fountain City House. Falkerson moved to Grand Traverse County in 1874, and Joseph Left bought Falkerson's island property. Left also owned property and fished on Beaver Island. Samuel Ashton of Chicago was an early South Fox Island property owner, but it is not known whether it was the fishing or other business that brought him to the island.

The Great Lakes fishing industry peaked in the 1880's, and upper Lake Michigan was the most fertile fishing ground in the world. Steamers were now collecting fresh fish for Chicago markets. In 1885 fresh whitefish sold for 3 1/2 cents per pound, and trout sold for three cents per pound. Salted trout went for about $3 a half barrel, and salted whitefish sold for between $3.50 and $4 per barrel.[15]

By that time, several other families had moved to South Fox. Hiram Beckwith was issued a patent for a lot in about the middle of the island in 1865. Beckwith was apparently quite a speculator, having already bought a lot near the lighthouse north of Northport and a lot in Northport, in addition to buying and selling the mouth of the river in Traverse City to Harry Boardman. Whether he fished while on South Fox or merely kept the fishermen company is not known. Beckwith was not always wise in his business dealings. Smith's diary records an account of Beckwith being arrested in Northport for illegal distribution of liquor. On June 18, 1858, the diary reads, "Had Beckwith up this morning, proposed if he would promise not to do the like again and destroy the liquor, he should be released. He came on his knees and promised to do better...."[16] Hiram Beckwith had a wife named Mary, according to the 1850 Census.

By 1870 all the fishing families were gone from North Fox, but there were, once again, families and men without families fishing from South Fox. Thomas Davidson came from Scotland, by way of New York, to seek his fortune, and Ole Goodmanson arrived from Norway. George Roe came from Ireland, and he and his wife Elizabeth settled on South Fox with their two sons, George and William. Other Roe families on the south island were in the wooding business and at the lighthouse. Christian Olson was another South Fox resident at that time, along with his wife Ingra, year old daughter Mary, and another relative, John Olson. Like Goodmanson, this family had come from Norway. Although Thomas Davidson had provided a good start for his family when he brought them from Scotland to settle on the Leelanau Peninsula, the sailor and fisherman Davidson died just two years after his name appeared on the 1870 Census for South Fox.

The men were gone in their fishing boats much of the time, traveling between the islands while the seasons for various kinds of fish changed. Fish was a staple food item in those days. Whitefish was the main catch, along with some lake trout, herring, suckers, perch, sturgeon, pike, pickerel and ling. The boulders off the northeastern shore of South Fox provided excellent bass fishing year round.

Another fisherman was Joe Palmer, who came from Scotland. He married Anna Williams at Mackinac Island, and they settled on Beaver Island but left at the time of the gentile exodus in about 1852. Joe Palmer helped to drive the Mormons away from Beaver after the assassination of the leader, James Strang. The Palmers then returned to Beaver Island for a time and lived in one of the deserted Mormon houses. They left Beaver Island before the 1860 census was taken, and the family was recorded in 1870 on South Fox Island. But Joe was no longer with them. Late in 1869 Anna Palmer and her children had received word that Joe had been washed overboard during a storm, and she went searching the mainland shore until she found his body near Manistique, in Michigan's upper peninsula. He was buried there, and the site was named *Scot's Point* in his honor. Anna's son Jeremiah was born two months later. Anna married again and moved to Traverse City. Her daughters Mary and Julia stayed on South Fox, marrying island residents — Mary to farmer Otto Williams in 1871, and Julia to fisherman Christopher Widerman. Otto Williams may have been related to South Fox property owner, Jerry Williams. Through death or desertion, Otto Williams disappeared from the scene, and his wife Mary wed fisherman and woodcutter John Floyd in 1874. Christopher Widerman died on South Fox in 1888, of tuberculosis. He and his wife Julia had owned property on Beaver Island, before 1875, and may have spent some time living there. By 1880 John and Mary Floyd were living on North Manitou Island, and by 1889 were back on Beaver Island where their families had lived years earlier.

Henry Longfield was living on South Fox in 1874 and was probably a fisherman like John Floyd, to whose wedding Longfield was a witness.

William Wyderman patented some South Fox Island property in 1877. He and his family had been living in Northport as early as 1872. Wyderman was a fisherman, originally from Germany, and his wife Elizabeth Retford (Redford) was from England. They arrived on South Fox with their two young children to begin island living. The Wyderman name for these island families was sometimes spelled *Weiderman* or *Widerman*. The William Wyderman family moved north of Northport by 1880 and then to the Dakota Territory in 1886.

In the early 1880's John (Johan) Nelson, a fisherman born in Sweden, bought property and fished off South Fox Island. Nelson had come to Manistee from Sweden at age 30. When his wife and two children died and were buried in Manistee, he returned to Sweden. He came back to this country in March 1884, and married Caroline Anderson. They lived on South Fox, where he fished for about 10 years, and then moved to Northport where he continued fishing for another 40 years. Others fishing off the Fox Islands in 1882 were Charlie Roe, George Johnson and Captain Budd. Roe operated a shingle mill on South Fox and also did quite a bit of fishing. The *Leelanau Enterprise* reported in November, 1889, that "Charles Roe brought 250 packages of salt fish from Fox Island (to Northport) last week."[17]

John Day was living on Beaver Island with his wife and two young children, in 1880. He owned property on the northwestern point of North Fox Island by 1885. The little point made an ideal base for fishing between the Fox Islands. Day was born in New York, and, apparently, moved to Beaver Island when his employer, James Dormer, moved his fishing business to Beaver. Day served as bookkeeper for Dormer's Great Lakes operation, based on Beaver Island's Whiskey Point. Dormer bought and sold fish from his Whiskey Point store, and John Day, most likely, used his fishing spot on North Fox to enhance the business. Day later acquired the Beaver Island store from Dormer and operated it for many years.

Another early South Fox fisherman was Robert DeGrolier (also spelled DeGolier or DeGolia). In September 1880 the *Leelanau Enterprise* reported that DeGrolier "removed his family to this place (Northport) and will close up his business on the island and come here to remain permanently next month."[18] In addition to fishing, DeGrolier was an assistant at the South Fox Light, and he left that post a month after relocating his family to Northport. His wife's name was Roxena.

Fisherman John Oscar Pierson (Peterson) owned property along the middle of the island's eastern shore. He is easily confused with two other Petersons, John and Oscar, who fished around the Fox Islands during the summer months. John and Oscar had a tug named *Fox* and also bought the *Two Brothers*. Pierson and the Petersons all settled in the Northport area, as did another who had fished off the Fox Islands, Ole Martinson.

The island fishermen were good suppliers of fish to the mainland. The steamer *Onekama* was one vessel scuttling from Northport to the Fox Islands and returning with barrels of fish.

In February, 1891, the *Leelanau Enterprise* announced, "The fishermen about Leland and the Manitou and Fox Islands will be able to sell their fish to a better advantage the coming season than ever before, as they will be able to dispose of them fresh, instead of salting them. A. Dahlmer of Northport has secured the Chicago tug *Babcock* and will buy fish for R. Connable & Sons, of Petoskey, and it is their intention to buy all the fish they can get in Traverse City, at the islands and at Leland, and for this purpose, the tug will visit the fishing stations. The *Babcock* is 65 feet keel, 16 feet beam, and has a 14 x 16 engine."[19]

Other fishermen who lived on South Fox just before and in the early 1900's were Native Americans Louis Bourisseau (son of Keeper Lewis Bourisseau and spelled differently); Enos Chippewa; Louis, August and Benjamin Ance; and John Andrews.

The life of a fisherman was not easy. He often was in his boat as the sun was rising and did not come home until sunset, or in some cases, for several day. But it was a comparatively prosperous life in these waters that abounded with such big catches of fish.

In the 1840's and 50's gill nets were used almost totally. The nets were usually made by hand during the winter months. Strips of wood were used as floats, and stones made good weights. The nets were tended every three to five days by the fishermen in their small Mackinaw boats. The size of fish caught depended on the size of the mesh. The fish were caught when their gills and fins were tangled in the mesh as they tried to swim through it. In 1852 James Strang reported in his *Ancient and Modern Michilimackinac* that nets had been set for whitefish as far as 1,400 feet deep near the Fox Islands.[20] He stated that the biggest fish were found in the deepest areas.

In 1890 evidence of over-fishing was apparent when the *Leelanau Enterprise* reported, "Eleven boats that were fishing from the Fox Islands this fall caught but 1,100 packages of fish."[21]

Seine nets were sometimes used in the spring and late fall. Two winches placed about 100 feet apart, about 150 feet in from the beach, held the net which looped out into the water. Floats and weights held it upright. The fishermen pulled the net in by cranking the winches. This method was used up until abut 1920. Very large catches of perch and other fish could be brought to shore in this way.

The pound net was invented in Scotland and introduced in Lake Michigan in 1856, followed by the trap net which was used in Lake Michigan mostly between 1903 and 1908.[22] Pound nets, often called *pond nets*, were stronger than the early gill nets and brought in a lot of fish. But the small mesh that made them effective also killed big numbers of immature fish. This waste of fish brought about Michigan's first commercial fishing law. Act 350 of 1865 set mesh regulations for pound nets used for whitefish and other species.[23] It also set mesh sizes for trap nets and required fishermen to return whitefish spawn to the water. Because fishermen were coming from other countries and taking fish, while not contributing to the economy of the state, the law also kept "persons not citizens of the state nor of the United States... from temporarily immigrating to the fisheries of the state ... for the purpose of catching and carrying away large quantities of fish... and thereby evading the payment of all taxes for the support of the state."[24]

Just as whitefish was the fisherman's favorite, sturgeon was the most hated. There was no market for the sturgeon, and they broke up the fishermen's nets because of their size, some being up to 400 pounds and nine feet long. As they were removed from the nets, the sturgeon were injured and soon died. The estimate is that more than ten million pounds of sturgeon were destroyed by Lake Michigan fishermen before the 1900's.[25] Some of the Native American fishermen did take sturgeon by spearing them.

The results of these abuses in commercial fishing began to be realized. In the bulletin *Seines to Salmon Charters*, produced by Michigan State University, we are told that, "Between 1880 and 1885 the number of fishermen in the entire Great Lakes fishing industry doubled, the gear investment tripled, but the catch was less than half again as large."[26]

Though the population of desirable fish began to decline before 1900, the improvements in equipment made the yearly catches greater. Catches of lake trout, chubs, herring, northern pike and yellow perch peaked during 1905 to 1909, amounting to 47 1/2 million pounds per year. This was the biggest average for any five-year period in the history of commercial fishing in Michigan.[27]

Fishermen had first used sailboats and rowboats; but when the steam tug came into being, the men could work in almost any weather and new grounds were accessible. A crew of a half-dozen men on a steam tug could set five miles of net, making possible a huge catch. The first fishing steamer was built on Mackinac Island in 1860. These steamers were first used in Lake Michigan in 1869. Automatic gill-net lifters appeared on some of these tugs around 1900.

A Booth Fishery operated on South Fox, just north of the sandy "fishermen's flat." Set near the gravely, southeastern shoreline, the fishery consisted of a long, narrow, wooden-pole building and a dock out in front. The Charlevoix-based business had fisheries on other islands as well. Inside the pole building, salted herring was packed into wooden barrels for transport to Charlevoix or other Lake Michigan ports. The pond net was one method the fishery used, fishing not far from the South Fox shore.

COURTESY CARLSONS' FISHERIES
Jacob Vannetter's Onward

South Fox property owner and fisherman, Jacob B. Vannetter, was master of the steam tug *Onward*, which he owned until 1895. This vessel went down at Bower's Harbor, near Traverse City, in 1910. Vannetter's years of fishing had been interrupted by the Civil War, from which he returned to live in Northport. During his years in Northport, he and his wife Harriet owned property on South Fox. Some of the fishermen on the island had small shanties on the "flat," just north of the lighthouse and before the Booth Fishery. By 1920 the Booth Fishery was reaching the end of its era. Down the shore at the lighthouse, the *Aida* was kept at the lighthouse dock, and during 1915-1920 it was used as a fishing boat for Keeper McCormick and assistants Nelson and Dame. Behind the carpenter shop, the keepers dried their nets on the net racks.

On North Fox, Joseph Gagnon was fishing off the Fox Islands in 1905, according to Traverse City's *Evening Record*, and had the only fish shanty on North Fox at that time.[28]

Another South Fox property owner and fisherman was Captain George Cleland Abbott, who was born on Manitou Island and moved to Northport as a child. He was a single man and quite a traveler. Some years found him fishing around the Fox Islands, but other years he could be found nowhere. In the 1940's, his brothers, assuming that he had died, wrote to the sheriff near Abbott's last known address, inquiring about his death and the settlement of his property. They promptly received a letter from their long, lost brother, informing them that he was quite alive. When Abbott did die in 1947, he was in Cheboygan, Michigan.

One of the steam tug owners was Beaver Islander Frank Left, son of earlier South Fox property owner, Joseph Left. Frank owned some of the first tugs around. Though the

Howard Steimel and Louis Stanwick lift their pound net near South Fox Island, about 1915.

fish were declining rapidly, it took several years for the fishermen to realize how much they were depleting the various species. In the early 1930's six steam tugs found the fishing off the Foxes too good to resist.[29] James Martin's *Evelyn M.*, Gus and Art Larsen's *Estonia*, and the steamers *Elizabeth G., Agnes S., Betty C.* and *LaFond* came from Beaver Island to the waters off the Foxes. The vessels' daily catches were loaded aboard the 65-foot package freighter *Rambler*, which took the fish to the Booth dock in Charlevoix and returned that evening with supplies. The fishermen celebrated their success aboard the *Rambler* each night. Gus Mielke of Beaver Island was that vessel's builder. The *Stella* also came from the Beaver Islands to fish around the Foxes, carrying its owner, Alex Cornstalk. Cornstalk also owned property on South Fox.

Just as fishermen came from Beaver Island, they came also from Leland, Northport, and other spots along the mainland to fish near the Fox Islands, as well as to other locations, in search of a good catch. Large clusters of boulders on the lake bottom off South Fox's northern bluff provided for good bass fishing. An underwater ridge of boulders west of the North Fox dune was also a good fishing spot.

Sometimes they found more than fish. Anyone who makes a living off the lakes is faced with the possibility of sudden storms, fog and breakdowns in equipment. In *The Journal of Beaver Island History*, historian Phil Gregg quotes William Belfy who owned the fish tug *Silver Star* with his brother Erwin Belfy: "I remember one December during this period (1925-35) when we were caught off the Fox Islands in foul weather for ten days. It was freezing too hard to lift our nets, so it was just a matter of waiting it out and shifting anchor from one lee to the other around the (south) island."[30] The Belfys made it back to Beaver Island safely.

The Carlsons of Leland were not so fortunate. On Tuesday morning, August 5, 1941, at about 8:30, William Carlson's tug, *Diamond*, caught fire and burned near South Fox

COURTESY CARLSONS' FISHERIES
Pete (Lester) Carlson, Warren Price and William Carlson lift a pound net as an unidentified couple looks on. The Carlsons' fish tug Diamond *burned off South Fox in 1941.*

Island. Will and his son Lester took off their boots and oilskins and attached life preservers before they were forced to jump into the water. They swam away from the boat, hoping someone would see the smoke from their burning vessel and come to their rescue. After drifting for some time, they decided to head for South Fox; but before they could make it, Will Carlson died of exposure. Even in the summer, eight hours in the water had been too much. At about seven o'clock, his son saw the Grosvenor mail boat passing in the distance, but it was too far away to be hailed. Three hours later Lester had to let go of his father's body and try to save himself by swimming to the island alone. After Lester and his father's body were separated, a Coast Guard cutter passed between them, but in the darkness the men were not discovered.

Toward morning, Lester's voice could hardly be heard as the weakened man, who had drifted toward the Manitous, called out to the fish tug heading toward him. Leland residents, Marvin Cook and Percy Guthrie, hauled the tired fisherman aboard the *Sambo*. On Wednesday afternoon the Coast Guard found the body of Will Carlson attached to the cork life preserver which his son had fastened tightly.

The *Smiling Through* carried fishermen to the waters off the Fox Islands in the 1930's and early 40's. In an Armistice Day storm in 1940, Captain and owner L. J. Strayer broke an arm and two ribs while being hurled out of the pilot house as he tried to hang on to the ship's wheel. His crew finally tied him in, as anxious family and friends watched the vessel make its frightful journey back into Northport Harbor.[31]

Captain Charles Bissell, a native of Beaver Island, also operated fish tugs between Charlevoix and Northport before 1950. According to his son George, Captain Bissell's last command was the *Evelyn M. Bissell*, which he used for fishing around the Fox Islands. Some of the other fishermen from the Northport area were: Albion Anderson in the *Two Brothers*; the Wilsons in their *Valentine* and *The Star*; fisherman Anderson in the *Hannah B.*; Ed Middleton in the *Grace*; Roy and Bruce Nelson in the *Major*, and Bill Hopkins in the *Flora*. Of course, there were many others.

Fishermen have a reputation for being a hardy lot. They have battled the elements since the first boat was launched in search of fish. Many of them met with misfortune, but more of them lived to tell stories to their children and grandchildren of the big catches from Lake Michigan. Unfortunately their fishing habits eventually wiped out the possibility of such adventures for their descendants. But this blame for the decrease in fish populations must be shared with others as well. *Seines to Salmon Charters* lists the four major human disruptions in the Great Lakes:

1. Intensive fishing
2. Extreme changes in the land and tributaries draining into the Great Lakes
3. Intentional introduction of alien fish and building of waterways that allowed ocean species to enter the Great Lakes
4. Physical and chemical changes in the atmosphere, surrounding land, and the lakes themselves that are due to urban, agricultural and industrial development[32]

By the mid-1900's the Department of Natural Resources had made many gains in replenishing the lakes with trout stocks, but recent over-fishing has once again made good catches scarce. Trout spawning observed around the Fox Islands in the 1990's resulted in the designation of a lake trout zone, with trout fishing prohibited in that area.[33]

Zebra mussels have added to concerns about lower Great Lakes fish populations, as the mussels clean the water of microscopic food on which the fish feed. And in 1994 a new threat was found to have arrived in Lake Michigan waters, that of the Eurasian ruffe. These fish are believed to have been introduced into Lake Superior in 1985 by way of ballast water from an ocean vessel and since then have spread to some of the other Great Lakes. The ruffe tend to "take over" and other species of fish are depleted. According to the *Traverse City Record-Eagle*, quoting Louis Kowieski, chairman of the Great Lakes Study Committee of the Wisconsin Conservation Congress, "I think the ruffe is going to be the most devastating thing to ever come down the pike.... Anyone with an interest in fishing should be extremely concerned about it."[34]

Lewis Bourisseau and Charles Nelson drying their nets in Northport.

America has often been called the "land of plenty." In the past, a bounty of wild animals and fish helped many families to establish themselves and survive in the Great Lakes wilderness. This God-given abundance should be viewed as a gift. Although there are regrets that our forefathers did not see the limits of these treasures, the present generation can learn and seek to protect and increase what remains.

[1] Andrew Blackbird, *History of the Ottawa and Chippewa Indians of Michigan* (Ypsilanti, Mich: Ypsilanti Job Printing House, 1887), p. 121.

[2] Chase and Stellanova Osborn, *Schoolcraft, Longfellow, Hiawatha* (Lancaster, Penn.: The Jaques Cattell Press, 1942), p. 54.

[3] Myron Vent, *South Manitou Island, From Pioneer Community To National Park,* (Springfield, Va.: The Goodway Press, Inc., 1973), p. 8.

[4] James Strang, *Ancient and Modern Michilimackinac* (1854; reprint, Mackinac Island: W. Stewart Woodfill, 1959), p. 6.

[5] Osborn, p. 53.

[6] "Reports on American Colonies," in *Michigan Pioneer and Historical Collections, Vol. 19*, 1891, p. 11.

[7] Osborn, p. 53.

[8] Strang, p. 93.

[9] Thomas Bates, *The Morning Record* 10 Dec., 1899, p. 13, microfilm.

[10] Orange Risdon in 1847 survey notes for North Fox Island.

[11] Ibid.

[12] George N. Fuller, ed., *Island Stories* (Lansing: State Printers, 1947), pp. 60, 61; collections of Marion M. Davis articles from *Michigan History Magazine*.

[13] Strang, *Northern Islander*, 9 Jan., 1851, reprint.

[14] Unpublished diary of The Rev. George N. Smith, June 23, 1852.

[15] Ibid, Nov. 30, 1856.

[16] Margaret Cronyn & John Kenny, *The Saga of Beaver Island* (Ann Arbor: Braun and Brumfield, Inc., 1958), p. 99.

[17] Smith diary, June 11, 1885.

[18] *Leelanau Enterprise* 28, Nov. 1889, p. 3.

[19] Ibid, 2 Sept., 1880., p. 3.

[20] Ibid, 26 Feb., 1891.

[21] Strang, p. 96.

[22] *Leelanau Enterprise* 18 Dec., 1890.

[23] John Van Oosten, "Michigan's Commercial Fisheries of the Great Lakes," in *Michigan History Magazine, Vol. 22*, 1938, pp. 107-145.

[24] Dean A. Brege & Niles R. Kevern, *Michigan Commercial Fishing Regulations: A Summary of Public Acts and Conservation Commission Orders, 1865 through 1975,* report, Nov. 1978, p. 2.

[25] Ibid, p. 5.

[26] William Cashman, "The Rise and Fall of the Fishing Industry," in *The Journal of Beaver Island History, Vol. One* (Lansing: Wellman Press, Inc., 1976), p. 75.

[27] Suzanne Tainter & Ray J. White, Extension Bulletin E-100, *Seines to Salmon Charters,* May, 1977, p. 5.

[28] Ibid, p. 5.

[29] "Hidden Wealth Wasn't Found," *The Evening Record* 9 Sept., 1905, p. 1, microfilm.

[30] Cashman, p. 80.

[31] Phil Gregg, "Beaver Tales," in *The Journal of Beaver Island History, Vol. Two* (Lansing: Wellman Press, Inc., 1980), p. 173.

[32] Wayne H. Mervau, II, "Smiling Through Barely Made It," *Leelanau Enterprise* 17, Aug., 1973.

[33] Tainter & White, p. 15.

[34] F. Glenn Goff and Phyllis J. Higman, *North Fox Island Development, Environmental Impact Report* (Vital Resources Consulting; Sept. 1990), p. 2-52.

[35] "There's a new danger to Great Lakes system," *Traverse City Record-Eagle* 5 March, 1995, p. 7B.

DOYLE FITZPATRICK COLLECTION
James Jesse Strang, "King of the Mormons," about 1843.

He hath chosen his servant James to be King: he hath made him his Apostle to all nations; he hath established him a Prophet above the Kings of the earth; and appointed him King of Zion: by his own voice did he call him, and he sent his Angels unto him to ordain him.

—James J. Strang in
The Book of the Law of the Lord

KING JAMES JESSE STRANG

One of the most colorful people in the history of the Lake Michigan islands is James Jesse Strang. This brilliant lawyer did much to influence the political history of North and South Fox and other islands. But an explanation of events preceding Strang's appearance is needed in order to understand what came to follow.

Native Americans who lived in northern Michigan before white settlers arrived were largely nomadic and had no need for government as we know it. They settled their affairs around the campfire or on the battlefield.

In 1534 Jacques Cartier discovered the mouth of the St. Lawrence River. This discovery paved the way for Samuel de Champlain, who established the Fort of Quebec in 1608, eight hundred miles inward from the mouth of the St. Lawrence. These men called this new territory *New France*. Under Richelieu, minister of foreign affairs for Louis XIII, Champlain was appointed governor of New France.

Champlain sent young Jean Nicolet on a westward expedition, expecting that he would find the Pacific Ocean, since the local natives talked of a great body of water in that direction.

In August of 1634 Nicolet and his seven companions arrived at present-day St. Ignace on the Straits of Mackinac. There at the Indian village of Taenhotentaron, the first treaty to be made in the Great Lakes country took place. The territory became known as the Province of Michilimackinac, and the King of France gained jurisdiction over the land of the Ottawas.

Over the next hundred years many British and French settlers arrived. As the fur trade flourished, the political scene was most confusing. Many settlers became rich, especially those who could exploit their power as governors or other officials. Native Americans were aggravated by unfair treatment and confused by not knowing whom to follow. The French and Indian War broke out throughout eastern North America and at its conclusion in 1763, the Straits came under British control.

Twenty years later, in 1783, the American Revolution came to a close with the Treaty of Paris. The Northwest Territory, which included Michilimackinac, became part of the United States of America. The British were slow to leave Fort Mackinac, however, and did not turn it over to the American authorities until 1796. The changes in possession of the land during this time by the French, English and the Americans resulted in name changes for the area: *The Province of Michilimackinac, Territory of Michilimackinac*, and finally in 1805, *The Michigan Territory.*

The British again held the fort at Michilimackinac for a time during the War of 1812, but the Americans regained control when the Treaty of Ghent ended that war in 1815.

In 1836 the Fox Islands and other lands were ceded to the United States Government by the Indians as Michigan prepared for statehood. Part of The Michigan Territory had been included within the boundaries of other states as they entered the union. In 1837 the Michigan borders were defined and the State of Michigan found its place in the United States of America. At that point, the islands began to develop their own political history.

Though fur traders and fishermen had already been visiting the islands off Lake Michigan's eastern shore, the nearby mainland began gaining white settlers with the arrival of The Reverend Peter Dougherty in 1839, on present-day Old Mission, at the end of the long peninsula jutting out from Grand Traverse Bay.[1] He came, bringing his wife and children, to work among the Ottawas and Chippewas. He was soon followed by more white families.

As settlements sprang up along the Lake Michigan shoreline, the Fox Islands, as well as other islands, became more politically connected to the mainland. Slightly less than half of Michigan's lower peninsula was included in Mackinac County, as was approximately one-fourth of the upper peninsula, The Beaver Island archipelago, of which the Foxes are a part, was included in this.

The most fascinating era of the islands' political history began in Voree, Wisconsin, in 1846. There James Jesse Strang lived as the leader of a community of Mormons. People in surrounding areas were suspicious of his strong rule and antagonized the Voree community.

James Strang had been converted to Mormonism in 1844 during a visit to the Mormon capital at Nauvoo, Illinois. Mormon leader Joseph Smith was assassinated just four months later, and Strang produced a letter from Smith appointing Strang as the successor. Some of Smith's followers called the letter a forgery, refused to follow Strang and went with Brigham Young to Utah. But those who trusted Strang settled with him in Voree. When hostilities toward the Voree Mormons peaked in 1846, Strang told his people about a "revelation" he had received from God which would lead them to "a land amidst wide waters, and covered with large timber, with a deep, broad bay on one side of it."[2] In May 1847, Strang and four others arrived at Beaver Island to explore it and prepare for a settlement. At that time Beaver Island was occupied by Native Americans and a few white fishermen and traders.

To understand the political history of the Fox Islands, it is necessary to explore the happenings at Beaver Island, for the events became intertwined.

In 1847 the Michigan State Legislature designated the Beaver Islands, which included the Foxes, into the township of Peaine. Although a part of the unorganized county of Emmet, the township of Peaine was attached to Mackinac for judicial purposes, to Newaygo for state representative elections and to Lapeer for the election of state senator.[3] Because of the geographical separation and the confusion of county authority, Strang was in a good position to set up his own rule.

By 1849 approximately 50 Mormon families occupied Beaver Island. On July 8, 1850, James Jesse Strang crowned himself King of the Mormon community, with a jeweled crown and a long, flowing robe. A man of small stature had managed his way to authority over his own kingdom.

At the coronation Strang read a decree given to him by a "revelation" appointing "the islands of the Great Lakes" as the "Kingdom of the Saints," and directing the "King" to apportion the land to his followers.[4] A few months before the coronation, Strang had written President Fillmore and Congress, describing the Mormon's persecution by others and the wish to live apart from their persecutors. Strang requested "a law giving the consent of the nation that the saints may settle upon and forever occupy all the uninhabited lands of the Islands of Lake Michigan and to cease to sell the same to other persons."[5]

Strang and his followers had believed that the remoteness of Beaver Island would allow them to practice their religion without interference or persecution from others. They also wanted to minister to the Indians, whom they felt were badly mistreated by many white people. But the Mormons soon discovered that their problems followed them even to the islands of Lake Michigan.

The officials at Mackinac were strongly opposed and hostile to the Mormon population. They, as well as others, looked with contempt upon a man who called himself "King of the Earth by direct appointment of God."[6] When Strang instituted the practice of polygamy, it did nothing for his popularity with the "gentiles," as Strang called non-Mormons. Strang himself had five wives and 14 children.* Strang charged that the real opposition came because the people of Mackinac were afraid that Beaver Island might compete with their own territory in importance, and especially that Beaver Island would become a bigger fishing center than Mackinac Island. In 1852 Strang stated that around 90 people in his township had been arrested on more than 200 criminal charges, without one conviction. He wrote, "Arrests without a single conviction, ought to satisfy our most violent enemies that we are maligned and falsely accused."[7]

In 1851 there were five families of Mormons living on South Fox Island, and Strang planned that there would be another twelve families arriving on that island the spring of 1852. Strang's followers on the Fox Islands were essentially farmers, but in winter they chopped wood, knitted fish nets, and made cedar staves for fish barrels. Strang thought his god was looking out for his people and gave them special talents as quoted in Strang's newspaper the *Northern Islander*. He wrote, "Navigating Lake Michigan in an open boat at mid-winter is considered a thing impossible by all but the saints."[8]

An apportionment act passed in 1851 by the State Legislature worked to Strang's advantage. The unorganized county of Emmet was separated from Mackinac and attached to the Newaygo representative district.[9] Strang announced his candidacy for legislator on November second, election day. No provisions had been made for carrying votes from Beaver Island to the appointed place for counting them, and the Mormons believed this was done deliberately to disenfranchise them. Since the mainlanders of the Newaygo District didn't know of Strang's candidacy, they were suddenly confronted with his receipt of 165 votes cast at Beaver Island and delivered in haste by a Mormon to the Newaygo District headquarters. Since the rest of the Newaygo District was sparsely populated, Strang was elected.

Strang was a gifted orator and was respected in the Legislature in Lansing. This didn't gain him any respect back in his own territory, however.

In addition to the Mormons who had settled on the Beaver and Fox Islands, there were many at Pine River, now Charlevoix; and the hostilities toward the Mormons in the area increased.

An act which passed in the Legislature, after being introduced in 1853 by Strang, included the Beaver Islands in the newly organized county of Emmet.

* Four of Strang's childern were born after his death.

> *All the islands, bars, rocks, and lands under water, contiguous to the said counties of Emmet and Charlevoix, and within the State of Michigan, not heretofore, by any legislative enactment, included within the body of any county in said State, together with so much of range 4 west, as was heretofore included in Cheboygan County, are annexed to said county of Emmet, and shall for all purposes be deemed and taken to be within and a part of said county.*[10]

Strang also introduced other acts of legislation which were passed: An act to organize the county of Cheboygan; another to organize the township of Drummond; one to complete the organization of Grand Traverse County; and another to complete the judicial organization of the state.[11]

Some mainlanders did not agree with Strang's legislative results in the organizing of Emmet County. In his newspaper, the *Northern Islander*, Strang wrote on November 2, 1854, that an effort was underway to divide mainland Emmet County, assigning half of it to Cheboygan County and the other half to Grand Traverse. Strang wanted to prevent this, if possible, by lining up opposition votes from the mainland Mormons. He wrote in the *Northern Islander* that "Before another election our settlements on that east shore will be large enough to control the politics of both Cheboygan and Grand Traverse. And having the power under such circumstances we should not fail to use it."[12]

In addition to Strang having Mormon settlers on the mainland and on the Beaver and Fox Islands, he had plans for the Manitous and for the small island in Grand Traverse Bay, near Traverse City. Of the latter he said, "There is a beautiful island, large enough for settlement, near the peninsula of Grand Traverse."[13]

Sentiments against the Mormons grew as their people settled in surrounding areas and their political power increased. Accusations were made by both sides against the other, and it's impossible to separate truth from overly zealous attacks as one reads written accounts of confrontations between Mormons and gentiles. Each accused the other of plundering and trying to force out others from Beaver and the surrounding islands and mainland ports.

In 1855 two gentile members of Emmet County carried through on a plan to separate Emmet County from the islands. John S. Dixon and Theodore Wendall went to Lansing and successfully secured the passage of an act reorganizing the county and excluding the Beaver and Fox Islands and other territory which had been attached to Emmet county.[14] Some writers mistakenly give Strang credit for introducing this act.

Strang was now in his second term of office when, on February 12, 1855, Manitou County was organized as a result of the breaking away from Emmet County. The new county of Manitou was made up of the Beaver Islands group, and included North and South Fox Islands and North and South Manitou Islands.[15] South Fox became the township of *Patmos* and North Fox was called *Paros*. The county seat was at St. James, Beaver Island.

Meanwhile, when the lands of Beaver Island had been put up by the government for purchase in 1848, Strang charged that the gentiles received notice of the sale first. There were many fishermen on the island for the new fishing season; and they marked the best quarter, according to Strang, before the Mormons knew the land was being offered. Claims were staked where Mormons had already built houses and had crops growing. The Mormons could do nothing but abandon the results of their hard work and turn their farms over to the gentiles.[16]

However, some historians argue that since the land was unavailable for public sale before surveying was done, the government had allowed that people living as squatters before that time had first claim to the land where they were living, at minimum price, without competitive bidding. They argue that Strang's charges are invalid.[17]

Discrepancies also occur in the accounts of plundering. Strang reports that his people were peace lovers and had migrated to Beaver Island to find freedom from persecution. They were robbed, he claimed, and their fishing nets destroyed, their boats stolen.

The gentiles accused the Mormons of the same crimes, both on Beaver and the adjoining islands and the mainland. Strang refuted these claims, saying that the gentile fishermen often stole from each other and arranged the evidence to indict the Mormons. The gentiles would give accounts to the press of treason, trespassing on public lands, stealing timber, counterfeiting, mail robbing and other misdeeds; and the stories were printed as truth, without any rebuttal from the accused.*

Strang won the approval of the Legislature as evidenced by this account in the *Detroit Advertiser*, February 10, 1853:

> *Mr. Strang's course as a member of the present Legislature, has disarmed much of the prejudice which had previously surrounded him. Whatever may be said or thought of the peculiar sect of which he is the local head, throughout this session he has conducted himself with a degree of decorum and propriety which have been equaled by his industry, sagacity, good temper, apparent regard for the true interests of the people, and the obligations of his official oath.*[18]

The people of Mackinac were unhappy with Strang's success as a legislator, and after a stop at Mackinac on his way to Buffalo, Strang wrote of an attempt by the people to kidnap him with the prospect of "Serving him as they did old Jo."[19] This was probably a reference to the murder of Joseph Smith.

In the end it was not the avowed enemies of Strang that removed him from power, however. On June 16, 1856, he was shot on Beaver Island while approaching the docked gunboat *U.S.S. Michigan*. He died on July 9 after being taken to Voree, Wisconsin. His assassins were in cooperation with Dr. Hezekiah McCullough, Dr. Atkyn and possibly Captain McBlair of the *Michigan*. Thomas Bedford was a fisherman who had married a Mormon and probably went along with the religion for the sake of the marriage. He was outspoken and antagonistic toward Strang, who had given him a public whipping after Bedford was caught in the act of adultery. Alexander Wentworth was, at first, a follower of Strang; but when Wentworth spoke out against Strang's practice and promotion of polygamy, Strang publicly shamed the young follower by revealing that Wentworth had been born of an incestuous relationship.[20] From that day forward, Wentworth was no follower of Strang. Wentworth had registered property on South Fox Island, either as part of Strang's influence over all area islands, or perhaps because of Wentworth's own separate ambitions.

* The truth about charges made against Strang and his followers is hard to judge. Most writers have made him a villainous creature. These accounts should be compared with a rebuttal such as Doyle Fitzpatrick's *The King Strang Story*.

Dr. McCullough, one of the disgruntled, was deprived by Strang of any public office because of his drinking habits in what Strang had made a dry settlement. Dr. Atkyn was a "professional visitor" to Beaver Island, and, according to Strang, a "cheap adventurer who sponged a living off the saints."[21]

The men plotted Strang's assassination, and Atkyn and McCullough waited aboard the *Michigan*, while Wentworth and Bedford fired the fatal shots. When all were safe on board, Captain McBlair told Sheriff Joshua Miller that he would take the assassins to Mackinac for trial, instead of turning them over to Miller as he should have done. The two were jailed at Mackinac for "about five minutes" and then set free as heroes.[22] Bedford, Wentworth and McCullough then returned to Beaver Island.

INSTITUTE FOR GREAT LAKES RESEARCH, BOWLING GREEN STATE UNIVERSITY
The United States Steamship Michigan *was built in Detroit and launched December 5, 1843. It was the first iron-clad warship of the United States on the Great Lakes. On June 16, 1856, Captain McBlair took Strang's assassins aboard the* Michigan *and transported them to Mackinac Island for trial, where they were quickly set free.*

So ended the reign of King Strang. Whether Strang and his followers were the corrupt ones or the targets of corruption is still debatable. Gentile accounts are generally against Strang and carry the same message as did an excerpt from the unpublished diary of The Rev. George Smith of Northport. At this time it was believed that Strang had already died.

> *June 25, 1856 —It was reported yesterday by John Maitland from N. Manitou that Strang was dead and buried — if so, one of the worst of men has taken his exit. He professed to be King of the latter day saints but was really the leader of a band of pirates of the worst kind.*

On July 1 the diary continues:

> *Troy reports Strang recovering — also that a large company have gone from Mackinaw to drive the Mormons from Beaver Island.*[23]

Strang did not recover, nor did the Mormon community of Saint James, Beaver Island. On July 5, 1856, the confused people were jeered and prodded onto vessels, being told, if they didn't leave, that their houses would be burned and their livestock killed. Reportedly, 2,600 Mormons were crowded aboard the vessels and subsequently left destitute on the docks of Chicago, Detroit, Green Bay, Milwaukee and Racine.[24] This Mormon uprooting has been labeled by historian Byron M. Cutcheon as "the most disgraceful day in Michigan history."[25]

The Mormons who were on South Fox Island abandoned their claims at this time. On August 1, 1860, census taker Philo Beers of Northport recorded the census on South Fox. After checking 21 dwellings, he concluded his report with the comment, "Good dwellings formerly occupied by Mormons, who have departed the island 'thank God'."[26] North Fox Island did still have a population in 1860 and the names appear in the previous chapter. Alexander Wentworth, James S. Douglass, and John and Minerva Pappenaw gained title to their South Fox property in 1859. We know that Wentworth was a former Mormon, and there is a good chance that he had some association with the Pappenaws. James Douglass may have been anticipating the Mormon uprooting, since his employer on St. Helena Island, Archibald Newton, was the organizer of the Mormon deportation on Beaver, and perhaps also on South Fox. Douglass quickly applied for and received a Military Bounty Land Warrant for Beaver Island property when the Mormons were ousted.

By 1890, discussions were being held on annexation of the Manitou County islands to other counties. The *Leelanau Enterprise* reported that "In speaking of the Manitou Island Project... Mr. William Gill thought the Fox Islands ought properly to belong to this (Leelanau) county, as the Fox Islanders do all their business with Northport."[27]

The islands continued to make up Manitou County until 1895, when the Fox and Manitou Islands were made part of Leelanau County, and the Beaver Island group was included with Charlevoix County. The act dividing Manitou County stated that all the books and records were to be taken to Charlevoix County and a transcript of the property records was to be delivered to Leelanau County. North and South Fox Islands are no longer Paros and Patmos townships, but are included with Northport, Omena and Gills Pier in the township of Leelanau and are part of the Thirteenth Judicial Circuit. Legal documents since 1895 have been recorded at the Leelanau County seat in Leland, Michigan.

[1] Ruth Craker, *The First Protestant Mission in the Grand Traverse Region* (1935; reprint, Mount Pleasant, Mich.: Rivercrest House, 1979), p. 50.

[2] George S. May, ed., Introduction, *Ancient and Modern Michilimackinac* (1854; reprint, Mackinac Island: W. Stewart Woodfill, 1959), p. vi.

[3] Milo M. Quaife, *The Kingdom of Saint James* (New Haven: Yale University Press, 1930), p. 141.

[4] Walter Havighurst, *Three Flags at the Straits* (Englewood Cliffs, N. J.: Prentice Hall, 1966), p. 177.

[5]Quaife, pp. 124-26.

[6] James Strang, *Book of the Law of the Lord*, Chapter 20.

[7] Strang, *Northern Islander*, 18 March, 1852, reprint.

[8] Ibid 9 Jan., 1851.

[9] "A Michigan Monarchy," in *Michigan Pioneer and Historical Collections, Vol. 18*, p. 635.

[10] "Reports of Counties," in *Michigan Pioneer and Historical Collections, Vol. 1*, pp. 162-163.

[11] Doyle Fitzpatrick, *The King Strang Story* (Lansing: National Heritage, 1970), p. 100.

[12] Strang, *Northern Islander*, 2 Nov., 1854, reprint.

[13] Strang, *Ancient and Modern Michilimackinac*, p. 87.

[14] "The History of Emmet County," in *Historic Michigan, Vol. III*, p. 73.

[15] M. L. Leach, *History of the Grand Traverse Region,* reprints from *Grand Traverse Herald*, (Traverse City, Mich,), p. 153.

[16] Strang, *Ancient and Modern Michilimackinac,* p. 41.

[17] *Michigan History, Vol. 56*, p. 89 et al.

[18] Strang, *Ancient and Modern Michilimackinac,* p. 90.

[19] Ibid, p. 73.

[20] Roger Van Noord, *King of Beaver Island* (Chicago: University of Illinois Press, 1988), p. 237.

[21] Fitzpatrick, pp. 110-111.

[22] Quaife, p. 172.

[23] Unpublished diary of The Rev. George N. Smith, June 25 & July 1, 1856.

[24] Havighurst, pp. 181-182.

[25] Robert P. Weeks, "The Kingdom of St. James and Nineteenth Century American Utopianism," in *The Journal of Beaver Island History, Vol. One,* p. 23.

[26] Philo Beers in 1860 Manitou County Census (microfilm).

[27] *Leelanau Enterprise* 18 Dec., 1890, p. 1.

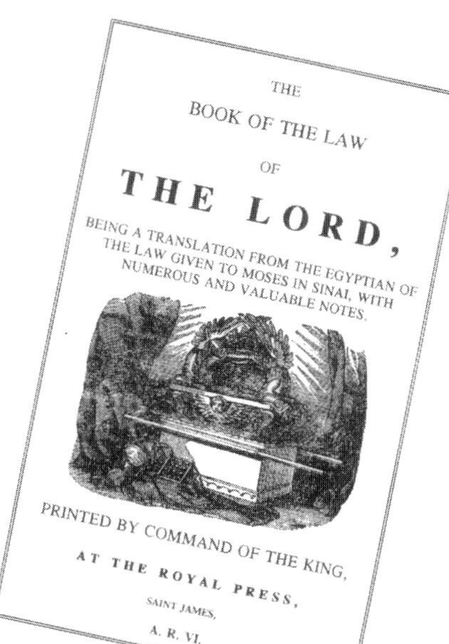
THE
BOOK OF THE LAW
OF
THE LORD,
BEING A TRANSLATION FROM THE EGYPTIAN OF THE LAW GIVEN TO MOSES IN SINAI, WITH NUMEROUS AND VALUABLE NOTES.

PRINTED BY COMMAND OF THE KING,
AT THE ROYAL PRESS,
SAINT JAMES,
A. R. VI.

James J. Strang's
Book Of The Law Of The Lord
Reprinted in 1991 by
Church Of Jesus Christ Of Latter Day Saints,
Burlington, Wisconsin.

CHAPTER XX.

CALLING OF A KING.

God is the only just and upright King over all; whosoever is not chosen of him, is a usurper, and unholy.

1. THE Lord your God hath made the earth and established it, and unto him the dominion thereof belongeth. He created man, and gave him dominion over it.[1] The nations are the workmanship of his hands; and he hath the right to rule.[2] [42 words, 179 letters.

2. He appointed Kings, and Rulers, and Judges; but man rebelled against them. He made laws, but man broke them, and trampled on them, and forgot them. [26 words, 114 letters.

3. Unto Noah gave he dominion over the earth: and to Shem after him; but the people rebelled against him, and established their own ways; and those that oppressed them were their Kings, and ruled over them in unrighteousness. [38 words, 179 letters.

4. Moses was King in Israel;[3] but the people kept not the Law of God; and, rebelling, set up a false god, and worshipped it. When God would make them Kings to rule the

1 Gen. i, 26. 2 Ex. xix, 5. Deut. x, 14. Ps. xxiv, 1. 1st Cor. x, 26, 28. 3 Deut. xxxiii, 5.

SEC. 4.] CALLING OF A KING. 169

earth, they despised his majesty, and went after other gods. [43 words, 173 letters.

5. Men have everywhere rebelled against God: nevertheless, the earth is his, and the fulness thereof. The dominion of it belongeth to him, and he conferreth it upon whomsoever he will. [30 words, 146 letters.

6. He hath chosen his servant James to be King: he hath made him his Apostle to all nations: he hath established him a Prophet, above the Kings of the earth; and appointed him King in Zion: by his own voice did he call him, and he sent his Angels unto him to ordain him. [54 words, 207 letters.

7. And the Angel of the Lord stretched forth his hand unto him, and touched his head, and put oil upon him, and said, Grace is poured upon thy lips, and God blesseth thee with the greatness of the everlasting Priesthood. He putteth might, and glory, and majesty upon thee; and in meekness, and truth, and righteousness, will he prosper thee. [60 words, 256 letters.

8. Thou shalt save his people from their enemies, when there is no arm to deliver; and shalt bring salvation, when destruction walketh in the house of thy God. Thou hast loved righteousness, and hated iniquity: therefore

22

COURTESY SALLY GREENE
Adolph Fick farm.

COURTESY JENS THOMAS
Paul Thomas farm.

PHOTO BY GRACE DICKINSON, 1983.
Robert Roe built this farmhouse in 1859. It was later owned by John Oliver Plank. Paul Thomas' wagon sits in the foreground.

ISLAND FARMING

Though fishermen were the first recorded settlers on North and South Fox Islands, they were soon joined by farmers. In fact, to say that fishermen did nothing but fish and farmers did nothing but farm would be incorrect. Many fishermen had garden plots, and many farmers spent some of their time fishing. The fish and the fruits and vegetables were placed together on the tables to make tasty meals for the families. Maple sugar and maple syrup were made by Native Americans who tapped the maple trees during the early 1900's. Many settlers also cut wood for steamer fuel, heat and cooking.

Some of the first farmers on the Foxes were Mormons who had come from Beaver Island. In the summer of 1850, James Strang was crowned a king to rule over the Mormons in the area. The greatest influence Strang had on the Fox Islands was political, as was recorded in the previous chapter. Part of this section will deal with the Mormon people themselves who lived on North and South Fox.

Strang called North Fox, *Paros*, and South Fox, *Patmos*. Of Patmos he wrote:

> *"Patmos is a mountain rising abruptly from Lake Michigan, to the height of two or three hundred feet. The summit is rolling and beautiful, and a most excellent soil. Towards the South-East the land is but moderately elevated, and exquisitely beautiful. There is the Mormon settlement. Several farms are opened, but there is room for more. No better farming land is found anywhere. There is no Harbor, but the shores are bold, and the landing good with any kind of craft....*
>
> *The island is to be laid out in farms, extending from the East to the West shore, and usually about two hundred acres in extent, and all intersected by a single road, from one end of the Island to the other, which rises to the summit by a very gentle ascent."* [1]

His description of Paros was more brief:

> *"Paros is a miniature of Patmos, though not quite equal in quality. The Mormons are just commencing a settlement upon it."* [2]

In 1851 Strang reported in his newspaper, the *Northern Islander*, that the South Fox Mormon community consisted of five men, five women and seven children.[3] There were also two families and two single men who were not members of the church. Wooding station owner Nicholas Pickard was probably one of those Strang referred to who was not a Mormon. The farms were not being developed quite as rapidly as Strang had hoped. He wrote in the *Northern Islander* in April, 1851, that although North and South Fox Islands were "well adapted to agriculture,"... "there is a lack of domestic animals and too little disposition to cultivate the soil." But Strang was hopeful, saying, "The colony gives full promise of prosperity."[4]

Nicholas Pickard supplied cordwood to the many passing steamers. The Mormon farmers are also reported to have done this and may have worked with Pickard. In addition, they made cedar staves for fish barrels. It is not known who the other non-

Mormons were. Fisherman Samuel Rice and his five young daughters were gone from South Fox by this time.

Strang wrote that he expected 12 new Mormon families would be added to the South Fox population the following spring. A young Mormon, William Chambers, took word back to Strang that the first growing season for the South Fox Mormons had given them an abundant potato harvest and corn of excellent quality, some stalks measuring 12 feet high.[5] Strang was ahead of his time in requiring his followers to be concerned about the environment. He demanded that refuse from fish cleaning be buried in garden plots. In this way, the grounds were more sanitary, and the Native American method of fertilizing crops was put into practice.

By 1854 more gentile fishermen had arrived on South Fox and so had more Mormon farmers. Strang reported an equal number of Mormons and non-Mormons. Some of these non-Mormons may have been Native Americans.

The Mormon farmers, as well as Mormon fishermen, gained notoriety on the islands and in the mainland settlement as troublemakers and robbers; and they were charged and hauled off to court over and over, although they were never convicted. Strang recorded one account of unfair charges against the South Fox Mormon farmers:

> *"Later in the fall (1851) the propeller* Illinois *went ashore on (South) Fox Island. The Captain went to Manitou for assistance, and was refused. He then went to Beaver, and asked Mr. Strang to furnish him assistance. He had been unfriendly to the Mormons, and several times treated them ill. Yet they turned out in force to save his boat, of which he was half owner. When they arrived there it was so much injured that he determined to abandon it. The Mormons refused to abandon it; saying, they would set their pumps and try the effect, whether he paid them or not. They did so, and in seven hours had her afloat. She was brought safely into Beaver Harbor, and saved.*
>
> *The settlers on Fox Island, who were an equal number of Mormons and Gentiles, took the job of saving the cargo on shares, and built a storehouse for the sole purpose of housing it; and put it up in the best possible order, and waited the Captain's arrival in the spring to divide it. This was at the back side of the Island, distant from, and out of sight of their dwellings.*
>
> *In the spring he came with the* Illinois *in the night and commenced moving the cargo, without consulting them. They accidentally discovered him in time to save part of their share. Yet he went off calling the Mormons robbers, and accusing them of plundering him, and has never shown them the slightest gratitude. Of the Gentiles who were equally concerned, he made no mention."* [6]

So it appears that the Mormon farmers on the Fox Islands experienced the same type of problems the Beaver Island Mormons encountered. When Thomas Bedford and Alexander Wentworth assassinated Strang in 1856, the Mormons on the Foxes departed.

The J. O. McNutt writings at the Clarke Historical Library in Mount Pleasant state that not long after this, Wentworth lived on Beaver Island and then moved to Minnesota.[7] Two-and-a-half years after Strang's assassination, Wentworth received his patent on some South Fox Island property. The patent had, apparently been in process as the Mormons established their farms on South Fox Island, along and inland from the eastern lowland shore.

Two other men who took out patents for South Fox Island property the same day that Wentworth did were James Douglass and John Pappenaw. Pappenaw and his wife Minerva moved to Emmet County and sold their South Fox property to Alexander Sample and Alfred Scovil, wood dealers based in Chicago. When James Douglass received his patent, he was living in Cheboygan County. After the assassination, he received bounty lands on Beaver Island, for military service. Another Mormon farm on South Fox was probably that of William Chambers, the one who had reported the successful crop to James Strang. Chambers apparently fell out of favor with Strang and was declared "apostate" about two months after Chambers had reported the good South Fox crop to Strang.[8] Alexander Wentworth ended his connection to islands when, after living a few years in Minnesota, he entered the Civil War and died a "good soldier and competent (non-commissioned) officer.[9] A conflicting report by J. O. McNutt says that Wentworth committed suicide.

Beaver Island historian, Shirley Gladdish, says that Galen Cole was a young Mormon who "became fairly important in Strang's eyes." Cole lived on Beaver Island, at Pine River (Charlevoix), and on one of the Fox Islands. He was lost on a Lake Michigan boat in 1855. If typical of other Mormons on South Fox, he would have fished and farmed.

According to Strang, there were also Mormon farms on North Fox Island. J. Wilder, or Wilbur (the record isn't clear), was the recorded owner of the northernmost part of North Fox in 1851, the same year Strang reported two families and two single men living on the north island. But, it is not likely that Wilder was one of Strang's followers or that Wilder even lived on North Fox. More about J. Wilder is found in a further chapter. The 1860 Census did show two families and two single men. Rushand and Harriet Roe had come from England and Canada. Their two children had been born in Illinois, a state from which some of the Beaver Island Mormons had come. John and Catherine Subnow were originally from Canada, but since their year-old daughter had been born in Wisconsin, they apparently had not arrived on North Fox much before 1859, and that was after the fall of Strang's Mormon kingdom. Robert Boyd was also living on North Fox in 1860, as was a small boy, John Fitz. Although no proof has been found that any of these people were Mormons, there remains a good chance that at least some of them were.

In 1862, six years after Strang's assassination, J. Haines Emery was granted land on North Fox "for the benefit of Agriculture and the Mechanic Arts." In 1868 Emery sold his property, in the middle of the island and to the western shore, to Thomas Bates and Jesse Cram, Traverse City land speculators.

When the Mormon lands were deserted on South Fox Island, Susan Zeller bought most, or all, of them through tax sale. She quickly sold them to John Oliver Plank of Chicago and Mackinac Island, just before 1900.

By the 1870 Census there were several families again living on South Fox. There were six in the Joseph Williams family. Farmer Otto Williams wasn't listed in 1870, but he did live on South Fox by at least 1872, when he married a resident of the island who had been born there—Maria Palmer.[10] Otto Williams had come from Norway before he began farming on South Fox. He disappeared from the scene a short time later, by death or by divorce, and in 1875 his former wife married John Floyd, another South Fox Islander. Floyd had stood as a witness to the earlier marriage of Otto and Maria. John and Maria (Mary Floyd) lived at their farm on South Fox for a while and, by 1880, were living on North Manitou and later on Beaver Island.

Robert and Catherine Roe owned property on both North and South Fox Islands. According to the 1870 Agricultural Census, the Roes owned about 650 acres on the two islands combined. Although most of their land was woodland or shoreland, about 70 acres was farmland. In 1870 the Roe farm was more productive than even those farms on the Manitou Islands. The Roes harvested 1,000 bushels of potatoes, slightly more than one-third of all the total potatoes raised on the Manitou and Fox Islands. They also produced one-third (500 pounds) of all the butter, two-thirds (400 bushels) of all the oats; and with six horses, six oxen, six milk cows and fifteen other cattle, the Roe farm was listed as the most financially valuable farm by far, at $5,880.[11]

This large Roe farm on South Fox Island was later abandoned and bought for tax sale by Susan Zeller. She sold it to John Oliver Plank in 1898, including the two-story house built by Roe. Plank and his wife Cora had 140 acres along South Fox's southeastern shore, containing the big farmhouse, a barn, and several outbuildings. Through the years, John Plank served as trustee for parcels owned by other property owners, on both islands. James C. Scott was one of the first South Fox property owners and probably engaged in farming and fishing. By 1907 Scott's property was in the care of John Plank. It is not known what happened to James C. Scott, but he may have been the same James Scott convicted of murder in Northport in 1855.[12] If so, that was the end of Scott's farming and fishing career.

The Planks also owned several other pieces of property on South Fox. Joining other farmers, fishermen, lumberjacks and Indian allottees on the island, Plank was appointed South Fox's first postmaster in 1905.[13] He traveled between the islands of North and South Fox and Mackinac and the City of Chicago, conducting business, while adding to his holdings tax sale properties on both North and South Fox. He awarded timber contracts on some of his island acres. On various documents, Plank's address is listed as Chicago, Ohio, Wisconsin, Mackinac Island or Pentwater, Michigan; but in December 1911, his address was given as South Fox Island.[14]

Plank's wife Cora died and in 1913 he took a second wife, Alma, who was about 30 years younger than he. Alma spent her first summer of marriage and seven or eight summers after that on South Fox. The Planks raised cattle and turkeys. The cattle grew fat off the land, without additional feed, and the turkeys grew to be the "best ever" by eating beech nuts and grasshoppers. When the cattle were ready for market, they were taken to the dock Plank had built and loaded aboard a vessel belonging to mainlander Joe Stevens.

The Planks also took domestic rabbits to South Fox, but these escaped and interbred with the wild snowshoe hares. Alma Plank planted many apple, cherry and other fruit trees and had a vegetable garden. Iris found themselves at home with wood lilies, wild roses, daisies and black-eyed Susans.

Jacob Vannetter is known mainly for being a fisherman, but he did try to bring a farm horse to the mainland from South Fox Island. Misfortune struck when Vannetter was preparing to move his family to their new farm near Omena. The *Northport Leader* reported in June, 1914, that Vannetter was bringing a horse from South Fox Island to Northport when the animal slipped off the boat and he couldn't get it back on board. Vannetter ended up cutting the rope and letting the horse drown. The newspaper recorded, "The loss strikes hard as the family had moved to their farm near Omena and the horses' services were badly needed for farm work."[15] It could be that Vannetter had purchased the horse from the Plank farm. In the first half of 1914, John O. Plank sold off his herd of cattle on South Fox, and some Northport residents, including Amos Bartlett and Isa Dame, went to the island to buy cattle from Plank.

COURTESY STELLA THOMAS
Left: Farmers Paul Thomas and Nels Ask store up wood and grow beards for winter. Right: Paul Thomas gets a "kiss" from his dog as his grandniece Louise looks on. His barn, wagon and fields appear in the background.

In about 1920 Paul Thomas also began acquiring South Fox property by purchasing tax-sale lands and parcels from individuals. He eventually owned 160 acres near the north end, where he raised cattle, allowing them to wander freely about the island. Thomas was a single man with ties in Ontario and Indiana. According to Bernice and Hildegarde Leo, who spent their childhood summers on South Fox, Thomas had "snowy-white hair and a belly laugh that could be heard from one end of the island to the other." Thomas had at least one horse that he used for riding and would stable it in the lighthouse "barn" when he did occasional work on the boatway.

Native American farmers Louis and Maggie Ance and their daughter and her husband, Enos Chippewa, had South Fox farms near Paul Thomas. Other Ance families also had small farms, as did the Raphael brothers and the Cornstalk family.

Another farmer in this area was Roger Kaley. Adolph Fick and his wife and Nels Ask had farms between the Plank land and the southeastern dunes. Sometimes Nels Ask's sister lived with him on the island farm.

In addition to their field crops and gardens, the farmers over the years raised horses, oxen, dairy cattle, hogs and poultry. The soil was good for growing, and the main crops were corn and potatoes. Just as the Mormons had recorded huge stalks of corn on South Fox, Alma Plank reported big potatoes. In a conversation with a later property owner, John Ingwersen, Mrs. Plank said that she didn't make any money selling potatoes because, as she put it, "Who wants three or four potatoes to the bushel?"[16]

Across the water, in the early 1920's, the North Fox Island Fur Farm was being developed. According to Robert Hatt's *Island Life*, the owner stated in 1922, "We already have 500 to 600 skunks on the island and they are doing fine. As everyone knows, the skunk is the most hardy and most prolific animal of the animal kingdom."[17] However, Hatt says, the company later stated that "a few" skunks had been introduced in 1920. During Hatt's investigations in 1938 no skunks were sighted.

Another South Fox farming adventure was that of two Northport natives, Magnus Fredrickson and Nels Nelson, who bought island property in 1923. Nelson later became a South Fox lighthouse keeper's assistant. Fredrickson, his cousin, owned a meat market in Northport. Their island farm was known to be in the area of the Fick farm and was probably one and the same. There they raised cattle for the meat market back on the mainland.

When Paul Thomas died in 1934, he left his South Fox property to Stella Thomas, the wife of his nephew. The Native American lands were eventually sold. John Oliver Plank's farmhouse remained until it burned in 1991.

A few traces of the farming years can still be found on South Fox, but North Fox is fully forested, except for an airstrip. A variety of apples hang from aging South Fox trees, and Paul Thomas' abandoned hay wagon sits inside a modern horse corral. Tumbled ruins and crumbling foundations give evidence of other farms, whose owners, with their dreams, have since departed.

PHOTO BY K. FIRESTONE
David V. Johnson with the first of several horses brought to Mirada Ranch.

In 1991 the first of several Tennessee Walkers were taken to South Fox Island by the island's owner, David V. Johnson. A working ranch was established, with a 10,000-square-foot stable overlooking the water on South Fox's eastern shore. The large corrals and the modern ranch house occupy land where Mormon farmers tried to establish themselves a century-and-a-half ago, only about

13 years after Michigan had become a state. The Johnson ranch is an oasis of peace, something the Mormons had hoped for, and something other island farmers did find throughout the years.

Old farm fields scattered about South Fox once again provide a harvest -- that of hay for the Mirada Ranch horses. Eggs are gathered each day to provide a hearty breakfast for the ranch hands. And some of the workers at Mirada have planted small gardens.

[1] James Strang, *Ancient and Modern Michilimackinac* (1854; reprint, Mackinac Island: W. Stewart Woodfill, 1959), pp. 85, 86.

[2] Ibid.

[3] James Strang, *Northern Islander*, 9 Jan., 1851, reprint.

[4] Ibid, 3 April, 1851.

[5] Ibid. 9 Jan., 1851.

[6] Ibid.

[7] Unpublished diary of James Oscar McNutt, 1848-1931, at Clarke Historical Library, Central Michigan University.

[8] Jerry L. Gordon, compiled records at Beaver Island Historical Museum.

[9] Roger Van Nord, *King of Beaver Island* (Chicago: University of Illinois Press, 1988), p. 270, quoting Civil War record of Alexander Wentworth.

[10] Marriage Record of Otto Williams and Maria Palmer, Leelanau County Marriage Records, Liber 1, p. 18.

[11] 1870 Michigan Agricultural Census.

[12] Rev. George Smith Diary, 1855 and *The Grand Traverse Region,* 1884, p. 52.

[13] Walter Romig, *Michigan Place Names* (Grosse Point, Mich.: Braun & Brumfield, 1976), p. 208.

[14] Leelanau County Tax Sale Liber No. 1, pp. 56 & 96.

[15] *The Northport Leader* 11 June, 1914.

[16] Letter to author from John Ingwersen, Feb., 1982.

[17] Robert Hatt, *Island Life in Lake Michigan* (Bloomfield Hills, Mich.: Cranbrook Institute of Science, 1948), p. 120.

PHOTO BY TED McCUTCHEON
This 1960 photo shows the remains of one of several cabins left by Native Americans. The cabins were built between 1900 and 1915.

NATIVE AMERICANS

Unlike the Beaver Island group, the Fox Islands are not believed to have had early Indian settlers. There are no Indian mounds or other archeological evidence of the Native Americans' existence on the Foxes before the white man came. Nevertheless, the Ottawas and Chippewas did play an important role in the history of the Fox Islands. Traveling with the French in the fur-trading canoes, they most likely did stop at the Foxes for rest and refuge on their journeys from place to place.

King Strang reported that Indians were living on South Fox during his rule (1850's), and perhaps the mingling of French and Native Americans did bring a small community to the island, since some former residents recall a small clearing on South Fox as being called *Frenchtown*. The French name of Pappenaw was registered on South Fox in 1859, but it is not certain whether either of the married couple was of Native American descent.

Chief Andrew Blackbird is reported to have brought his bride to South Fox Island for a honeymoon visit. His native name was *Me-ka-te-bi-neshi,*[1] and he was the son of an Ottawa chief. Blackbird was a government interpreter and was appointed postmaster at mainland Harbor Springs.[2] It was in Harbor Springs where he met the Robert Roe family. Roe had a wooding station, which supplied cord wood to passing steamers, and a shingle mill on South Fox in the 1860's and 70's; and when Blackbird visited the island, he and his wife were the house guests of Robert and Kate Roe.

The most common Native American name for the Fox Islands is *Wau-goosh-e-min-iss* or *Wau-goosh-e-min-issing,* which is roughly translated as "Foxes, Their Island(s)."

Early Native Americans traveled the Great Lakes in their birch-bark canoes, which were light and easily maneuvered. Waterproofed with pine pitch, these were much longer and wider than present-day canoes. Though the French and Indians traveled in these together as they carried on their fur trading, the Indians were still using this method of transportation when schooners began bringing waves of white settlers. Some of these canoes soon began to appear with small sails. The first documented Indian settlers on South Fox used what was the modern mode of transportation for that day — the Mackinaw boat.

In addition to transportation, lake travel was used for trading and fishing. Though Native Americans fished the same species as the white men did, they also sought the sturgeon — a fish their white brothers discarded as a nuisance. On a calm day when the water was glassy and the bottom could be seen, an Indian fisherman would take his canoe or Mackinaw boat to deep water in search of sturgeon lying quietly on the bottom. Twenty-five to 30-foot spears were lowered while the fishermen kept a close watch on the white quill which marked the detachable point of the spear. When the point was plunged into the fish, the handle became separated, and the fisherman held on to the line attached to the point. Both were then in for a tiring battle. If the fisherman won, he took home a huge sturgeon, usually several feet long. What couldn't be eaten for supper could be salted down for other meals.

When more Ottawa and Chippewa settlers came to South Fox Island in the early 1900's, fish was one of their main sources of food. Fishing was a way of life for them, and so was farming.

The first documented Native American settlers to South Fox, in about 1900, were the families of Bourisseau, Ance, Pabo and Cobb. The government made trust allotments to some of these people and to other Native Americans who arrived soon after, many of them from the Beaver Island area. According to Frances Densmore in *A Study of Some Michigan Indians*, published in 1949, Native Americans living on the Beaver and adjacent islands were not incorporated under the Reorganization Act. Densmore wrote that parts of both North and South Fox Islands were included in property to be granted as Indian allotment lands.[3] Although several Native American families have been identified as living on South Fox, no records have been discovered granting them land on North Fox.

The land was to be held in trust for them for a period of 25 years from the date of the allotment. But in order to show that he or she wanted control of the land, the allottee had to occupy it continuously for five of the first several years. After that the owner was free to sell the property if that was desired. (This five-year requirement was also placed upon white settlers in other parts of the United States because Europeans had been arriving, receiving property, and then returning to their native lands.) The 25-year trust agreement on the Indian properties insured that they would remain in the Indian family's name for that period of time whether or not the land was "proven" (occupied for five years). If the allottee was still living at the end of the 25 years, a patent would be issued to him or her for the land. If the allottee had died, either the legal heirs would be issued a patent or the Land Office would sell the property, with the proceeds going to their heirs.

The Bourisseau family did not apply for an allotment and may not have been able to receive one, since they were already living in the government lighthouse at the southern tip of South Fox Island. Lewis Bourisseau was the sixth keeper of the lighthouse, appointed 1891, and assisted the crews of several stranded or wrecked vessels during the number of years he was stationed at the light. More details of his work there are given in another chapter.

Lewis, born in Michigan, was half Chippewa, and his French heritage gave him the Bourisseau name. Like her husband, Susan had roots in Canada and was half Native American and half white. Her maiden name was Josephine Susan Packau. In 1900 their oldest son Louis was a fisherman, and son William was a day laborer, probably working in the logging operations. Sixteen-year-old Josephine was still at home at the lighthouse, but Gertie and Philaman were away at school in Northport. Six-year-old Frank was to become an assistant keeper at the light when he was grown.

About three miles to the north lived the Ance family, and the Cobb family was close by. These people often walked the woodland paths to visit each other and their white neighbors.

Louis Ance received allotments on the island for himself and his children on January 2, 1900. He and his wife Margaret (Maggie) had a small farm and Louis also did some fishing. He was three-quarters Indian, and Maggie was half Ottawa and half white, having come from Canada. Their oldest son Julius had died four years earlier, and daughter Lizzie was married and living on the mainland. Their second son August, and his wife Christine, lived with them on the island and helped with the farming and fishing. Also living in the house were daughter Marceline and her husband William Pabo. Because of the lack of a school, Louis and Maggie's

COURTESY DOROTHY WEBB
Grandmother Maggie Ance at her South Fox Island home, with grandchildren Julius and three others.

teenage sons, Ben and Casper, were away at the mainland school. Ten-year-old Abbie completed the island family.

Needless to say, the small log cabin was crowded with its many occupants. Marceline and William soon built their own cabin, and August and Christine also built one where they raised four children. Lizzie came to South Fox later with her husband Enos Chippewa; and when Abbey grew up and married John Andrews, these two families also had cabins nearby. By Louis and Maggie's house there was a log barn, chicken coop and ice house. Like other island residents, these people chopped down the trees for their houses and barns and fitted them together by notching the ends. Chinking for the cracks, as well as glass windows, were brought from the mainland.

The Cobb family was also there in 1900 but did not spend as many years on South Fox as did the Ance family. John and Jane Cobb *(Cobb-mo-washa)* were Ottawas and had a son James. Father and son worked as day laborers, probably for one of the logging concerns. Jane died in 1932 at mainland Omena, at age 68. Her son James died in 1941 and is buried in the Omena cemetery.

The people lived simply, with fishing and farming their mainstay. Louis and Maggie Ance's barn was filled with hay for the horses and cows, and the chickens were well tended. In the garden they grew mostly potatoes, beans and squash. The beans were canned, as were rhubarb, sand cherries and currents. Apples were peeled, cored, sliced and hung around the kitchen to dry. Sap was gathered from the maple trees and cooked down to make maple sugar and maple syrup.

Just as the Ance women worked together to preserve the food, the men often fished together. Louis had a sailboat which he used for fishing and transportation. He built a dock by constructing an underwater fence and then filling it with rocks. He soon had a gasoline-powered boat with a small skiff aboard, and he did deep-water fishing with the help of his sons and sons-in-law. The men cut ice from the Big Lake in the wintertime and stored it in the ice house at Louis' homestead. This helped preserve some of the fish, while other catches were salted and taken to markets in Suttons Bay and Northport.

Louis and Maggie complied with the five-year residency and received a patent for their land in 1908. Unfortunately, Louis Ance fell off his sailboat and drowned near Suttons Bay five years later. He is buried in the village of Lake Leelanau. Maggie Ance died in 1921 at Northport and is buried there. Before their years together ended, however, their children made their own way into the history of the South Fox Island settlers.

COURTESY DOROTHY WEBB Left: August and Christine (Raphael) Ance bought property on the mainland as soon as their Fox Island allotment was "proven" in 1908. Right, Josephine Chippewa and Marceline Ance as adults, living on the mainland.

Their son August was 24 when he received his allotment in 1900, the same time as his parents. His land was also proven in 1908. He was married to Christine Raphael, whose family also received allotments on South Fox. August helped his father fish, and Christine was kept busy caring for their children and tending the garden. After their land had been proven, this family moved to the Bingham area of Leelanau County, along with their four children. Six more children were born there, and one of them, Louis, later spent some time working at South Fox Island. Christine Ance died in 1951 and August in 1953.

Louis and Maggie Ance's daughter Marceline was 23 when the family moved to the island. She was married to William Pabo. Clara Pabo was William's daughter by a previous marriage, and William's other heirs later received payment for the sale of Clara's allotment.

Elizabeth (Lizzie) Ance Chippewa was living with her husband Enos on the mainland when her parents went to South Fox in 1900. Enos received an allotment on the island in 1902, and they moved close to the rest of the Ance family there. Enos was a fish dealer, and his wife joined the other Ance women in gardening, doing farm chores and raising the children. John,

Dorothy and Josephine were born to Lizzie and Enos. Enos outlived all of his family and spent about 16 years on South Fox Island. His land was proven in 1907.

When Louis and Maggie Ance's daughter Abbie grew up, she married John Andrews, who was an Ottawa born on High Island, part of the Beaver Island group. They lived on South Fox, where their sons, Henry and Raymond, were born. Abbie was a fine seamstress and had a treadle sewing machine at her island home. She made clothing for her family and was also hired by other island residents to make dresses and shirts for them. As late as 1918, John Andrews was working as a fish dealer between South Fox and the mainland.

COURTESY DOROTHY WEBB In 1906 Benjamin Ance was killed in a logging accident at age 23 and was buried in the small Indian cemetery near the property. His wife Jeanette returned to her people on High Island. Their son Julius was left in the care of his grandparents, Louis and Maggie Ance, and daughter Emaline lived with her mother.

Louis and Maggie Ance's children and grandchildren made up a small community all by themselves. There were happy days of large catches of fish, quiet farm life, afternoons on the beach and evenings of father Louis playing his homemade fiddle. But there were also times of sadness. Their oldest son Julius had died of tuberculosis four years before they went to South Fox, and their 16-year-old son Casper died early in 1900.

Another son, Benjamin, was killed in a logging accident on the island in 1906 at age 23. Ben was buried in a small cemetery near the Ance settlement; and his wife, the former Jeanette Oliver, soon returned to her people on High Island, taking her daughter Emaline with her. Jeanette was a half sister to John Andrews, who married Abbie Ance. Ben and Jeanette's son, Julius Benjamin Ance, was only three years old when his father died, and his mother left him in the care of his grandparents, Louis and Maggie Ance, when she went to High Island. Jeanette later married Jonas McSawby in Charlevoix. She and her children inherited South Fox Island property alloted to her deceased, firstborn son, Oliver Benjamin Ance, who is probably buried near his father on South Fox.

The Native American and white population of South Fox Island reached its peak just before the 1920's, numbering about 60. Several people were farming and fishing, and the Leo shingle mill was going full speed. John Plank was trying to turn the island into a resort area, and some of his friends were spending summers on the island. Of course, the lighthouse quarters were occupied by the four keepers and their families.

The Raphael brothers had allotments and worked in the mills, first for the Leos and then for the Zapf Fruit Packaging Company. Joseph, Ambrose, Mitchell and Peter were the sons of Raphael and Rose Gagaishe. Their sister Christine was married to August Ance. The Gagaishe name had several other spellings *(Gogogashee, Gahgohzoshe, Gagegagshoe)* and meant "crow" in the Native American language. Rose didn't like the name, and the family began using her husband's given name, Raphael, as their surname.

This group of Fox Island residents lived on Indian allotments in the early 1900's. Left to right are: Back row; Lizzie Ance Chippewa (wife of Enos), unidentified woman, Lucy Chippewa Simon, unidentified man, John Andrews (husband of Abbie Ance). Middle row; Rose Chippewa Raphael (wife of Joseph), Helen Blackman Ance (wife of William), Susan Miller (a visitor who did not live on the island), Enos Chippewa. Front row: Josephine and John Chippewa (children of Lizzie and Enos).

Joseph Raphael worked at several lumber mills on the mainland and also for a time at the mills on South Fox. During his time on the island, he sometimes visited the lighthouse residents. In the parlor at Assistant Keeper William Green's quarters, Joe enjoyed playing Mrs. Green's pump organ. The Green's daughter Zella recalled that Joe played the organ so hard it would wobble. The Raphaels enjoyed music and often held square dances at their log cabin near the northern tip of the island.

Apparently, Rose was a popular name for women at that time. The Raphael brothers' mother was named Rose. Peter married Rose Anthony McKinney and Joseph married Rose Chippewa. Peter and a previous wife, Hattie Pewash Raphael, had a son Benjamin, who died and was buried on South Fox in June, 1913, at age four.

Ambrose was the first of the brothers to leave South Fox. Needing more adventure, he entered the merchant marines. He never returned to the island nor to Leelanau County. When he died, while working in Cleveland, there was no money to bring his body home, and he is buried there. His son Enos was adopted by Tom Kingbird.

Mitchell Raphael worked as a sawyer in Leo's South Fox mill, and later worked on the island for the Zapf Fruit Packaging Company. His knowledge of wood came in handy when his wooden leg needed replacing; he made his own. While Mitchell (called Mike) lived in the men's quarters at the lumber camp, his family was back on the mainland.

Peter Raphael was mainly a farmer. He raised cattle and had a big garden and took care of the horses for the Zapf Fruit Packaging Company. Peter married Rose Anthony McKinney who had two daughters by a previous marriage. Peter and Rose's son Joseph was born on South Fox in 1916. It seemed a good life for Peter, even though an accident in the mill had taken some of his fingers, and an old injury caused him to walk with a limp. But the solitude

COURTESY EDITH ANCE
Peter and Rose Raphael lived on their farm near the South Fox Island dune.

of island living was no guarantee against tragedy. Peter's wife died three years after giving birth to their son. After that, Peter and little Joseph moved often between South Fox Island and the mainland villages of Shingleton, Harbor Springs and Peshawbestown, wherever there was work to be found in the mills.

There were property allotments made to other families, also, just after 1900. The Chippewa family was one of these. In 1903 Samuel Chippewa signed up for allotments in the names of his children, Jennie, Lucile and Lozrana (also called Lorenzo, she died in 1918 at age 25, and her property was inherited by her brother and sisters). Sam and Angeline's son Enos had already registered for a South Fox homestead and lived there with his wife Lizzie.

Though Sam Chippewa's wife was named Angeline, he also had a daughter Angeline. The younger Angeline married Simon Ance, and their son William inherited and lived for a short time on an allotment at the northern tip of South Fox Island, while he worked at the Leo shingle mill.

Daniel Cornstalk, then living in Northport, took out an allotment for his minor child Alex in 1903, and this was proven in 1908. The Cornstalk farm was near the Ance family settlement, just a little north of the middle of the island. Sometimes this name was spelled *Comstock*. The name seems to have originated on Garden Island where Native Americans raised fields of corn and squash. According to Keewaydinoquay in *The Journal of Beaver Island History, Volume Two*, the Garden Island natives were called Cornshocks, to distinguish them from Native Americans of other islands.[4] As an adult, Alex Cornstalk lived on High Island and fished along the Beaver chain in his boat *Stella*.[5] As late as 1958, Alex Cornstalk was living on Beaver Island.

William *(Shaw-we-ben-saey)* Southbird received an allotment near the northern tip of the island, about 25 acres. However, he died in Suttons Bay in 1906 as a young man, and his father Paynick Shaw-we-ben-saey claimed his South Fox property.

For various reasons the Native American people left South Fox Island, just as the white people did. The Cobb family moved to Northport in the early 1900's. Sam Bird had received an allotment just after 1900, but in 1911 informed the Office of Indian Affairs that he wanted to relinquish his land. He did not state a reason for this move and was encouraged not to go through with it. Joseph Bird retained land not far from Sam. Isaac McAndrews, apparently a relative, later claimed some of this land.

August Ance bought property in Bingham, Leelanau County, where he moved the same year he proved his South Fox property. At least his property on the island was securely in his control, as was the property of other allottees who complied with the five-year residency. Fred Ance, son of August, bartered his 40 acres on the island to pay for haircuts from a Suttons Bay barber. Most of the Ance property was kept for many years after the family's departure from South Fox. August Ance's son Louis spent some years there in the late 1920's and was one of the last Native Americans to reside on the island. Those who had proven their land were free to sell the property if they wished. As the years went by, many of the Ance family members expressed a desire to sell the land and waited for buyers. August Ance sold his deceased father Louis' property to Leo Brothers' mill. Leos also bought the properties of Peter Raphael and Sam Bird.

Other families who had not completed their five-year residency still had property in their names but had lost control over it. In 1945 Mitchell Raphael and other council members in the Peshawbestown settlement on the mainland tried to work out a plan whereby the Native Americans would receive back control of this South Fox land. They were unsuccessful, however, and in 1953 the land office advertised for bids on about 700 acres of the island. The office appraised the property at $16,628. Alex Cornstalk, the only living original allottee, was free to sell his own property and transferred a deed. In cases where there was a multiple ownership through inheritance, a patent in fee was issued to the purchaser by the government.

The Bureau of Land Management thought the land should be sold because on most properties "there has not been an Indian residing for the past forty years. The land is only valuable for the timber that it has and it is believed that the land should be sold in order to avoid future heirship complications."[6]

There was only one reply to the advertising of this land. In 1954 Sterling Nickerson and his sons, all of Kingsley, Michigan, bought the property for about $1,400 above the appraised value. This money was paid to the Great Lakes Consolidated Agency in Ashland, Wisconsin, and the agency subsequently divided it among over 40 heirs of the original Native American allottees. Those of the Ance family who had maintained ownership made a private sale of their South Fox Island property to the Nickersons.

PHOTO BY TED McCUTCHEON, 1960 Ivan Miller, left, and Elijah Wanegeshik on South Fox Island during their years of employment at the Nickerson lumber camp.

This ended the Indian ownership of lands on South Fox. However, it did not end their involvement. When the Nickerson sawmill was put into operation in the fall of 1954, many Native American men began coming to work in the lumber camp. For about ten years, they walked the same trails their brothers had walked. Several years later, in 1985, Archie Miller was quoted by Kathleen Stocking in *Traverse, the Magazine* on his feeling for islands, especially for South Fox, "Seems like you always have what you need on the island. You don't crave anything. Seems like on the mainland, there's always something you want. Gotta get in your car. Gotta go get something all the time. I'd be at peace out there. I wouldn't know what was happening on the mainland. I'd be just as happy not to know."[7]

It is peaceful on South Fox. And only the remains of several log cabins, crowded by saplings and underbrush, provide evidence of the earlier Indian community — a community which played a large part in the history of South Fox Island.

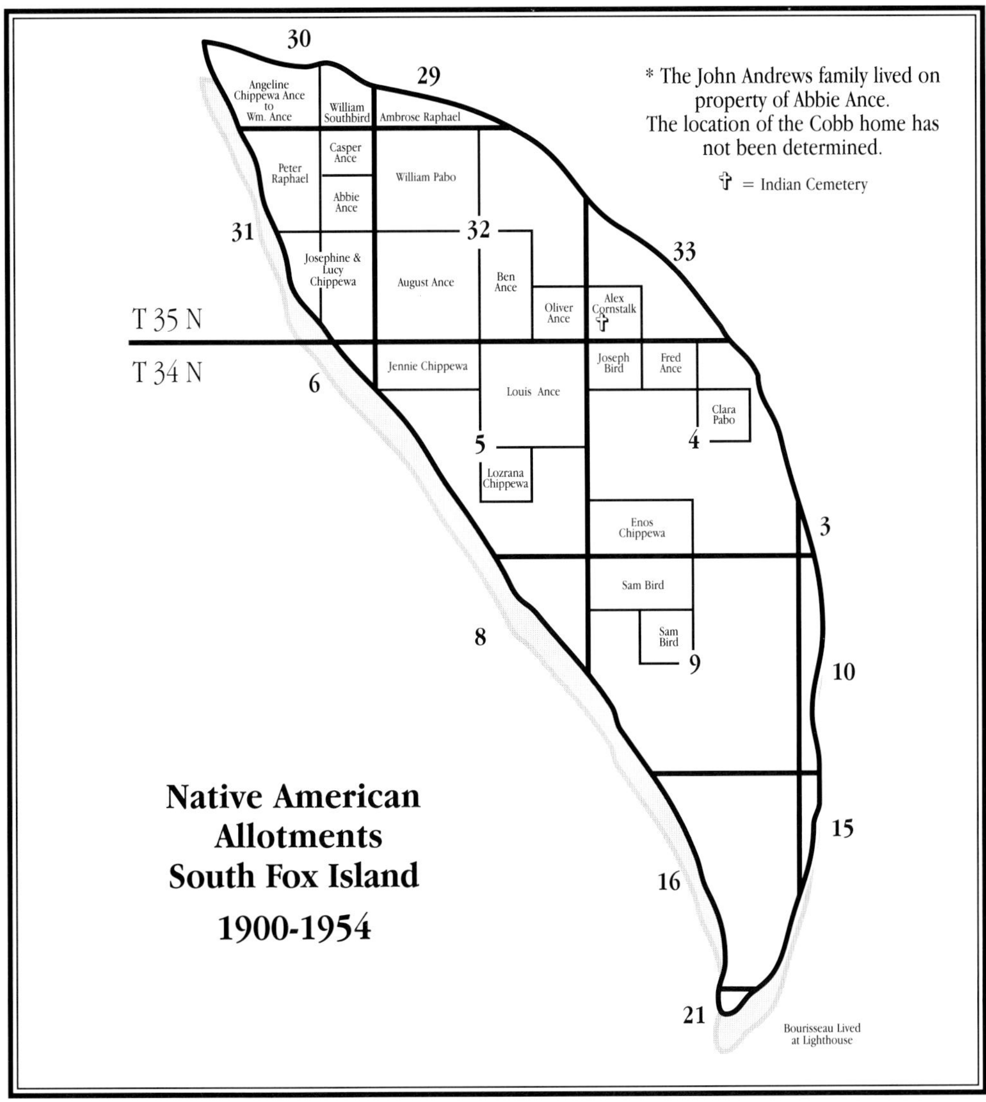

[1] Ruth Craker, *The First Protestant Mission In the Grand Traverse Region* (1935; reprint, Mount Pleasant, Mich.: Rivercrest House, 1979), p. 23.

[2] Ibid, p. 24.

[3] Frances Densmore, *A Study of Some Michigan Indians* (Ann Arbor: University of Michigan Press, 1949), pp. 1 and 35.

[4] Keewaydinoquay, in "Miniss Kitigan," *The Journal of Beaver Island History, Volume Two* (St. James, Mich.: Beaver Island Historical Society, 1980), p. 29.

[5] John V. Runberg, in "Boat Building and Builders on the Islands," *The Journal of Beaver Island History, Volume Three* (St. James, Mich:. Beaver Island Historical Society, 1988), p. 157.

[6] Letter from E. J. Riley of the Great Lakes Field Office, Bureau of Land Management, to K. W. Dixon, Acting Area Director; 1953.

[7] Kathleen Stocking, "A visit to Archie's Islands," *Traverse, the Magazine*, August, 1985.

(Top) COURTESY DOUGLAS McCORMICK
The 1934 tower and 1867 lighthouse are both visible from the pier, and "Old 63" is in front of the boat house.
(Bottom) COURTESY LAVERNE SWENSON
The Bourisseau children play on the pier, before the 1934 tower is erected.

MARITIME MEMORIES

Native Americans had braved the unpredictable waters of Lake Michigan long before New World explorers arrived. Their birch-bark canoes became the pattern for the French trading canoes. Loaded with furs and other goods, the 30- to 40-foot French boats were paddled between the islands and their mainland posts.

The era of sailing ships on the Great Lakes began with the appearance of La Salle's *Griffin* in 1679. Square-riggers and two- and three-masted schooners soon became the mode of travel. By 1850, schooners made up 80 percent of all sailing vessels.[1] The steamers arrived in the early 1850's, bringing side-wheelers, paddle-wheelers and propeller steamers. These carried settlers and freight between the big cities and smaller ports. According to Lawrence and Lucille Wakefield in *Sail & Rail*, by 1860 there were 139 side-wheel steamers, 197 propellers and 1,112 sailing vessels on the Great Lakes.[2] Many traveled through the Manitou Passage, also called *the channel*, stopping at various islands to pick up cordwood and to board and drop off passengers.

During this time, the Mackinaw boat was the favored vessel of fishermen and local travelers. The most common Mackinaw measured 26 feet and had a 7 1/2-foot beam. Two masts of about equal height rose behind a long bowsprit holding a single jib. The Mackinaw was easy to beach because of its rather flat bottom, and this was an advantage in a time when there were few harbors and docks. The Mackinaw was the prevalent boat of fishermen on the Foxes and other islands up until about 1920.[3]

The hidden rocks and sandy shoals of the channel east of the Beaver Island archipelago have brought disaster to many a vessel. Though neither of the Fox Islands has a natural harbor like the Manitou or Beaver Islands, the holding ground around them provided some shelter from the winds. Ships were often spoken of as "a-laying-to" behind the Foxes.

SHIPWRECKS OF NORTH FOX ISLAND

The Great Lakes hold many sunken ships, some with gold and silver, some with bones of seamen. Although numerous vanished vessels will never be found, the water-logged skeletons of others can be seen from the air or on beaches where they have washed ashore. The waters around North Fox Island have swallowed more than one vessel.

In 1855 the schooner *Crescent City* was wrecked off North Fox.[4] And the 174-foot, three-masted schooner *Frank Perew* was driven ashore on North Fox in October, 1873. Although the captain and crew were taken aboard another vessel, the *Perew* sat there, lodged in the shallows, throughout the rest of the fall season and then was surrounded by shoreline ice until spring. In June the wrecking tug *Magnet* freed the *Frank Perew* and took the schooner to Detroit for repairs. The *Perew* remained in service until the end of 1891, when it foundered off Whitefish Point and six of the seven crew members were lost.

West of the North Fox dune lies a long underwater ridge of boulders. On this reef the three-masted schooner *Sunnyside* lies after being wrecked in 1883. The twenty-year-old vessel was 164 feet long and weighed 563 tons, unloaded.[5] According to the *History of The Great Lakes, Volume 2*, first published in 1899, Captain Robert Kerr of Cleveland bought the bark *Sunnyside* about 1881.[6] The vessel left Escanaba bound for Cleveland with a load of iron ore on August 19, 1883. It was being towed by the steamer *William H. Barnum*, accompanied by the *Samuel H. Foster* and the *Dewey*. That night during a heavy Lake Michigan squall, Kerr's *Sunnyside* broke free from the *Barnum's* tow line and struck the *S. H. Foster*. The bow of the *Sunnyside* was stove in, but some of the *Foster's* crew jumped to the *Sunnyside's* deck, fearing that the *Foster* would sink. They soon jumped from the *Sunnyside* back to the *Foster*, and Captain Kerr's wife, a *Sunnyside* passenger, was lowered into a life boat and taken aboard the *Dewey*. Captain Kerr, his son Robert W. Kerr, and the rest of the crew abandoned ship and were taken aboard one of the other vessels. They could only watch through the darkness for a glimpse of the *Sunnyside* as the vessel filled with water, rolled over and sank. In the captain's thirty-two year experience as master, it was his only loss of a vessel. The *S. H. Foster* fared better and remained in service until late in 1906.

INSTITUTE FOR GREAT LAKES RESEARCH, BOWLING GREEN STATE UNIVERSITY.
The Samuel H. Foster *collided with the* Sunnyside *in 1883.*

INSTITUTE FOR GREAT LAKES RESEARCH, BOWLING GREEN STATE UNIVERSITY.
Illustration of the Sunnyside *by Loudon Wilson.*

The scow-schooner *Minuet* was wrecked near North Fox in October, 1886. Captain William Smith was hauling a load of lumber, but the vessel never reached its destination. The horrible tragedy was recorded in *The Detroit Free Press*, October 17, 1886, and is partially recounted as follows:[8]

> ...*The* Minuet *had a crew of seven and a female cook named Mary Poule, who belonged in Charlevoix. All hands were forced to take to the rigging by the heavy seas washing over the schooner, which was beached at a point hidden from the sight of the few people living in the neighborhood. Shortly after dark the cook cried out that she was unable to hold on any longer. One of the men was just about to go to her assistance when the unfortunate woman, uttering a terrible scream, let go her hold and fell into the boiling surge. A moment later the survivors thought they heard a faint cry, but nothing more was seen of the cook. Some time after, the survivors clinging to one of the masts saw another form go over the side with a frightful crash. Drenched with spray and shivering with cold the men held on desperately till morning broke, when it was discovered that one of their number, known as Scrubby, but believed to hail from Milwaukee, had disappeared, having fallen from the rigging during the night. The gale moderated in the morning and the half-dead survivors were finally rescued by a boat and taken to Glenhaven....*

The 821-ton schooner *Helena,* of Cleveland, and the 365-ton steamer *Hubble,* of Chicago, went down near North Fox in 1888; but little is known of these events.[9]

There were no lighthouses or lifesaving stations on North Fox Island, so men and women on vessels in distress near this island had little hope of rescue, except by other ships whose crews may have happened to sight the foundering craft.

Frank Kalchik and his crew had at least one frightening experience about 1960, as they left North Fox when a storm came up. It was time for a trip to their base of operations on the Leelanau County mainland, while working on construction at North Fox. Somewhere between the islands of North and South Fox, it seemed they would not make it to the mainland and rode with the waves to South Fox. Once alongside the big lumber dock at the Nickerson camp, it was nearly impossible to tie up. With each rolling wave, the *Ace* would rise above the dock planking and then ride again several feet below the dock. Each rope tied to a piling would break with the stress, and the *Ace* could not be secured. Kalchik's employee, Clayton Thomas, jumped to the dock and ran up the small bank to the sawmill, where he found heavier rope. Back at the dock the rope was tied to a lose piling which had a little "give" to it. Finally the rope held, and Kalchik's crew was able to walk on dry land.

THE SOUTH FOX LIGHTHOUSE AND ITS KEEPERS

With the increase of lake travel and the subsequent disasters, lighthouses began to appear on mainland points and on the islands of the Great Lakes. In 1867 a federal appropriation of $18,000 was made for a light at South Fox Island.[10] Part of the southern tip of the island was already owned by the federal government, and the rest was purchased from the State of Michigan for $421.86 that same year, bringing the total acreage to about 115. In the summer of 1867, construction was begun. The tower with attached keeper's dwelling was made of yellow Milwaukee brick, which was laid 13 inches thick. The square tower rose 45 feet and was a little over nine feet in diameter at its cylindrical top.[11] A keeper had to climb 48 steps in order to tend the lamp.

On the night of November 1, 1867, the light cast its first red beam across the channel. The lens enclosing the lamp made four-minute revolutions, gliding across 20 metal ball bearings at its base, and an oil lamp lighted the 10 ruby-red, 36-inch-high panels. Every two minutes "bullseye" panels on opposite sides of the lens varied the steady beam by making a bright flash. This flashing code indicated to the passing mariner which lighthouse he was near, so that he could better figure his location.

PHOTO BY CHARLES STAFFORD
Forty-eight steps lead to the top of the South Fox Island lighthouse, built in 1867.

The first lighthouse keeper on South Fox was Henry J. Roe, who served from September 14, 1867, until the middle of 1871.[12] Although they may have all been related, this Henry Roe should not be confused with the son of Robert Roe, who was yet to be born, nor with Henry Roe who had lived on North Fox as a child, ten years earlier. There were at least three Henry Roes on the Fox Islands by 1870. The light keeper Henry Roe and his wife Marie and two young daughters, Florence and Mabel, had occupied a house near the lighthouse before accepting the South Fox Island post in 1867. In 1869, ninety-seven ships were lost on the Great Lakes during a four-day hurricane.[13] In 1871 the steamer *Diamond* burned and sank between South Fox and North Manitou,[14] (just as the fishing boat *Diamond* did 70 years later).

Keeper Henry Roe, no doubt, kept a watchful eye for troubled seamen, as each of his successors would do. Roe and his family later moved to Northport, as did one of his assistants, Robert DeGrolier (DeGolier, DeGolia). The next keeper was William Bruin, who served until 1876.[15] One of the shipwrecks recorded off South Fox Island during Bruin's tenure was the burning of the 40-ton, propeller tug *U. S. Grant* in 1875.[16]

The work of these men was inspected quarterly by the U. S. Lighthouse Service. The inspectors would arrive unannounced, ready to hand out reprimands for such minor infractions as a messy kitchen or fingerprints on the brass. Such things could even be cause for a formal complaint against a keeper. In addition to seeing that the dishes were washed and the brass polished, the keepers had the daily duties of cleaning and polishing the lens, cleaning and filling the oil lamp, dusting the framework of the apparatus and trimming the wicks. By ten in the morning the light had to be ready for the next lighting. A linen curtain kept it clean during the day. After the daily duties were done, the keeper had to see if the buildings or grounds needed attention. For their labor, the early keepers received $150 per quarter.[17]

Left: Keeper Willis Warner, his wife Sarah, and children Lillian and Clarence were at the lighthouse 1876-1882. Right: In later years Warner told many maritime adventures to his family. Bottom: He constructed the board fence around the lighthouse in 1880, to keep out the sand and snow drifts.

COURTESY MARION SIMONS

In June of 1876, the keeper's duties were handed over to Willis Warner[18] when he and his wife Sarah and family came from Algonac, Michigan. Warner's father had been a sea captain, and Warner himself was a marine engineer. At least three generations followed the family tradition when Willis Warner's sons also became sea captains. During Warner's years at South Fox, his son George became an assistant keeper there, replacing Robert DeGrolier.

George Warner married Elizabeth Leslie while he was employed at the lighthouse. Her brother Morris Leslie spent some seasons during the early 1880's at the light with the Warners, and the two families traveled frequently between South Fox Island and the Leslie home in Northport. The lighthouse closed up for the worst part of the winter when lake travel all but ceased. During that time, the keepers and their families often made their homes in Northport. The women and school-aged children stayed on the mainland throughout the school year.

One of Warner's summer projects for 1880 was to construct a board fence a few feet away from the outside walls of the lighthouse. High winds caused sand and snow to beat at the structure's windows and doors and to chill its interior. The boards were placed tightly together to form a five-foot-high, 320-foot-long barrier around the building. This partially solved the problem, but sometimes drifts of sand or snow managed to accumulate even higher than the fence. Though the winds caused difficulties for the land dwellers, they caused even more for the seamen.

During the 1800's large steamers and schooners were in their hey-day on the Great Lakes. The Warners experienced many exciting adventures during their years on South Fox Island. Records from the Life Saving Station of North Manitou Island list four vessels stranded off South Fox between April of 1880 and May of 1881: the steam ship *Conestoga* off the west side, April, 1880; the steam barge *Fletcher*, November, 1880; the schooner *Champion*, May, 1881; and the three-masted schooner *Monquagon*, May, 1881.[19] The wreck of the *James Platt* in November 1881 also took place during Willis Warner's years as keeper. Newspaper accounts tell of Warner's heroism in the *Fletcher*[20] and *James Platt* episodes.[21]

The steam barge *Fletcher* left Chicago on November 19, 1880, headed for Buffalo, carrying 34,500 bushels of corn. A blinding snowstorm struck, and the vessel was driven ashore at South Fox on Sunday, the 21st, at 5:30 in the morning. Island residents were apparently unaware of the plight of the *Fletcher*, probably because of the low visibility. All day Sunday the crew was tossed by the heavy seas, and attempts to get ashore were futile. The smokestack and rigging had been carried away and the rudder was unshipped. Finally, on Monday morning another attempt succeeded, and a message was taken to Keeper Willis Warner. The *Fletcher* was stranded in 10 feet of water, and although the snowstorm remained just as fierce and the seas just as heavy, Warner persisted and was successful in rescuing Captain Graves and the remaining crew members. Though the entire cargo was lost and the barge was a total wreck, there was no loss of life. Early in December the tug *Smith* was scheduled to tow the disabled *Fletcher* away, but the *Leelanau Enterprise* reported on December 16, 1880, that the *Fletcher* was "a total wreck, having gone almost entirely to pieces since she struck."[22]

The *James Platt* had been stranded on North Manitou in May, 1875, and had been abandoned at the Mackinac Straits for a time in 1874, but this 441-ton schooner, built in 1863, continued its Great Lakes service until it met its fate off South Fox in 1881. The shipping season was about to close when Captain Henry Turner tried to get in one more run. November 25, 1881, ended in disaster for the *Platt*. Thirty-five hundred barrels of salt were being transported from Bay City to Chicago when another of Michigan's infamous November snowstorms hit. After becoming stranded off the island, Captain Turner attempted to loosen a life boat, was washed overboard and drowned. While five other of the crew clung to the wreckage, the female cook was also lost overboard. The wreck was discovered two days after it happened, and Willis Warner and his assistants went to the aid of the crew. Warner swamped his boat twice in attempting to make his way to the stranded vessel. But his family tradition of struggling against the sea succeeded on the third try, and he was praised by a thankful crew for his heroic and skillful efforts in rescuing them from the same fate as their captain. When the weather calmed, the survivors were taken to Northport in one of the lighthouse boats. Two weeks later, Willis and George Warner and Morris Leslie joined their families in Northport for a well-deserved winter's leave.

As if to add a final chapter to Warner's years at South Fox, the *City of Green Bay* was driven ashore off the island in May of 1882, while carrying a load of lumber. The captain was taken to Northport, probably by the lighthouse workers, and he telegraphed the vessel's owners in Chicago. One of Warner's assistants at this time was S. Ramsdell.

Willis Warner was a skilled boat builder, and his sailboat *May Cornell* was often anchored at Northport Bay. Morris Leslie took command of the sailboat for use in the fruit

COURTESY MANITOWOC MARITIME MUSEUM
The City of Green Bay *at a mainland port.*

INSTITUTE FOR GREAT LAKES RESEARCH, BOWLING GREEN STATE UNIVERSITY
Steamer, Side-wheeler Chicago

trade when the Warners finished their term at South Fox Island. In July of 1882, Willis Warner sailed for Algonac aboard a schooner he had also built. Back in Algonac he became a steamboat engineer.

While Warner lived a long life and told many stories to his descendants, his successor was not so fortunate. William Lewis arrived at South Fox in July of 1882.[23] It appears that he came from Leelanau County, where he was shown owning property in Kasson Township in 1881.[24] Whatever memories he had of his island years died with him after he suffered a fall three years later. A Civil War grave marker behind the lighthouse, showing Post 899, may be on the grave of William Lewis. It is known that, during Lewis' years of service, the passenger steamer *Chicago* caught fire eight miles southeast of South Fox Island and was a total loss. That occurred August 24, 1882. Lewis made several repairs to the lighthouse property during his short tenure. Boatways constructed of logs were used for landings, and these were damaged almost yearly by the ice and winds. Lewis and his assistants made a new boatway and sank a crib to protect it. In subsequent years, the boatways needed seasonal repairs, and new cribs were added, some being 20 feet long and 10 feet wide

COURTESY LAVERNE SWENSON
Lewis Bourisseau and his wife Josephine Susan on the mainland, in later years.

William Lewis' successor, Joseph Fonntaine, headed the construction of some of these. Fonntaine served from July 1885, until the spring of 1891.[25] During Fonntaine's first summer on South Fox, the schooner *Jarvis Lord* went down with a load of coal, somewhere between the islands of South Fox and North Manitou.[26] Because of the distance of the wreck from the South Fox light, Fonntaine was probably unable to help the crew of the *Jarvis Lord*. And because of the distance of South Fox from the mainland, lighthouse workers were also at a disadvantage. In the spring of 1886 assistant keeper Lewis Bourisseau took a small boat to Northport to report that the island residents had been living on half rations for some time and that no mail had been delivered to South Fox for several months.

Often an assistant keeper was promoted to head light keeper. Lewis Bourisseau was an assistant to Joseph Fonntaine and succeeded him as head keeper in March of 1891.[27] He was the sixth keeper of the light and the only one known to be of Native American descent, though his son later became an assistant. Bourisseau's wife Susan and their children spent part of the time on the island with him and part of it in Northport.

During Bourisseau's second year as keeper, he laid 600 running feet of plank walks, connecting the various buildings. A few summers later he and his assistants built a brick oil storage house which could hold about 360 gallons of oil for the tower lamp. This oil house was necessary because the old lard oil fuel was replaced with kerosene, a much more flammable fuel.

On October 18, 1892, the 300-foot, steel-hulled steamer *W. A. Gilcher*, carrying 3,200 tons of coal, was lost on Lake Michigan, apparently, somewhere between South Fox and North Manitou Island.[28] It was only the second trip for the *Gilcher*, and when bodies and wreckage began washing ashore on North Manitou, the ship's fate appeared sealed.

Charles Roe, a previous resident of South Fox, found the midship spar of the *Gilcher* while sailing about twelve miles northeast of the South Fox light. Roe (also spelled Rowe) towed the spar to South Fox, where it was inspected by the lighthouse crew. Because the spar was split, it seemed evident that the *Gilcher* had broken in two before going down. A center hatch cover found later was also split across the middle. All of the 21-member crew were lost.

Lifesaving records show another mishap off South Fox at about that time. In June, 1893, the 300-ton schooner *C. A. King* collided with the *Imperial*.

COURTESY STANLEY DEFORGE
The fog signal house, with iron walls, was built in 1895.

Always trying to reduce the hazards of navigation on the lakes, in the summer of 1895, the government commissioned Charles Tilley of Northport (later of Beaver Island) to construct a steam-powered fog signal at the South Fox Light. A concrete floor was laid and two steam boilers put into place, housed in a 22-by-40-foot frame building. Because of the heat the boilers would generate, the building was covered with corrugated iron on the outside and smooth sheets of iron inside. The walls between the wooden studs were filled with sawdust and lime. This signal was first operated by Keeper Bourisseau. When fog began to appear, fires were built from coal or wood in the boilers, and about an hour later, the whistle had enough steam behind it to send out its three-second warnings. Keeper Bourisseau and his assistants put down another 115 feet of boardwalk to connect this building to the others.

Lewis Bourisseau seemed never to run out of things to do. The boathouse was rebuilt in 1897 and the water supply crib lengthened. The next year a well was dug, covered by a pumphouse, to supply water for the steam whistle. More boardwalk was laid, boatways and a new dock were built, and a derrick for lifting spars from the sailboat was built next to the boathouse. Constant repairs and updating of buildings and equipment were normal duties for all of the keepers and their assistants.

In 1892 the pay for a keeper was $580 per year, while an assistant received $420. The keeper's salary was to be used for actual salary, rations, fuel for the keeper's quarters and fuel for towers where "temperature is often such as to frost the lantern glass and prevent the light from being useful unless the tower be warmed by stoves."[29] Such pay does not seem, by modern standards, equal to the dangers and responsibilities the keepers and their assistants faced. But Bourisseau, the men who worked with him and those who followed, continued their watch of the Big Lake.

Bourisseau's assistants between 1898 and 1900 were: William Wilson, George Chamberlin, Thomas Wright, Burton Keith, Ulysses Cornell, Edward Cornell and Frederick Stebbins. During Bourisseau's years of service and those of Dame, Wilson, Green and McCormick, who followed him, there were more changes — and more mishaps.

In February 1899, the schooner *Morning Star* became stranded off the South Fox shore. After providing for their immediate safety, Keeper Bourisseau transported the four crew members to Northport aboard the lighthouse boat.[30] The 122-foot, two-masted schooner *Mars* was also stranded off the island in November, 1903, during Bourisseau's time and that of Assistant Will Green. The 31-year-old vessel was declared a total loss.

COURTESY MANITOWOC MARITIME MUSEUM
The schooner Mars *was stranded off South Fox Island in 1903.*

From 1902 through 1908, a railroad car ferry service ran between Northport and Manistique, sometimes stopping at South Fox Island to transport workers or summer residents. The lighthouse families often traveled on the ferry. In 1905 the ferry *Manistique* was locked in the ice for 30 days off South Fox. Transporting food and fuel to the crew was a major undertaking, but a necessary one, since the desertion by the crew of the four-million-dollar vessel would be disastrous to the ferry service.[31]

Also while Bourisseau was head keeper, the wreck of the 301-foot propeller *Vega* occurred. On November 28, 1905, a destructive storm sank or caused heavy damage to 30 ships on the Great Lakes.[32] As told in *The Detroit Free Press*, the twelve-year-old *Vega* sailed from Escanaba for South Chicago, carrying a load of iron ore; but this Gilchrist Transportation Company's vessel never reached its destination.[33] The violent snowstorm caused the *Vega* to break in two as it struck bottom off the east side of South Fox Island. The fore and aft parts of the vessel were separated by more than twenty feet, but the crew clung to the wreckage as the cold waves washed over them. Native American fishermen from South Fox tried to reach and rescue the vessel's nineteen crew members, but their fishing boats could not fight the angry waves. Shortly after noon, the lake calmed enough that the seamen could launch lifeboats from the broken *Vega* and make it to shore. When the storm was over, the fishermen transported the *Vega's* crew to Northport, and the vessel's captain, A. M. Williams, left for his Cleveland home. The fishermen who helped were, most likely, from the South Fox families of Ance, Cobb or Raphael; and lighthouse keeper, Lewis Bourisseau may have assisted.

INSTITUTE FOR GREAT LAKES RESEARCH, BOWLING GREEN STATE UNIVERSITY
The propeller Vega *was wrecked off South Fox in 1905.*

COURTESY LUJEAN BAKER
William P. Wilson in his keeper's uniform.

William Porter Wilson took his oath in the lighthouse service on November 9, 1895, and began working on South Fox as an assistant to Keeper Bourisseau in 1898. He moved his family into the frame keeper's assistants' quarters and set to work helping Bourisseau in lighting and caring for the lamp, standing watch, operating the steam whistle, replacing damaged cribs and other equipment and performing the various other duties required at the light. The men took turns standing watch, the first taking the dusk until midnight shift and the second tending the light from midnight until dawn. By rotating with the other assistants, each man had a regular night off. Every few hours, the keeper or assistant on duty turned the hand crank that kept the clockwork mechanism wound, so that the lens would continue its rotation. At some point, the red flashing light was converted to a white beam, and the whistle of the fog signal was changed to a low-pitched horn.

In November 1899, Wilson began working at the Grand Traverse Light at Cat Head Point. He served other terms at South Fox, one beginning in 1903, and another beginning in 1906. He served back and forth between both lights, and he and his wife Mary were at Cat Head for his last appointment. Wilson died in 1943 at age 86 and is buried in Northport.

William Franklin Green was no stranger to Lake Michigan when he took his post as third assistant to Keeper Bourisseau at the lighthouse in March of 1900. His predecessor, Frederick E. Stebbins, was promoted to second assistant and then transferred two years later. Born near Northport in 1875, Will Green had spent some of his early adult years operating a scow, carrying fruits and vegetables from the Leelanau Peninsula up the lake to Escanaba. When Green first arrived at South Fox, it was probably aboard the post's open sailboat, which was old and not very safe. A few months later this outdated craft was replaced with a new steam launch.

COURTESY SALLY GREENE
William F. Green worked for 31 years at the South Fox Island Light.

Later that year Green married Katherine Thomas, also of Northport, and she accompanied him to the island. The Greens, like other assistant families, lived in the frame quarters near the brick lighthouse where the head keeper lived. Both dwellings had five rooms each, and sometimes more than one family shared the assistants' quarters, until two smaller buildings were erected. A summer kitchen was located behind the main assistants' house.

Though the many buildings on the lighthouse grounds were constructed of a variety of materials, nearly all had red roofs. Water for these families was pumped from the lake and stored in cisterns until later wells were dug. An outdoor hand pump was used for drinking water.

Around 1910, spacious, new, red brick assistants' quarters were built next to the lighthouse, and the yellow brick of the lighthouse was painted white. Lou Comfort of Charlevoix brought a work party to the island for the construction of the new building. The assistants' quarters even had indoor plumbing, something many mainland homes didn't have.

Will Green was promoted to second assistant and then first assistant, both in 1902. Other assistants from 1900 to 1906 were Owen Gallagher, Oscar Dame, Conrad Strain, John Stibitz, Alphonso Tyres, Wallace Hall, Paul Walter, George Brown and William Conan.

Green was transferred to the Grand Traverse Light, north of Northport, in 1903, but returned to the island station again in February 1907, with his wife and small daughter,

COURTESY STANLEY DEFORGE
Taken in front of Assistant Keeper Green's frame quarters about 1909 are Assistant Edward Graves' wife, with Mrs. Bill (Kate) Green and little Zella Green.

Zella. The family soon numbered four and lived at the South Fox Light until 1919 when Green was moved to Old Mission. Two of the assistants at South Fox during this time were Edward Graves and his replacement, Frank L. Moore, the latter arriving in late 1911.

While the men had their duties, the women were also kept busy with household chores. A special challenge was that of providing food. Fresh milk was usually not available, and soil near the lighthouse wasn't suitable for a garden. Potatoes and apples were stored in the basement, along with home-canned foods prepared in Northport; and the men occasionally shot rabbits on the island. When there was enough, Adolph Fick would bring fresh vegetables from his small farm near the dunes. Bread was baked by the women, using a bit of "mothering yeast" kept from the last batch. It was a special treat when fishermen stopped in, bringing gifts of fresh fish, and also being welcome excitement for the isolated families. Sometimes, when fishermen were seen offshore lifting their nets, lighthouse residents would row out to watch and would be given part of the catch. When the weather was bad, fishermen often pulled into the boatway and visited with lighthouse families until the wind died down.

The women also worked hard to keep the homes clean, since the government inspector, Mr. Stoddard, could arrive at any time. When someone at the light spotted a vessel in the distance with a secretly placed, tell-tale flag flying, word spread fast that the inspector was arriving. Women scurried to put away out-of-place articles, and men who were out of uniform quickly dressed in their regulation duds. When the lighthouse tendern *Sumac* or *Hyacinth* pulled up to the boatway and Inspector Stoddard stepped off,

COURTESY DOUGLAS McCORMICK

The tender Hyacinth *came to the South Fox light for regular inspections and to bring supplies. The* Hyacinth *was a single-screw steamer, 165 feet in length, with a crew of twenty, including six officers. All of the tenders were named after flowers, bushes or trees.*

COURTESY DOUGLAS McCORMICK
A winter scene, showing the assistant keeper's quarters, where there were three apartments, and the South Fox Island Lighthouse, where the head keeper and his family lived.

the lighthouse residents were ready. Sometimes they were relieved to see that the distant vessel was not carrying an inspector but only the needed supplies—fuel, machine parts and other equipment. It was a cause for celebration when these materials arrived and were carted in wheelbarrows to their proper storage places. At other times vessels came from headquarters in Milwaukee, carrying building materials and supplies. Lou Comfort would travel from light to light around Lake Michigan, bringing work parties and project orders.

From March 11, 1906, to November 30, 1917, a post office was located at the Plank farm on South Fox's southeastern side. Lighthouse families received mail at the post office address when it was not delivered by lighthouse tenders. In other years, all of the island mail was delivered to the lighthouse by mail boat, and the other South Fox settlers would have to go to the southern tip of the island to receive and send mail. The mail boat came about every two weeks. In the 1950's a Coast Guard tender from Charlevoix delivered mail to the lighthouse families.

COURTESY DOUGLAS McCORMICK
Assistant Keeper, Oscar Dame

Oscar Dame of Northport served as "acting" third assistant at the light during the summer of 1902, when there was a vacancy. Beginning about 1907, he worked as an official assistant and continued until 1928 when he and his wife Ella moved on to the Grand Traverse Light. During his years at the island, the Great Storm of 1913 occurred. With the Great Storm, cyclone-force winds played havoc for 16 nightmarish hours. Ten Great Lakes ships were sunk, more than 20 others driven ashore and 235 seafarers were drowned.[34]

James McCormick served at many of the lighthouses on Lake Michigan, for a total of 34 years. He and his wife Mary and their 10 children became accustomed to moving. McCormick arrived on the island around 1915, replacing Lewis Bourisseau as head keeper, and worked at the lighthouse until 1924. He, Will Green and Oscar Dame served part of their time together, along with Nels Nelson, Ray Buttars, Emil Johnson and Llewellyn Vannetter. Vannetter, known as "Van," was the son of an earlier South Fox Island fisherman, Jacob Vannetter, and was transferred to the Cat Head station in 1921. Buttar's father was the head keeper at Cat Head (Grand Traverse Light).

When Keeper McCormick's children were grown, they recalled that assistant Nels Nelson used to play the violin to entertain his wife Augusta and the others at South Fox. He would sing as he played, and his favorite tune was "Over the Waves." These times of enjoyment were reprieve from the hard work of the keepers and their assistants.

The gratitude for the work of those who assisted seafarers in distress was expressed in the following letter written by the Swedish captain of the steamer *Ishpeming*, operating out of the Detroit River station, in 1920.[35]

Dear Sir:

I vill vrith you a feue linse to tel you vad Brav faitful and kyarfull man you have in you Servis. I kan not in vord price dem enofe. 2 Weks agaa I vas on May Way from Manistee to Cleveland vith a gaselin Boat that I boat in Manistee and hven I kom infront of Travers Laithous Stasion the Engen stopt and I kod not get it going. Mr. Johnson the Laithous keper had no Gaselin Boat saa hee kod not do eneyting for mee and I vendt on the Pondt and the 2 Laithous men vas Out in the Water up to the Nek to get hold of Mee and Mey Boat and Hvi godt Blok and takle on hem and puld hem saa fare up that hee vas resting Eisee and after 48 Hours the See and Wind vendt down and hvi godt hem turnd around and den the Laithous keper from South Fox (James McCormick) kom along and hee puld mee of and Chards Mee noting. and hven I vas reddey to live I askd Johnson how much the Bell vas and hee sade noting The ters kome in Mey Eyse I did not now vad to say saa I kan not in vords explain how much I tink of dem and I onley vich that I shudd have a Chans to do dem a fever Plece do not forget to hare in Maind Man laiks that you dodt in Serwis Deserw a god turn of der is a Chanse.

I am Yours Respectfulley

George Olsen

COURTESY DOUGLAS McCORMICK
James and Mary McCormick, soon after his retirement from lighthouse service.

McCormick and his assistants and their families spent their winters in Northport, as most of the other lighthouse employees had done.

COURTESY STANLEY DEFORGE
Albert Kalchik, from the Leo Brother's mill, is standing between two unidentified men aboard "Old 63," around 1918.

The winter of 1922-23 was an especially long one, and in May, McCormick was still waiting for the ice to break up enough for him to return to the island. He finally started out in a small boat, along with his assistants. The *Traverse City Record-Eagle* of May 10, 1923, reported that "anxious watchers peered toward the island till the first light beam came and knew that McCormick and his three assistants were safe."[36]

Those who served the Great Lakes lighthouses often risked their own lives in order to carry out their duties. During McCormick's years at the South Fox Light, the lighthouse boat, "Old 63," was taken to Milwaukee for repairs. When the vessel was put back in good shape, it was towed to South Fox by the tender *Hyacinth*. The weather became very stormy, and, about a half-mile from the lighthouse boatway, Mate Brown of the *Hyacinth* fell overboard and drowned. Trips which were not so unpleasant were made by McCormick, Nelson, Dame and Vannetter in their private, open launch, *Aida*. From this vessel they fished off South Fox Island and brought home many meals for their families.

Douglas McCormick, son of Keeper McCormick recalled that John (Cap) Roen occasionally came from Charlevoix to the lighthouse grounds to pick up scrap metal. Roen soon began the Roen Shipyard in Sturgeon Bay, Wisconsin, aided by profits from the metal salvages. McCormick also recalled farmer Paul Thomas riding his horse down from his farm north of the lighthouse, to help dredge and move stones at the lighthouse boatway.

Will Green once again served at South Fox, this time as head keeper, from 1924 until his retirement in 1940. For 40 years he was a light keeper, and 31 of them were served at South Fox. He was the last South Fox keeper to serve his entire duty under the U. S. Lighthouse Service. During this time he saw many advancements, including the changing of the light from oil burning to electric.

Some of his assistants during his last tour at South Fox were: Nels Nelson, Frank Bourisseau, (son of Lewis), Irving Carlson, Fred Leslie, Franklin Noonan, William Goudreau, and a Mr. Brotherson. Nelson was involved in a cattle-raising venture with Northporter Magnus Fredrickson during his stay on the island.

Though travel back and forth to the island could sometimes be uncomfortable, the quarters were not. The well-built, red brick house had spacious rooms with three separate apartments for the men and their families. The first assistant had the left half of the house, both upstairs and down. The building was divided in the middle with the second assistant living on the main floor of the right side and the third assistant in the apartment above. Fine, wood floors and freshly painted walls made these quarters as nice, or nicer than, many homes on the mainland. The yellow brick lighthouse building, with its roomy home attached to the winding staircase which led up to the light tower, was still the home for the head keeper and his family.

Fred Leslie, son of Morris Leslie, who visited Keeper Warner in the 1880's, began his duties at the South Fox Light in 1926 as an employee of the U. S. Lighthouse Service. Serving for 20 years, Leslie joined the Coast Guard when the lighthouse was turned over to that branch of the service in 1939. In 1940 he replaced Will Green as head keeper. Nels Nelson, Frank Bourisseau, Franklin Noonan and Pete Timmer served with him. The wives and children of the men spent summers with them on South Fox. The men stayed on the

COURTESY STANLEY DEFORGE
Left:Assistant Keeper Nels Nelson. Right: This 1932 photo shows Third Assistant Irving Carlson, First Assistant Fred Leslie, Keeper Bill (Will) Green, and Second Assistant Frank Bourisseau.

island year round during this time, but each had a monthly turn at visiting his family and picking up supplies in Northport.

The South Fox Station was modernized in 1934, and a work party arrived to help put up a new 132-foot tower which had arrived from Sapelo Island, Georgia. Ada Brown from Northport cooked for the extra hands. Her husband, Earl Brown, and son-in-law, George Clark Craker, along with Ivan Shimmell, Don McCormick, Dan Flees and Harry "Swede" Anderson were among those who came from Northport and, with the help of the other

COURTESY LAVERNE SWENSON *COURTESY STANLEY DEFORGE*

George Clark Craker of Northport helped to construct the new light tower in 1934, raising it to 132 feet high. Walkways connected the lighthouse to the paint shop (right), past the new tower, and to the fog signal house.

lighthouse employees, poured nine feet of concrete into holes they had dug, making supports for the tower's new foundation. After chipping paint from the tower sections, they erected them, using identification numbers as a guide. One hundred and five steps circled to the top of the tower. A diesel engine was put into operation for generating electricity for the new 160,000 candlepower light,[37] and compressed air operated the fog horn. The original light and its equipment were still maintained in just as strict a manner, and the 1867 structure kept its vigil as a back-up for the new tower.

The South Fox Island Light was known as one of the loneliest on Lake Michigan. Some men who applied for lighthouse service did not accept their appointments to South Fox, because they wanted to be nearer to civilization. Leslie said that, with the remodeling, the Fox Island Light had "all modern conveniences except neighbors."[38] The Zapf sawmill on the island had closed down, and the farmers had all gone by the time Leslie had first arrived. The isolation was combated by keeping the outpost in top shape. Leslie made so many improvements that the Coast Guard inspectors rated it one of the best kept and most efficient in the Cleveland District. When there just wasn't anything to do, whittling knives were taken from pockets, and assistants made patterns of wood shavings in the white beach sand.

There was the occasional excitement of a vessel in distress to keep the employees busy. Though high winds were the biggest danger to Great Lakes travelers, heavy fog could be almost as hazardous. Leslie recalled a barge being stranded off the island after it came too close to shore during a heavy fog. "The fog was so dense, that from our pier, we could see no part of the ship, though it was only a few hundred yards out," [39] he said. After Leslie rowed out to the barge and went aboard, the captain told him that the fog was so dense it had made the fog signal sound farther away; and doubting his compass, he had changed course and hit the rocks. The barge was carrying 7,000 tons of hard coal. Two Coast Guard lifeboats and a cutter soon arrived, followed by a tug and a freighter. Enough coal was taken off to float the barge off the rocks, and then it was towed away by the tug.

PHOTO BY TED McCUTCHEON
The South Fox Island Light, at the southern tip of the island, operated from 1867 to 1968.

Experience was no guarantee that a seaman could win out over the many hazards of the lakes. At least two men of experience lost their lives off South Fox during the 1940's. Unfortunately, both of these accidents occurred too far out to be within range of help from Leslie and his assistants. One of these men was William Carlson, whose story is recorded in Chapter 2. The other was Captain Jack Oling of the *Badger State*. Oling sailed his 50-foot, diesel-powered tug out of Thunder Bay in Lake Huron and went through the Mackinac Straits, heading for Chicago. But he hit a Lake Michigan storm. After being damaged by heavy seas, the tug was being towed to the port of Cal-Cite, Michigan, by the steamer *Carl D. Bradley*. The weather was so stormy that it was impossible to transfer Oling and his crew to the *Bradley*, so a tow line was shot and fastened to the *Badger State*. When the tug suddenly started to sink three miles off South Fox, its occupants jumped overboard. The engineer and deck hand were rescued; but Oling, who had been a sailor for 30 years, could not be found. His body was later recovered. Ironically, in the late 1950's, searchers visited North and South Fox Islands when the *Bradley* was also lost.

Life at the lonely outpost of South Fox continued. Though days were easier than they had been when the lighthouse opened in 1867, there was still much to do. The electric generator provided electricity, but the tasks remained of getting the lenses cleaned, brass polished, quarters painted, machinery tuned and yards tended. The 25-foot boat also had to be kept in good repair.

Assistant keeper Nels Nelson was transferred to the Point Betsie station in Frankfort in 1931, and Fred Leslie went to the Grand Traverse Light in 1946. Mr. Kruell took over as head keeper, briefly. Pete Timmer was promoted to that position about a year after Leslie's departure. Timmer returned a short time later, and Allen Pearsen Cain, who had arrived as an assistant in 1946, became the last keeper of the South Fox Island Light. His wife Anna lived in the lighthouse building with him, as did his small granddaughter. Cain spent a total of 32 years serving various lighthouses. In 1958, when the Fox Island station was converted to an automatic light, Al Cain was transferred to Alpena.

So ended the lonely vigil of keepers and their assistants at South Fox Island.

COURTESY ANNA CAIN Shown near the assistants' quarters in 1951 are (L-R) Mr. Kruell and wife, Anna Cain and her husband, Keeper Allen Cain, Mrs. Timmer and Assistant Pete Timmer. The Cain's granddaughter, Cheryl Davis, stands in front.

Ready to go rabbit hunting are Keeper Al Cain and an assistant, Claude Finch.

Assistant Bob Harris is shown playing with dog.

Tied at Northport is the 25-foot South Fox Island lighthouse boat, used during Keeper Cain's years of service.

Occasionally, Coastguardsmen spent brief duty at the light, seeing that things were in order and changing batteries when needed. The battery-operated light was turned off automatically when hit by the sun. When that light burned out, one of three waiting bulbs rotated in to take its place.

Bob Harris and David Markle were some of the last to serve at the South Fox Light, under the Coastguard. Ron Loebich, from Ohio, was the very last Coastguardsmen to tend the light. When he left, the rotating bulbs were changed by owners of the Nickerson Lumber Company, which operated a sawmill a short distance up the shoreline. In 1968 the light was shut off permanently, and the beacon of South Fox Island ended its work of guiding seamen through the channel. Now only buoys at strategic points warn large craft when dangerous shoals or rocks are being approached.

COURTESY ERWIN GALE
Island owners Erwin Gale and Tom Stevens examine an old maritime wreck near the tip of South Fox Island, 1987.

The 1867 lighthouse, which served the mariners so faithfully, is, unfortunately, on its way to ruin. If the Michigan Department of Natural Resources does not plan to preserve this light, it would be better placed in private hands where restoration of this historic sentinel could occur.

Additional Maritime Notes

[1] Lawrence & Lucille Wakefield, *Sail & Rail* (Traverse City, Mich., Village Press, 1980), p. 5.
[2] Ibid.
[3] Ibid, p. 2.
[4] *History of The Great Lakes, Vol. 1* (1899, reprint, Cleveland, Ohio: Freshwater Press, Inc., 1972), p. 854.
[5] Ibid, p. 891.
[6] Ibid, Vol., 2, p. 854.
[7] "A fearful experience," in *The Detroit Free Press* 17 Oct., 1886.
[8] F. Glenn Goff and Phyllis J. Higman, *Environmental Impact Report: North Fox Island Development*, (West Branch, Mich: Vital Resources Consulting, 1990), p. 2-56.
[9] *Lighthouse Establishment, Statement of Appropriations & c.: from March 4, 1789 to June 30, 1882,* printed in 1886.
[10] U. S. Lighthouse Board, *Description of Light-House Tower, Buildings, and Premises at South Fox Island Light Station, December 1st, 1907.*
[11] National Archives Coast Guard Records, *Register of Lighthouse Keepers Through Fiscal Year of 1912* RG. 26.
[12] Harlan Hatcher & Erick Walter, *A Pictorial History of the Great Lakes* (New York: Bonanza Books, 1970), p. 95.
[13] George Weeks, *Sleeping Bear, Yesterday and Today* (Franklin, Mich.: Altwerger and Mandel Publishing Company, 1990), p. 139.
[14] National Archives Coast Guard Records.
[15] *History of The Great Lakes, Vol. 1*, pp. 728-31.
[16] Barbara Hamblett, "Lighthouse Keeping: A Womanly Art," in *Michigan History Magazine Vol. 65*, No. 6, Nov./Dec., 1881, p. 29.
[17] National Archives Coast Guard Records.
[18] North Manitou Island Lifesaving Station Records, microfilm.
[19] *Leelanau Enterprise* 25 Nov., 1880, p. 1, microfilm.
[20] Ibid, 8 Dec., 1881, p. 1.
[21] Ibid, 16 Dec., 1880, p. 3.
[22] National Archives Coast Guard Records.
[23] *Atlas of Leelanau County, 1881*, in Leelanau County Register of Deeds Office.
[24] National Archives Coast Guard Records.
[25] Steve Harrington, "North Manitou: A step back in time," in *Michigan Sportsman*, April 1986, p. 67.
[26] National Archives Coast Guard Records.
[27] *History of the Great Lakes,* Vol. 2, p. 480.
[28] U. S. Cong., Senate, 15 Feb., 1892, Doc. 38, pp. (52-1) 2892.
[29] *Leelanau Enterprise* 21 Feb., 1899, p. 1.
[30] Edmund M. Littell, *100 Years in Leelanau* (Leland, Mich.: The Print Shop, 1965), p. 25.
[31] Dana Thomas Bowen, *Memories of the Great Lakes* (Daytona Beach: by author, 1946), p. 241.
[32] "Vega's Crew Drenched By Icy Water For Hours," *The Detroit Free Press* 2 Dec., 1905, p. 2.
[33] William Ratigan, *Great Lakes Shipwrecks & Survivals* (Grand Rapids: Wm. B. Erdsmans Publishing Co., 1960), p. 135.
[34] Letter from George Olsen to "Milwaike Supertendent of Laithuse," 24 Aug. 1920, copy on file at Grand Traverse Light.
[35] *Traverse City Record-Eagle* 10 May, 1923, microfilm.
[36] "Chief Leslie of Northport Light Retires After 28 Years Service," unidentified newspaper clipping, 1950.
[37] Ibid.
[38] Letter to author from Fred Leslie, March, 1982.

PHOTO BY L. DAVID HOLLISTER
Sterling Nickerson, Sr, filing the fine-toothed saw.

WITH AX AND SAW

Probably more people have been brought to the Fox Islands, Manitou Islands and Beaver Islands because of the timber than for any other reason. David Gladish in *The Journal of Beaver Island History, Volume One,* says, "Virtually all the islands have contributed to the logging industry in one way or another."[1]

The first recorded land certificate on South Fox was issued to Nicholas Pickard, who was born in New York in 1817. He took out a claim on the southeastern side of South Fox in 1850. This was just before the Mormon settlers arrived. Pickard had already established a wooding station where schooners could pick up cooking fuel, on North Manitou Island in 1846,[2] and Manitou had the biggest wooding port of the islands off Leelanau County. At that time there were no white settlers on the nearby mainland, although boats traveling the Manitou Passage stopped at North Manitou daily. Pickard obviously found this to be a profitable business, extending his wooding operations to South Fox Island, and later to Leland and Northport. His business "Nicholas Pickard & Company" was owned in partnership with Edwin Munger of New York. Munger was probably a financier of the company. When steamers on the Great Lakes were at their greatest number, between 1870 and 1880,[3] Pickard was well equipped to provide cordwood for their steam boilers and cooking stoves. The hardwoods on North and South Fox, when cut into four-foot-lengths, made ideal fuel for the steamers when they stopped by. During most of these years, Pickard and his wife, the former Nancy Buss, made their home in Leland and on North Manitou Island. Nicholas Pickard died in Leland in 1876, at age 59. His death was sudden, listed as a stroke, and his final inventory included "125 cords shipping wood on bank," along with a propeller launch, a Mackinaw boat, wood-cutting tools and farm animals.[4] In the property settlement, the name of Wilder appeared as an heir to Edwin Munger, who had died before Pickard. It is interesting to note that J. Wilder owned property on the North end of North Fox in 1851, at the time of the early Mormon occupation of that island.

Robert Roe, a sea captain, came from Ireland to New York to Beaver Island, and then arrived at South Fox sometime between 1859 and 1861. He bought property next to Pickard, to the north. Over the next 20 years, Roe bought and resold parcels of property as he cut the wood needed for his own wooding station. Roe sold a piece on South Fox's northeastern shore to Alexander Sample and Alfred Scovil of Chicago. Scovil did not continue his involvement in the island property, and Sample and Roe combined their wooding businesses and bought additional joint property. Roe already had quite a business going before Sample joined him in his venture. Employees of Roe listed on the 1870 and 1880 Censuses for South Fox were William Chase from England, Francis Boyle from Ireland, Andrew Olson and Powel Johnson from Norway, James McGregor from New York, and Josiah Boyce. Some of these men are listed as married servants of Roe, but their families were not living on the island. For their labor, wood choppers got fifty cents a cord for four-foot lengths. One person could cut about a cord a day. The wood was then sold to steamers for $1.50 a cord.[5]

Robert Roe also owned more than a mile of shore frontage along North Fox Island's

COURTESY JAMES & HARRIET ROE
This 1892 photo shows old pilings remaining from the Roe wooding station dock on South Fox. The schooner Ida Keith *is at left, with the tug* Favorite *directly in front of it. The steamer* Thomas Friant *and Roe sailboat* Islander *are to the right.*

east side, which he registered in 1864. This was the best place on North Fox to operate a wooding station, away from the westerly winds.

Though a wood chopper didn't get rich, his job would keep him alive until he found something better. Steiner Garthe came with his widowed father from Norway to Michigan, in 1868, and found a job on the Leelanau mainland as a farm hand. He agreed to work for a year for $150, plus board and washing. Garthe claimed he got the board and washing but not the money. He thought he might do better as a woodcutter on South Fox Island and signed up at one of the wooding stations. His sister Mary went to the island with him, and they lived with another Norwegian, Ole Goodmanson. Presumably, Steiner Garthe received his pay, and experience helped him to clear some 40 acres around 1870, back on the mainland near Cat Head Point. From his first job as a farm hand, Garthe worked his way through woodcutter, railroad man, farmer, Leelanau County Supervisor, and in 1902, Judge of Probate.[6] From such humble beginnings, many settlers in America left their mark as Steiner Garthe did. A common job such as woodcutter could be a stepping stone for an ambitious immigrant.

COURTESY CHRISTINE GARTHE
Steiner Garthe worked as a woodcutter on South Fox Island and later became Probate Judge of Leelanau County.

Perhaps some woodcutters weren't so willing. Stan Floyd of Beaver Island and Charlevoix claimed that his grandfather, John Floyd, was shanghaied to South Fox to cut cordwood. According to the grandson, John Floyd arrived in Milwaukee after the Civil War and got a little drunk from celebrating. He woke up later on South Fox Island. It's not known which wooding station John Floyd worked for; but he made friends on the island with Mary Palmer and her sweetheart Otto Williams. John Floyd was witness to their 1871 wedding, and when Mary Palmer Williams became a young widow or was deserted by her husband, John Floyd married her in 1874. Henry Longfield, who probably was a woodcutter, accompanied Mary and John to Northport, where the marriage took place. After most of their children were born on South Fox, the Floyds were found to be living on North Manitou in 1880, where Mr. Floyd, most likely, worked in one of the lumbering operations there. The family soon moved to Beaver Island, and descendants became part of that island's community. Another of Roe's woodcutters, William Chase, also married and raised a family on Beaver Island.

Marriage was on the mind of a friend of John Floyd. John Malloy, who was called "Buffalo," was a woodcutter on South Fox with Floyd. Malloy was scheduled to marry a girl from Beaver Island, but it seemed that the thin, spring ice was slow to break up, preventing travel by boat. Malloy said he would crawl if he had to, to get to his waiting bride. Stan Floyd related that Malloy kept his promise and did crawl much of the way across the melting ice between South Fox and Beaver Island, and the wedding took place on schedule.

By 1880 most of the Great Lakes steamers were converted to coal, and the wooding business began to decline. Eventually, Sample, Roe and Pickard left the islands that had been so good to them. Roe sold some of his property on the northeastern shore of South Fox to fisherman, John Oscar Peterson (Pierson). Some property on North Fox Roe sold to Sample. The gravely lots on North Fox's eastern side passed from Roe to Elijah Harpold of the Garden City Sand Company.

Robert Roe and his wife Catherine, or Kate, had raised a large family during their years on South Fox. It was a good life. Their large farm and the vast wood supply on the Fox Islands had provided them a good living during these years. In *A Child of the Sea*, Elizabeth Williams says that Robert Roe bought the

COURTESY JAMES & HARRIET ROE
Charles Roe, son of Robert and Kate Roe, continued to operate the South Fox mill for several years after his parents moved to Harbor Springs. Roe shingle mill on South Fox Island, about 1895.

land on South Fox where the Mormons had lived. Property records and Strang's description of South Fox support this. Mrs. Williams also says of Roe, "He put out a dock, built a comfortable house...."[7] The house later became known as "the Plank house", the oldest standing building on South Fox, until it was struck by lightening and burned in 1991.

In 1880 or 1881 Robert Roe and his family moved to Harbor Springs. Wood from the South Fox Island mill was used to build their new home, modeled after their island residence. In Harbor Springs the lumbering tradition continued, and the family also raised horses. As late as 1895, Robert and Kate's oldest son, Charles, was still operating a South Fox shingle mill and saw mill, employing several men. Shingles from the mill were used to cover the steeple roof of the Holy Childhood Church in Harbor Springs. Some wood products from the mill were also taken to Northport. Although a larger vessel may have been used to transport shingles, Charlie Roe used his sailboat *Whitecloud* for fishing and personal transportation. The fishing business was still going strong in the area, and Charlie Roe's cargo sometimes contained packages of salt fish from the waters of the island chain.

In the late 1880's Mann Brothers of Milwaukee and Two Rivers, Wisconsin, began operating a logging business in Leelanau County. Charles Mann had Ed Johnson serving as his agent in the Suttons Bay area, and Peter Possing was in charge of the Leland and Carp Lake business. The Mann Brothers' scows and tug *Temple Emery* transported lumber from the Leelanau County shoreline to Wisconsin. On at least one occasion, the weather overcame them, resulting in extra men being hired to pick up logs that had been lost in the storm. Charles Mann sent a scout to look for available timberlands on the islands. From

COURTESY MILWAUKEE PUBLIC LIBRARY
Mann Brothers' tug Temple Emery *transported lumber across Lake Michigan to Wisconsin in the late 1800's and early 1900's.*

1895 to 1898 the company owned a wide strip down the middle of North Fox Island, in association with Gottlieb Patck, also of Milwaukee. In 1898 and 1900 Mann and Patck bought small parcels on the northeastern and southwestern shores of South Fox. The small amount of property held on South Fox hardly seems enough to provide much logging, but Mann Brothers may have also bought timber rights from other landowners on the bigger island. Some of their North Fox property was gained by tax sale of land owned by William B. McCreery. Property records show that Mann Brothers, through its agent Gottleib Patck, also owned on Beaver Island, in 1886, and on North Manitou.

Around the turn of the century, the property inland from Pickard's on the southeastern shore of South Fox was purchased by tax sale by John O. Plank. While Plank was dreaming of how to turn both of the Fox Islands into resort areas, he made timber contracts with several parties on behalf of his wife, himself and South Fox property owner Jennie Horton. Some of Horton's property on South Fox touched the water and was the site of an earlier sawmill, probably that of Charles Roe. Jennie Horton also owned property on the Leelanau County mainland, and it appears that John O. Plank, Jr., son of the elder John O. Plank, had a timber interest in this property. As far as this author has been able to determine, Jennie Horton did not live on either of the Fox Islands but did buy or inherit properties on the mainland and on the island. On the timber contracts, her residence was listed as Tiffin, Ohio.

In a 1902 contract John O. Plank, Sr.'s, house, barn and shingle mill on South Fox were leased to Archibald Bunting and John O. Plank, Jr., along with permission to cut timber. Payment to the owners was to be 20 percent of the sale of such timber. At the same time, a timber contract was awarded to Bunting and Plank, Jr., for nearly all of North Fox Island, with the exception of the southern point and a small area about mid-shore on the eastern side of the island. The trees on either island were not to be cut unless measuring at least ten inches at the base, except for cedar, which could be as small as six inches.[8] John Plank, Sr., wanted the lumbering to be completed within three years on North Fox and within five years on South Fox. The logging does not appear to have been done within that time frame, if at all. One unconfirmed source reported that John O. Plank, Jr., drowned, and that may have occurred soon after the timber contract was recorded.

The Kelley Lumber Company purchased timber rights on North Fox Island in 1906 and hired E. A. Kildee to do the lumbering, apparently not undertaken or completed by Plank, Jr., and Bunting. Kelley Lumber's president was Walter N. Kelley, who worked in the main office in Traverse City, dealing in lumber and shingles. The business also operated in Benzie County's village of Frankfort. The Traverse City *Evening Record* reported on July 21, 1906, that E. A. Kildee had left for North Fox on the tug *Maggie* and would do large-scale lumbering on North Fox, which was "covered with valuable timber."[9] Kildee took with him fifteen men and four teams, expecting to add about 45 more workers and three additional horse teams. Tents were taken for shelter for

Walter N. Kelley, President of Kelley Lumber Company.

the woodsmen, along with a large amount of equipment and provisions. The *Maggie* made regular trips to Manistique, allowing for nearly daily communication with the island.

The Kelley Lumber Company bought property on South Fox from Paul Thomas in 1908, and from the estate of August Ance. Kelley also entered into a timber-cutting contract with Plank and Horton. The Plank contract again stipulated to a time limit, all logging to be completed by May, 1912.

A 1957 letter written by Alma Plank, second wife of John O. Plank, Sr., stated that on North Fox Island "The timber has not been sold since before 1913, and then the people didn't cut much as they went broke trying to boom logs and tow them."[10] This coincides with the bankruptcy declaration of the Kelley Lumber Company in 1909 and Mr. Kelley's resignation from the company in 1910.[11]

A third contract was sold to William and Herman Leo and John Diepenbrock. The Leo brothers were from Suttons Bay and had established their mill on South Fox in 1904. From then until 1921, they manufactured lumber, shingles, lath and railroad ties on a rotating basis. John Diepenbrock of Grand Rapids was taken into the business in 1914, and the name was changed to Leo Brothers & Company. In March, 1909, the *Evening Record* reported the burning of the Leo Brothers mill in mainland Suttons Bay and that "Leo Brothers are lumbering North Fox Island."[12] This appears to have been a mistake, noting North Fox where it should have said South Fox.

The Native American families of Chippewa, Ance and Raphael were on South Fox at that time, as was farmer Paul Thomas and lighthouse workers Bourisseau, Dame, Green and McCormick. John O. Plank, Sr., would sometimes arrive from Chicago aboard his yacht, and Plank's son and family were living in the big farmhouse. The Leo's uncle, Roger Kaley, homesteaded a piece of property and worked in the Leo Mill.

COURTESY BERNICE LEO
Roger Kaley, an uncle of the Leo brothers, worked at Leo's mill and homesteaded this piece of property nearby.

A family named Williams lived near the beach at the "landing" north of the mill. They had two teen-age sons who worked for Leos. Bernice Leo recalled that the Williams family sometimes had visitors from High Island and that they had long hair in the "House of David" fashion. Perhaps the Williams family was related to those on High Island.

Other Leo employees were Nels and Henry Ask, Louis and Albert Kalchik, Dennis McKee, James Cobb, Fred Brehmer, Fred Kurtzel, Dick Boston, Jack Murray, Oscar Borgeson, Benton Oleson, William Ance and Rollie McDole. Lee Manigold of Kingsley was the head sawyer. The Raphael brothers worked at the mill, and their mother did the cooking for the hands for a time. Other cooks were Herman Leo's wife Cora; Mrs. Frank Stafford, whose husband worked at the mill; a Mr. and Mrs. Bumgartner, and Nellie Steimel, the wife of a fisherman.

Piles of logs were made into stacks of shingles at Leo Brother's mill, which operated from 1904 to 1921.

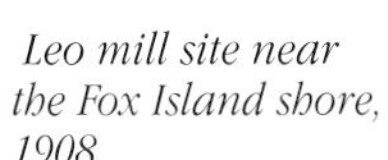

Left: The Leo crew washes up for supper, Left to right are: William Leo, Anna Leo with daughter Hildegarde, Katie and Andrew Stallman, Jack Murray, Roger Kaley, _________________ Raphael, others unidentified.

Leo mill site near the Fox Island shore, 1908.

PHOTOS COURTESY OF BERNICE & HILDEGARDE LEO

In 1910 the Leo Brothers had to rebuild the South Fox Island mill after it burned, just a year after fire had destroyed their mainland mill. Saw mills had a way of doing that from time to time. There was also the Big Lake to contend with. A Mr. Knight from Charlevoix carried shingles from the South Fox mill on his boat for a time; and once, due to an overload, the boat sank and shingles were found all the way from Charlevoix to Pentwater.

PHOTOS COURTESY OF BERNICE & HILDEGARDE LEO
A winter view of the Leo mill, as seen from the dock.

Part of the Leo mill crew. Left to right are: Herman Leo, Howard Steimel, Oscar Borgeson, unknown, ________________ Anderson, two Williams brothers, Pete Raphael, Nels Ask, Fred Brehmer.

One of the difficulties of operating a lumbering or shingle business on an island is that of transportation for the product. For the wooding business that was no problem, since the steamers were the buyers; but other lumbering concerns had to hire vessels to carry the lumber and shingles, and that sometimes made the profits questionable. One of the transporters of shingles from South Fox was the steamer *Chequamegon*, one of the finest of her kind, though only about 100 feet long.[13] The Leos sometimes hired this vessel. There was a long dock on the east side of South Fox where the mill was. Logs cut on the western hills were rolled down to the beach and then towed around to the mill on the eastern side.

Wells-Higman moved the Leo home to former fisherman Nelson's property (where Kilbourns' had spent summers) and connected the various buildings together. The Leo family is shown during a later visit.

The Wells-Higman Company of Traverse City began cutting on South Fox Island shortly before 1920. The company gained property on the north end of the island from Martin Brown of Leland, from the government and from Frederick Kilbourn of Chicago. The fruit business was going strong on the mainland; and Wells-Higman made fruit packing boxes and baskets, in addition to hardwood veneers from the island's resources. The logs were skidded by horses into the water and then rafted to Traverse City, where they were made into the final product.

Charles Zapf was manager of Wells-Higman, of which the Zapf Fruit Packaging Company became a division in 1921. In that year, Leo Brothers sold its South Fox holdings to Zapf. One of the notable events of the island's history occurred soon after and was recorded in the *Traverse City Record-Eagle* as it happened.[14]

The winter of 1923 was an especially long one, and supplies were getting short at the Zapf logging camp. Near the end of March, some of the employees started across the ice but were forced back to the island by drifting ice and open water. About a month later, on April 15, when things were even more desperate, three men spent more than two harrowing days making their way across 22 miles to the mainland. Edward Horn (McIntosh) of Suttons Bay and Carl Cooper and Ellis Ayers of Traverse City left South Fox at 7 a .m. on Monday the 15th in a small skiff, carrying a pair of oars, an ax and a pole. After hauling the skiff over mounds of ice, they finally reached open water and launched their boat. But the men reached new ice, which cut their light vessel to pieces, forcing them to abandon it as they reached solid ice again. One man had broken through the thinner ice and had to save himself, as the others couldn't get close enough to pull him out.

In the evening the wind came up, blowing the ice and forcing the men to jump from floe to floe. At one point they gave up and lay down to rest. When they woke up, they saw that the wind was blowing them toward the shore, and with new hope, they continued their journey, reaching land between Cat Head Point and the Grand Traverse Light at about nine o'clock Wednesday morning. Exhausted, they were taken to Northport, where they told citizens of conditions on the island, leading Northporters to believe the remaining island residents were in immediate danger of starving.

When Gilman Dame heard of their plight, he arranged for a plane from Selfridge Field to carry food to the nine men and a woman still on the island, even though there was no established airstrip there. Later, when Ed Horn reported in at the Traverse City Zapf office, he handed the superintendent a note from Nels Ask, the island camp's foreman. The note read in part, "In regard to food, I leave it to you, but the last week it has been slim, beans and potatoes ... bread and black strap for butter ... we got enough beans and potatoes for six months, and flour." Horn denied that they had told the Northporters of eating frozen potatoes or butchering the work ox, but he did say that supplies were low. Mr. McAlvay at the Zapf office told reporters the story of the starving people was "quite puzzling" in light of the fact that a good supply of food had been put up at the beginning of winter.

Nels Ask, left, and Albert Kalchik worked the island mills in the 1920's. Here they display a cow's skull, possibly from the Paul Thomas farm.

Plans for the Selfridge plane continued, however, and the people of Northport set to work gathering a thousand pounds of food to be picked up by the plane and transported to the island. But when the plane attempted to land on the slush ice in Northport despite the waving hands of onlookers, it broke through the surface. The two occupants were safely pulled ashore, but the disabled plane was not able to deliver the supplies. In the next few days other attempts to reach the island by plane failed: A French Briquet plane from Chicago, a government mail plane and two other Army planes either suffered broken landing gear or were temporarily reported lost. Meanwhile, the controversy continued. Were the people on South Fox Island starving or not?

COURTESY MANITOWOC MARITIME MUSEUM
The car ferry Ann Arbor No. 5 *reached the stranded Zapf workers May 23, 1923, and took them to Frankfort.*

On Sunday the 23rd, the 360-foot *Ann Arbor Carferry No. 5*, also called the "Bull of the Woods," plowed through the ice toward South Fox Island. The biggest ship of its kind in the world and the fastest on the Great Lakes, the railroad car ferry reached the stranded islanders and took them to Frankfort. Alfred Clark was left on the island to care for the horse teams; and a provision of food from the car ferry was left for him, despite the protests of Nels Ask, who insisted that no one was starving. The eight people taken from the camp were: Foreman Nels Ask and Howard Smith of Leelanau County; Mr. and Mrs. Ed Morrow, Louis Baudette and Joe Ramsey of Traverse City; Robert Husted of Ithaca; and Jack Garvey of Chicago. Ask continued to deny that they had been in danger of starvation but admitted that some things were scarce. He charged that those who had come across the ice were only tired of the isolated island life and didn't want to work. He said they had taken, without permission, the boat of summer resident Paul Thomas, and had deserted the rest of them.

Others substantiated the earlier reports of Cooper, Horn and Ayers, however. Mrs. Morrow the cook said, "You don't get hungry on the kind of food we had, you get faint. That's the way with all of the men. That's why they couldn't work. I cried about it often. I was sick of it and I couldn't stand it. I heard there were 800 bushels of potatoes at Nels Ask's place on the island, but I never saw any of them." Mrs. Morrow reported that they had killed Paul Thomas' cow in February but hadn't had any meat since that was gone.

The employees were taken to the Zapf office in Traverse City, where they could tell their stories and collect their winter's pay, each getting "well over one hundred dollars."

While there were plenty of close calls, no lives were lost among the stranded or the rescuers. But even in good weather, logging can be a dangerous business. About a year after the lives of the Zapf people were saved, an employee of the steamer *M. H. Stuart* was killed as he was crushed between two logs while they were being loaded from the Zapf

INSTITUTE FOR GREAT LAKES RESEARCH, BOWLING GREEN STATE UNIVERSITY
The steamer M. H. Stuart *of the Traverse Bay Transportation Company hauled logs from the islands to the Zapf factory in Traverse City.*

dock onto the vessel tied up at South Fox.[15] Martin Hansen had been taken aboard the ship as a wheelsman only nine days earlier in Milwaukee. Although *"Stewart"* was the newspaper-reported vessel in that incident, it was, apparently, the steamer *M. H. Stuart*, a boat known to have carried logs and other goods from the local islands to mainland ports. Captain Charles Anderson of South Manitou Island piloted the *M. H. Stuart* for the Traverse Bay Transportation Company, and one of the company's regular customers was Zapf Fruit Packaging Company. The newspaper did report Captain Anderson at the wheel that day.

Zapf also suffered bad luck that spring when, just at the beginning of the new harvest season, the newly completed baskets and packaging were destroyed by a fire at the factory in Traverse City.[16] Fortunately, the loss was covered by insurance. Another loss was the death of the company's president, Charles Zapf, two years later, in 1926.

About 10 years later, Zapf sold out to the Berrien County Package Company, the largest manufacturer of fruit packages in Michigan. Its main office was in Benton Harbor, but the logs from South Fox Island were destined for the Traverse City plant. President LaVerne Lane and his company eventually owned about half of South Fox. Numerous attempts were made to raft the logs and tow them by boat to the mainland, but the rough waters of Lake Michigan broke the logs apart with each try. Finally, the logging operations were given up and the property was sold, about half of it to the State of Michigan and the rest to others.

PHOTO COURTESY ELAINE BEARDSLEY John Ingwersen, owner of Manitou Logging Co.

The next logger tried the same process for getting logs off the island. The Manitou Logging Company began operations on South Fox in 1952 as part of the dream of John Ingwersen of Traverse City. Ingwersen had previously done logging on South Manitou Island. He inquired of the government the possibility of logging state lands on both North and South Fox Islands but was told there were no state lands on North Fox and none available for logging on South Fox. On South Fox, he bought 40 acres from a Suttons Bay barber, John Send, who had taken a deed to some of the Indian property as payment for several years of haircuts. But having no real use for it, he sold the land to Ingwersen for $50. With that parcel and another 40 acres, the Manitou Logging Company began its work. Charles Stevens, of Northport, had cleared farm acreage to be used as an airstrip, and some of the logging company men pulled a birch log behind a caterpillar tractor to smooth the strip. Some of the logging equipment was transported to South Fox by barge, with the help of Lester Carlson of Leland.

COURTESY REGINA LAWSON Regina Leemaster driving the "cat."

Ingwersen's men took to the woods and cut only the best, saving the tops for charcoal. The logs were then skidded with tractors to the shore at about the middle

PHOTOS COURTESY OF REGINA LAWSON
Sam Brown & Elvie Burroughs with a pile of John Ingwersen's logs. Since Ingwersen had no dock, his boats came close to shore when logs were being attached for rafting. In this photo the Major *is beached, a problem the* Arrow *also encountered.*

of South Fox's eastern side. During this part of the work, the first mishaps occurred when Sam Brown had his leg broken as he worked with the logs, and then Archie Miller injured his shoulder badly when a tree limb fell on him. The shoulder injury improved and Brown's leg mended, and these men and Elvie Burroughs, the "cat" driver and pilot for the J3 Cub plane, took up residence in the Roe/Plank house. Regina Leemaster cooked for them, and, during that time, she and Sam Brown were married.

The next stage of the work was getting the product off the island. Sometimes cables were threaded through holes drilled in the logs; and other times, big screwhooks were forced into the log ends and cables were threaded through them. They were then ready for rafting across the water. Ingwersen bought Roy and Bruce Nelson's fishing boat, the *Major*, which had been built by "Big John" Johnson of Northport. Louis LaFreniere, of Beaver Island, set up a mill at Leelanau County's Good Harbor Bay, on the mainland, and the logs were to be processed there as the *Major* brought them in. Some of the men who towed logs for the Manitou Logging Company were Charles Stevens and Roland Dame of Northport, Ben Peshaba and Archie Miller of Peshawbestown, and Bruce Price of Lake Leelanau.

But Ingwersen and his men discovered the same thing the Berrien County Package Company had learned — that rafting wasn't the way to do it. No matter how well the logs seemed to be secured, the rolling seas had a way of tearing them loose. Ingwersen recalled that his company "scattered logs all over upper Lake Michigan," and was "an announced hazard to the Mackinaw (sailboat) race."[17]

He thought a bigger boat might work better and bought the 65-foot steel fish tug *Arrow* at Ontonagon. The boat was severely damaged by the weather, after being brought down from Lake Superior to Traverse City. It was rebuilt, and the coal-fired boiler was replaced with a diesel engine, which was rejuvenated in the garage behind Ingwersen's Traverse City home. With this boat, Ingwersen tried rafting logs across the lake to Escanaba; but still they broke loose. According to Ingwersen, he and Ernie Chippewa wrapped one raft around the lighthouse at the entrance to Big Bay de Noc. Another was lost in a storm, and as Ingwersen spotted it later from the air, he saw the water-soaked logs being pulled to the bottom by the long cable. He dreams were going down with it.

But, being determined, he made another attempt, using a 230-foot scow rented from Cap Roen of Sturgeon Bay, Wisconsin. Ingwersen recalled that it held a crane that was started by "jumping and hanging all your weight on the high crank handle."[18] Having no dock, his crew tried to maneuver the scow close to shore, and it washed up on the beach. Before they were through, the *Arrow* also became beached, and the east wind gave them a fight before the two vessels were set free.

The Manitou Logging Company was short-lived because of the hazards and loss of money, but John Ingwersen recalled that there were also good memories: "Dick Golden coming up out of a smoky engine room, Ernie Chippewa dancing with a grapple on a jackstrawed pile of logs, Elvie Burroughs up on the D6 (caterpillar tractor), Mack Barr patting a tree as it fell, Sammy Brown cussing his broken leg, Ike, Al Krumlauf, Al Bussa, old Jake Spencer, Jim Reichart, Regina Brown and others still vivid in the light coming down through the big timber."[19]

Ingwersen deeded some of his property on South Fox to John Frost of Birdseye Veneer of Wisconsin, as payment for money advanced to him by that company. His other property, caterpillar tractors, and supplies were sold by Ingwersen and his creditors to Sterling and Eva Nickerson, who with their sons Quentin, Max and Sterling, Jr., formed the Sterling Nickerson & Sons lumber company. In the fall of 1954 they began constructing a modern sawmill on South Fox Island, bringing machines and tools from their mill in mainland Kingsley. While living in a tent, and then the Plank house, the men got the mill into operation and then put up a cookhouse, bunkhouse and office.

Since 1848, when the government first offered lands on South Fox Island for sale, the island had been divided into many parcels among those who had arrived and staked

PHOTO BY L. DAVID HOLLISTER
The Nickerson mill was built in 1954 at the site of the earlier Pickard and Roe wooding stations on South Fox.

their claims. The Nickersons bought the large properties of John O. Plank from his widow, Alma, and the properties of Paul Thomas, which he had left to his nephew's wife, Stella Thomas. The lands of the early fishermen, farmers and wood merchants were bought by the Nickersons, along with several pieces of government property, including Indian lands from the Bureau of Indian Affairs. About two-thirds of the island became the property of the lumber company, and the other third was owned by the government. The sawmill, other buildings and a dock were erected in the same area where Nicholas Pickard had begun his wooding station a hundred years earlier.

NICKERSON FAMILY PHOTO
The Miss Manistee *was used to transport workers between South Fox Island and the mainland.*

From this land the company cut maple, birch, ash, basswood, oak, hemlock and cedar. The Samples, Roes and Pickards had used the two-man saws and axes, but chain saws in the 1950's helped the Nickersons cut 15,000 board feet a day. At first the lumber was carried off South Fox by Captain Dick Lyons with the *White Swan* and the *North Shore* of Charlevoix, while the *Miss Manistee* carried workers back and forth between the island and the mainland. When the 60-foot *North Shore* ran aground at Northport, carrying 70 tons of hard maple, the Nickersons decided it was time to get their own lumber boat. They bought the 65-foot tug *Tramp*, a fish tug from Charlevoix. Sterling Nickerson, Jr., obtained a boat pilot's license and transported much of the lumber to Northport, where it was loaded into railroad cars by anyone in town who wanted to earn a few dollars. The lumber was sold to several firms and used for pallets, hardwood flooring, pianos and other furniture. A pleasant sight on Grand Traverse Bay was the 33-foot sailboat *Witchcraft*, built from South Fox Island white cedar and ash, by Northport boatbuilder Bill Livingston, for his wife Betty.

PHOTO BY GUYLES DAME
Bill Livingston constructed the Witchcraft *from South Fox Island timber.*

Many men were employed over the years to work in the South Fox woods and in the sawmill. During the height of operation, about 20 men were working at a time. Some of the cooks who kept the lumberjacks fed were Eve Nickerson, the wife of Quentin; Myrna Souvinouen, wife of the head sawyer; and Elmer Bergeron of Sault Ste. Marie. The cooks normally peeled and cooked a half-bushel of potatoes a day, baked bread and pies, fried four dozen eggs and always had a pot of coffee brewing.

NICKERSON FAMILY PHOTO
On the South Fox Island dock, built by the Nickersons, are Eva and Sterling Nickerson and two of their sons, Quentin and Max.

The men who worked in the woods and in the mill came across the water from Kingsley, Northport, Peshawbestown and other mainland towns. The place was sometimes called "alimony island" because some of the men thought they could escape paying it there. When a worker got homesick, a three-hour trip on the *Tramp* or a 15-minute plane ride would take them back to civilization. Two-way radios were used by the Nickersons to communicate with Sterling Nickerson, Jr.'s, house in Northport, where messages were relayed to Kingsley. The South Fox Island office could also radio the *Tramp* at sea.

In 1957 the Nickersons inquired of Alma Plank, who had gained title to all of North Fox Island by 1951, about purchasing timber rights on the smaller island. After a positive response from Mrs. Plank, the island was inspected by Quentin Nickerson, but the timber was not viewed as of sufficient value to be of profit to the Nickerson camp. It appeared to Quentin that the North Fox Island timber had been "cut very close years ago, and fire must have gotten into the small growth, for there is nothing of any size ...."[20]

When the Mackinac Bridge was completed, Sterling Nickerson, Jr., went to St. Ignace to inspect one of the tugs that had been used for bridge construction. In 1958 the steel-hulled, 65-foot *Bridgebuilder X* was bought by the Nickerson company. It was reconstructed at Burke's coal dock in Suttons Bay and at the Sears dock in Greilickville and put into operation, making it possible to haul a day's sawmill output in one load.

COURTESY PETOSKEY NEWS-REVIEW
Quentin Nickerson, left, and his brother, Sterling Nickerson, Jr., sit atop the Tramp *in this 1956 photo.*

PHOTO BY L. DAVID HOLLISTER
The 65-foot lumber carrier Tramp *at the island dock. North Fox is seen in the background.*

Photo by L. David Hollister
Part of the Nickerson crew Left to Right: Front row: Bill Moran Carl Benninghaus, Wayne and Myrna Souvinouen, Eve and Quentin Nickerson, Sterling Nickerson,
Hugh Edgerton, Elijah Wanegeshik, Jesse Kewaygoshkum, Chippewa,

PHOTO BY L. DAVID HOLLISTER
Eve Nickerson and Myrna Souvinouen prepare a meal in the cookhouse.

PHOTO BY L. DAVID HOLLISTER
Nickerson employees loading logs on the truck, to be taken to the sawmill.

NICKERSON FAMILY PHOTO
Loading lumber from the Fox Island dock onto the Tramp.

COURTESY MACKINAC BRIDGE AUTHORITY
The 65-foot Bridgebuilder X *was used to help build the Mackinac Bridge. It was purchased by the Nickersons in 1958 and converted to a lumber carrier.*

About once a week Sterling, Jr., hauled a gross of 53 tons of hardwood to the J. W. Wells Company and the M and M Box Company in Wisconsin.

The lumber business was going well for the Nickersons, but on December 15, 1959, a shadow fell on their good fortune. About ten in the morning, Sterling Nickerson, Jr., and a relative, Glen Roop, left Sturgeon Bay, Wisconsin, aboard the *Bridgebuilder X*; and when they didn't show up at South Fox Island, a search was begun by the Coast Guard and pilots in private planes. Though the search was continued for several days and was joined by people walking the mainland shores, no trace of the boat was ever found. A day after the disappearance, an oil slick was sighted about 15 miles southwest of South Fox Island but

The remodeled Bridgebuilder *was lost on Lake Michigan December 15, 1959, and never recovered. Sterling Nickerson, Jr., and Glen Roop perished with the vessel.*

was quickly dispersed by the waves, preventing further investigation. Roop's body washed ashore in Wisconsin the following summer.

There had been 11-foot waves several hours after the *Bridgebuilder* had pulled out into the Big Lake, but Nickerson had battled worse than that before. Earlier in the season, during heavy fog, the *Bridgebuilder* had scraped bottom. She was repaired at the Roen Shipyard in Sturgeon Bay and was sailing back into operation from there the day the vessel was lost. Cement had been removed from the hull in order for repairs to be made, and the repairmen had questioned Nickerson about whether the boat had enough ballast. He replied that he had plenty of heavy chain back in Northport and could place that inside the vessel when he arrived there. The only reasonable explanation for the boat's disappearance seemed to be that the ballast was needed sooner, when the sudden, heavy seas hit.

COURTESY BETTY ROOP SHAW
Glen Roop was lost with the Bridgebuilder, *1959.*

In *A Child of the Sea*, Elizabeth Whitney Williams tells of the loss of her husband and others, expressing the grief which she felt — a grief with which the Nickersons and others who had lost loved ones on the seas could identify. "The bodies were never recovered, and only those who have passed through the same know what a sorrow it is to lose your loved one by drowning and not be able to recover the remains. It is a sorrow that never ends through life."[21] The loss of Nickerson and Roop on the *Bridgebuilder X* left two widows and nine fatherless children.

Ironically, while the search was going on for the missing *Bridgebuilder*, government documents were in the mail on their way to the lumber company, certifying that the name of the vessel was officially changed from *Bridgebuilder X* to *Nickerson*.

COURTESY BETTY ROOP SHAW
Sally, Charlene, John and Glen Roop, several months after their father was lost on Lake Michigan.

The lumbering on South Fox Island continued for a few years after this, until the cutting was completed. Max Nickerson transported the lumber aboard the *Tramp*. In October, 1964, he and his crew faced the anger of Lake Michigan between South Fox and Northport. About half way between, a storm forced them to alter course. The bilge pump and the *Tramp's* engine both shut down. With the boat taking on water, two-thirds of the lumber cargo assigned to Atlantic Lumber Company had to be thrown over to lighten the load. When the engine started an hour later, the *Tramp* was able to find refuge at Charlevoix. Some of the lumber was salvaged from the beach north of Charlevoix. Although the South Fox lumbering venture was considered a financial success, the Nickerson family met the same dangers many other islanders had faced through the years. The *Tramp* survived numerous voyages but was later purchased and sunk intentionally near Traverse City by a group of scuba divers. It rests 45 feet below in Grand Traverse Bay.

The South Fox property was put up for sale, and the island was uninhabited except for the cook, Elmer Bergeron, who stayed on as caretaker. A sale of the land was made to Lynn Dillin in 1965. Ten years later Dillin's property was sold to Stanley Riley, Erwin Gale and Tom Stevens of Hart, Michigan.

Upon recommendation of the Michigan Department of Natural Resources, a decision was made to do further logging on South Fox Island, since the recently established deer herd had eaten much of the underbrush, and logging would bring about new growth. According to Erwin Gale, the DNR wanted to clear-cut the timber, but the island owners didn't want to destroy the island's natural beauty and appeal. They made an offer to the DNR that the State of Michigan handle all the logging (without clear-cutting) of the island, with the state keeping all profit from its own property and half the profit from the private property. The DNR rejected managing the logging, however, and the island owners were left to find a timber company to log the private properties only. J. W. Timber Harvesting of Frederick, Wisconsin, accepted the challenge. And what a challenge the operation proved to be, especially for the South Fox Island property owners!

PHOTO BY ERWIN GALE
J. W. Timber Harvesting loading South Fox logs aboard the barge, 1986.

Although thousands of logs were moved by barge to a market in Canada, profits which were to be split equally between the private property owners and the logging company proved questionable. The operation got off to a bad start in late 1985, when three of the loggers narrowly escaped the burning cookhouse, where they had been sleeping. The building was uninsured and had to be replaced before the following deer hunting season. J.W. Timber bought its own transport vessel to cut contract costs, but the boat, loaded with costly acetylene tanks, became lost in fog and ended up sinking. In 1986 the DNR charged that 130 acres of state forest timber, over 700,000 board feet, had been taken without any agreement with the state. A value of up to $155,000 was placed on the removed timber. The loggers argued that they were unaware they were on state land, and charges were dropped when the company agreed to pay restitution of $28,000. The island owners also had to forfeit the last two barges of lumber.

When pieces of yellow-orange Styrofoam began washing up on mainland beaches, along with battered barrels, an investigation found that the South Fox loggers had used dynamite in an effort to destroy the no-longer-needed barge that had been used as a loading platform in the logging effort. Pieces of steel and boulder-sized chunks of foam littered the island beaches. The company agreed to clean up the debris on South Fox, but small pieces of Styrofoam could still be found on mainland beaches for several summer seasons.

According to Erwin Gale, neither the island owners nor J. W. Timber Harvesting company made any money from the timber cutting. He said that "Only the deer benefited" by allowing for new growth of vegetation.[22]

Although South Fox Island still has much of the appearance of a wilderness, changes in vegetation have resulted from logging operations over the years. In old photographs, tall pine trees are evident. In a 1945 report by I. H. Bartlett to the Michigan Department of Conservation, a listing of trees found on South Fox showed "hemlock, balsam, spruce and cedar are occasionally present on the eastern edge of the island, mixed with the hardwoods. They increase in number toward the center and become more plentiful in the sand dune area along the western portion." Nearly forty years later, in a letter from botanist James Wells to Dr. Thomas Stevens, Wells stated, "We were especially impressed in not finding any red, jack or white pine, no hemlock nor white spruce. We wondered if these species never grew there or may have been eliminated through lumbering activities."[23]

On North Fox Island the forests are considered valuable because of their habitat types. Northern Swamp, Mesic Northern Forest and Boreal Forests rival virgin woodlands in other parts of North America, according to ecologists Dennis Albert and Gary Reese.[24] While ecologists and conservationists believe these forest acreages should be protected, there is always the possibility of North Fox being lumbered, and even clear-cut, unless public ownership of this island is acquired.

[1] David Gladish, "Notes On Island Logging," *The Journal Of Beaver Island History, Vol. One* (St. James, Mich.: Beaver Island Historical Society, 1976), p. 101.

[2] George N. Fuller, ed., *Island Stories* (Lansing: State Printers, 1947), p. 53; collection of Marion M. Davis articles from *Michigan History Magazine.*

[3] Lawrence & Lucille Wakefield, *Sail & Rail* (Traverse City, Mich.: Village Press, 1980), p. 6.

[4] Leelanau County Probate Records, 1887.

[5] James Strang, *Gospel Herald* 17 May, 1849, reprint.

[6] *Northport Leader* 27 June, 1912, microfilm.

[7] Elizabeth Whitney Williams, *A Child of the Sea* (1950; reprint, Beaver Island Historical Society, 1983), pp. 218, 219.

[8] Miscellaneous Records, Book 2, Leelanau County Register of Deeds, p. 605.

[9] "To Lumber North Fox," *The Evening Record* 21 July, 1906, p. 1, microfilm.

[10] Letter to Quentin Nickerson from Alma Plank, July 25, 1957.

[11] "W. N. Kelley Has Resigned," *The Evening Record* 14 Jan., 1910, p. 10, microfilm.

[12] *The Evening Record* 8 March, 1909, microfilm.

[13] Wakefield, p. 40.

[14] *Traverse City Record-Eagle* 19 & 23 April, 1923, p. 1, microfilm.

[15] Ibid, 16 July, 1924, p. 1.

[16] Ibid, 1 May, 1924, p. 1.

[17] Letter to author from John Ingwersen, Feb. 1982.

[18] Ibid.

[19] Ibid.

[20] Letter to Alma Plank from Quentin Nickerson, July 20, 1957.

[21] Williams, pp. 214, 215.

[22] Erwin Gale in telephone interview with author, May, 1995.

[23] Letter to Thomas M. Stevens, from James R. Wells, Cranbrook Institute of Science, July 23, 1984.

[24] Dennis A. Albert and Gary A. Reese, *An Overview of the Plant Community Ecology and Natural Area Significance of North Fox Island, Leelanau County, Michigan,* 29 Nov. 1989, p. 3.

Points of Interest

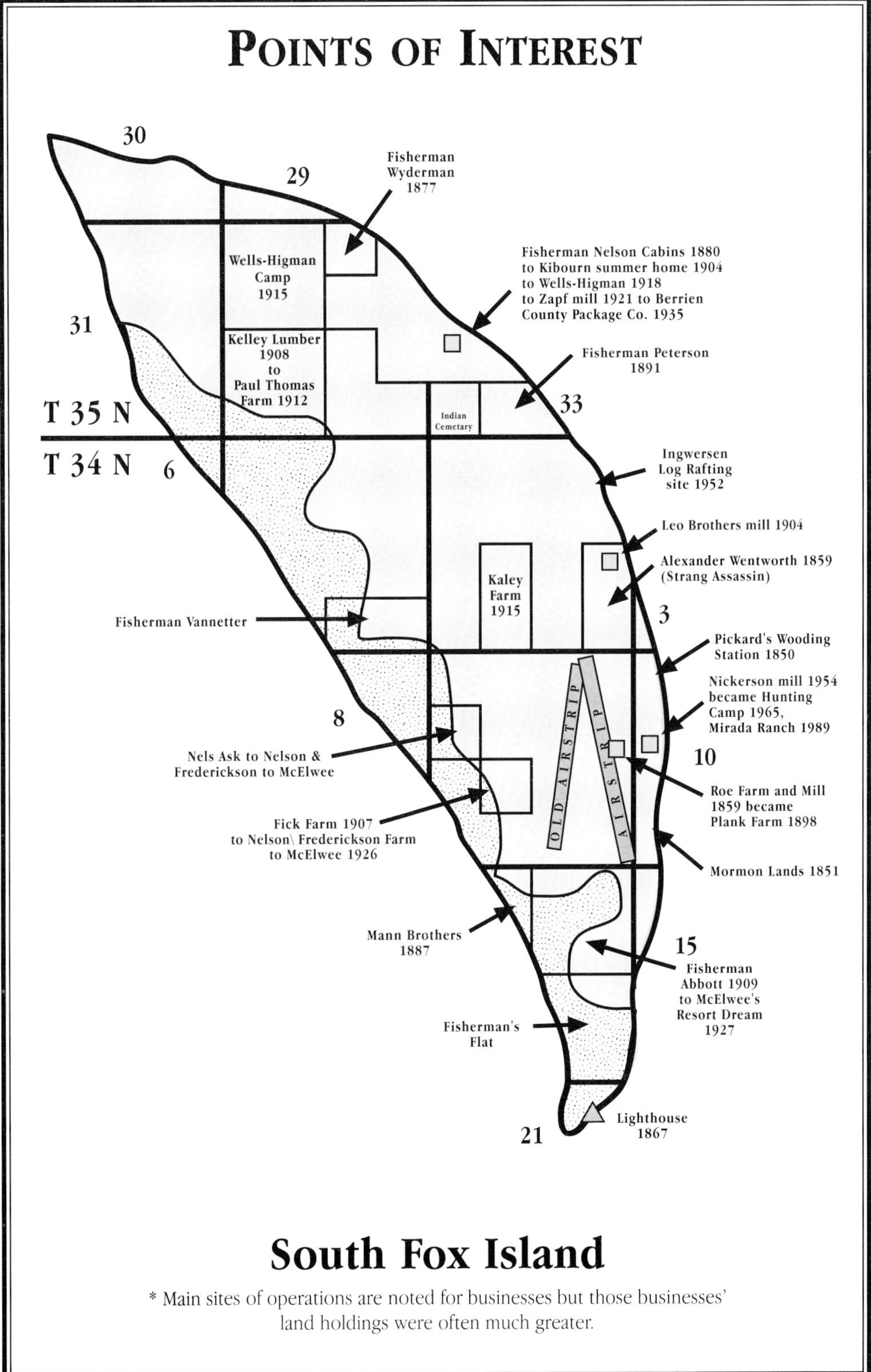

South Fox Island

* Main sites of operations are noted for businesses but those businesses' land holdings were often much greater.

PHOTO BY GORDON CHARLES
Hunting camp on public lands on the north end of South Fox Island, about 1989.

DEER HERDS AND HUNTERS

Except for dogs, hogs, cattle and horses brought by humans throughout the years, the Fox Islands have had limited species of larger animals. Hare populations have risen and fallen in cycles, and foxes have continued their presence on both islands. The winter ice or a floating log has brought an occasional beaver, but this animal has never become established. Coyotes began appearing in the 1990's on South Fox, but, as yet, there are no wolves or bears on either island. The one larger animal that has had an impact on the Fox Islands is the whitetail deer. Deer are not native to these islands but have been introduced by island owners, at least once on North Fox and twice on South Fox.

Francis D. Shelden, who purchased North Fox Island in August, 1959, planted deer on the island that same fall, partially to add to the assets of a small resort development plan. Two bucks and five does were purchased from a private deer farm in Charlotte, Michigan. Shelden had contracted with Frank Kalchik of Omena, Michigan, to construct an aircraft runway and unloading dock on the island, and Kalchik's fishtug *Ace* transported

PHOTOS COURTESY FRANK KALCHIK
In 1959 seven deer were transported to North Fox Island aboard the Ace *and then released from their crates to produce a new herd on the island.*

the crated deer to North Fox. Foul weather delayed delivery of the deer to the island, and they first spent a week in the garage at Kalchik's Omena farm and then another week aboard the docked *Ace*. Finally, the weather cleared. Frank Shelden was also aboard the *Ace* that day and helped unload the crates from the boat, anchored at the sandspit on the western side of the island. Some of the deer were slow to move into their new surroundings, away from the humans and the crates to which they had become accustomed. One young buck decided he didn't want to stay on his new island home and bolted into the water. The frightened deer made it about half way to South Fox Island before Frank Kalchik and the crew of the *Ace* were able to lasso the buck and pull it back on board. Again crated and back on North Fox, the run-away deer was carried, crate and all, on the front of Kalchik's bull dozer to be set free on higher ground. Gradually the new herd settled into its island habitat.

Feasting on their favorite browse, ground hemlock, the deer began to multiply. While it was obvious that the herd was increasing, the actual number of deer was hard to estimate, since the rabbit population was in its high cycle in the early 1970's, and both the deer and the rabbits were devouring the ground hemlock. In the spring of 1972, Francis

Shelden sent ground hemlock twig samples to the Michigan Department of Natural Resources for analysis. District Wildlife Biologist, Donald Y. McBeath, from the Cadillac post, responded that the browse sign comparisons of the years 1971 and 1972, from snowshoe hare activity on North Fox, was "a phenomenal sight."[1] Since a cyclic "crash" of the hares was expected, McBeath predicted that browsing pressure from the animals would "soon decrease." He also stated that the deer herd was showing an impact on the ground hemlock, but that a harvest of about 12 whitetails would be beneficial. In subsequent reports for 1972, Shelden recorded 13 deer killed in the hunt.

In October and November of 1973, the deer harvest increased to 30, with one being a 22-point buck, which was recorded as a trophy by Commemorative Bucks of Michigan. The number of deer killed was a surprise to the DNR, which reported that "our estimate of 50-60 deer on the island may have been conservative."[2] Even with the greater number of deer being taken, there was concern about possible disappearance of the ground hemlock. In his letter to Frank Shelden, DNR Biologist Robert Huff recommended that hunters "harvest the deer very close." He stated that, in order to keep the ground hemlock, "you may have to keep the deer herd at such a low level that deer hunting will be far less attractive than at the present (1974)." At the same time, the snowshoe hare population was still at the high curve of the cycle.

According to Frank Shelden, "It soon became obvious that introducing deer onto the island was a mistake."[3] He even considered introducing wolves to North Fox Island, wolves being a natural predator of deer. Shelden was not a deer hunter himself, but he invited friends from Charlevoix and Leelanau Counties, and from Canada, to harvest the whitetails.

By the 1974 fall hunting season, the ground hemlock was disappearing at an alarming rate. From October 1974 through January 1975, 144 whitetails were harvested. Some deer were taken as hunters walked in a transverse line from the south end of the island, driving the deer one-and-a-half miles to the northern airstrip, where other hunters waited beside the flat clearing. During one "drive" 15 deer escaped into the Lake Michigan waters and headed for South Fox Island. Shelden reported to the DNR that he didn't know if they "returned, made it or drowned!" Even with the increased number of deer taken, Shelden said that hunters estimated 50 or more deer remained on the island. Shelden transported some of the dead deer in his plane, landing in Charlevoix. Others were taken off the island by aviators such as Joe McPhillips and Ray Wood of Charlevoix and George Stevens and Jim Niessink of Leelanau County.

Robert Huff again expressed his surprise at the number of deer killed and acknowledged his underestimation of the population numbers. It was the DNR's position that the deer herd be removed from North Fox, if vegetation was to be preserved. In a 1975 letter to Shelden, Huff wrote, "Ground hemlock is mostly gone in several areas — all ground hemlock has been reduced through browsing. The hardwoods and elderberry on the south end of the island have been severely browsed. I suspect that many of the flowers, forbs, and herbaceous growth has been altered from summer browsing.... I would expect the deer to eventually use the (white) cedar if all the ground hemlock was gone."[4] Huff suggested that if deer were to remain on the island, the population should be kept at no more than 25.

Since all of North Fox Island was Frank Shelden's private property, the deer could be taken in any season, without bag limits. He continued to allow hunting in the off-season, and to the delight of ecologists, by 1976 there was no sign of any deer on North Fox Island. Gordon Charles, well-known outdoor writer and hunter, questioned that the deer could have been completely wiped out in so short a time. A whitetail carcass was reported on North Fox Island in 1989.[5] It may have been the last of a remnant herd, or just a lonely whitetail which wandered across the ice or swam from other island shores. Since the elimination of deer from North Fox Island, the ground hemlock has made a recovery and browse lines on the cedar trees have disappeared.

According to scientist Robert Hatt's 1948 publication *Island Life*, whitetail deer were introduced on South Fox Island about 1915.[6] This was during John Oliver Plank's residency on the island, and he is the one believed to have taken the deer to South Fox. Perhaps it all tied in with his dream for a resort. Hatt says the deer increased to about 40 by 1925 but were soon wiped out by some means. Some reports say that other residents began harvesting the deer before they became well established.

The second introduction of deer to South Fox took place in September of 1962, three years after Francis Shelden planted deer on North Fox. At that time, the Nickersons had just finished their logging operation on South Fox Island, and there was an abundant growth of ground hemlock, mountain maple, white ash and red elder, which had sprung up where the timber had been harvested. This was ideal food for deer, and Game Division Chief Harry D. Ruhl, of the Michigan Department of Conservation, agreed to a request from Sterling Nickerson and arranged to have 17 deer brought to the island. To prevent interbreeding, deer were selected from the Houghton and Cusino experimental feeding pens in Michigan's upper peninsula, from the Traverse City Zoo and Baldwin's Porter Ranch, in Michigan's lower peninsula.[7]

In 1962 fifteen deer were unloaded from a DNR truck and loaded aboard the Nickersons' Tramp, *bound for South Fox Island.*

Six male and 11 female deer were crated and loaded aboard the Nickerson's lumber carrier *Tramp* at Northport. Max Nickerson piloted the boat to South Fox, accompanied by other family members. According to Quentin Nickerson, the weather was rough, and almost everyone became sick except the deer. When they reached the island dock in the middle of the night, the deer crates were taken onto land and opened. The adult deer bolted off into the darkness, glad to be free; but the fawns were frightened and kept returning to the crates. They finally had to be pushed out from their security, and the crates were nailed shut to prevent the young deer from returning. Slowly, they joined the others and found comfort among the tangles of underbrush. The new herd fed on the lush vegetation and thrived, though two does were found dead the following spring. From the remaining 15 deer, the present deer population descended. Because of the excellent food supply and the absence of predators, the deer herd exploded rapidly, just as it had done on North Fox Island.

PHOTO BY GORDON CHARLES
Because of the excellent food supply and absence of predators, the deer population exploded rapidly

In 1965 Keith Chappel of Kingsley arrived on South Fox as caretaker. That same year, the first deer, an 18-month-old buck, with a dressed weight of 193 pounds and displaying 10 points, was shot during the first South Fox Island deer season. It was to be the first of hundreds of deer Chappel would see taken from the island. Sterling Nickerson spoke to game officials the following spring, "Years ago I was against killing does and fawns; now I know I was wrong... after only three fawn crops, we've had a deer explosion. If we don't shoot some of those antlerless deer this season, we're going to have starvation...."[8]

Later that year, the Nickersons sold their property, which amounted to two-thirds of South Fox Island, to Lynn Dillin, an industrialist with business operations in southeastern Michigan and Nashville, Tennessee.

During Dillin's first year of ownership, the Department of Conservation began allowing antlerless deer seasons on the island. Dillin and his friend, George Gee, converted the logging camp into a hunting lodge. The cook shanty that had served woodsmen now became a place where hunters traded stories of the day's adventures. In 1966 three bucks and three does were taken. In 1967 thirteen bucks and two does were killed. Outside the cook shanty, between the trees, poles were placed and the deer strung from them. As newspaper photos of the large and plentiful deer were published and the whitetails began coming off the island, it became evident that South Fox was no ordinary hunting ground. Earl Harger and Jack Cook's *South Fox Island Deer Story* relates," In 1967, at a highway checking station, department biologists happened to examine a large buck which had been shot on the island.... Information provided by the new owner in 1968 and a quick reconnaissance of the island by Dr. R. King and other department biologists clearly revealed that the deer herd was erupting."[9] In 1970, one of the best hunting seasons, 612 licensed hunters took 382 deer — seventy-six per square mile![10] How many additional deer were taken by archers or by poachers is not known.

PHOTO BY GORDON CHARLES
Keith Chappel, left, with Louis Reno of Kingsley, admiring one morning's kill of deer at South Fox Island. Note fox on right, also shot by a deer hunter.

North and South Fox Islands are part of the Beaver Island Wildlife Research Area, which meant that the Natural Resources Commission could authorize experimental hunts. These were begun on South Fox in 1969 and permitted a hunter to take two deer, one of which had to be antlerless. One hundred and eighty-eight deer were taken in that first experimental season.[11]

The fur trade and fishing had brought people to the islands 100 years earlier, and now the deer population brought others to South Fox, if only for a short season out of the year. Keith Chappel continued to manage the hunting camp for Dillin and was assisted for several seasons by Chuck Stafford, who first came to the island on a television assignment. Eager hunters who had heard of the large deer population came by boat and by plane, with hunting gear in hand. But, most of them didn't find the hunting as easy as they had imagined. While the dunes and dense foliage are beautiful to look at, they are difficult to conquer, especially in a foot of snow, while the hunter is wearing several layers of clothing and carrying a gun and other gear. Some city folks expected indoor toilets and hot showers at the hunting camp but were sadly disappointed when their lodging fees didn't cover such luxuries.

PHOTO BY GORDON CHARLES
Keith Chappel and a hunter load a deer for transport from South Fox to the mainland.

PHOTO BY GORDON CHARLES
Aerial view of western dunes and cedar area on South Fox Island shows difficult hunting territory.

If the hunters at the South Fox camp had a tough time, it was much harder on those who had not paid the fee and were hunting on state lands. They could come only by boat or sea plane, since the private landing strip was off limits to them. They also had to take their drinking water from the lake, sleep in their cold tents, and contend with patrolled lines bordering Dillin's property. A controversy arose between the mainland taxpayers and the Dillin camp. Citizens claimed that since the original deer had been placed on South Fox by the State of Michigan, one man shouldn't reap so much of the benefit. Dillin counterclaimed that he had a right to protect his property from vandals and trespassers. Tempers flared and several legal squabbles ensued.

The biggest was between Dillin and Lloyd Spears of Northport. Spears and Dillin apparently had a verbal agreement that the *Isle Royale Queen II*, piloted by Spears, could dock at the hunting camp. There was no other dock on the island. Dillin changed his mind after Spears had already received payment from several hunters, and legal exchanges followed,[12] resulting in Spears pulling his people off the public lands before the season was over.

Seasons were less controversial after an exchange of hunting rights was made, allowing the public to hunt on about the northern third of the island, with a solid boundary line dividing it from the paying hunters. The government lands and Dillin's private property on the other two-thirds were hunted by Dillin's camp. No hunting was allowed on the state-owned lighthouse property, eliminating the crossing of Dillin's land by non-paying hunters.

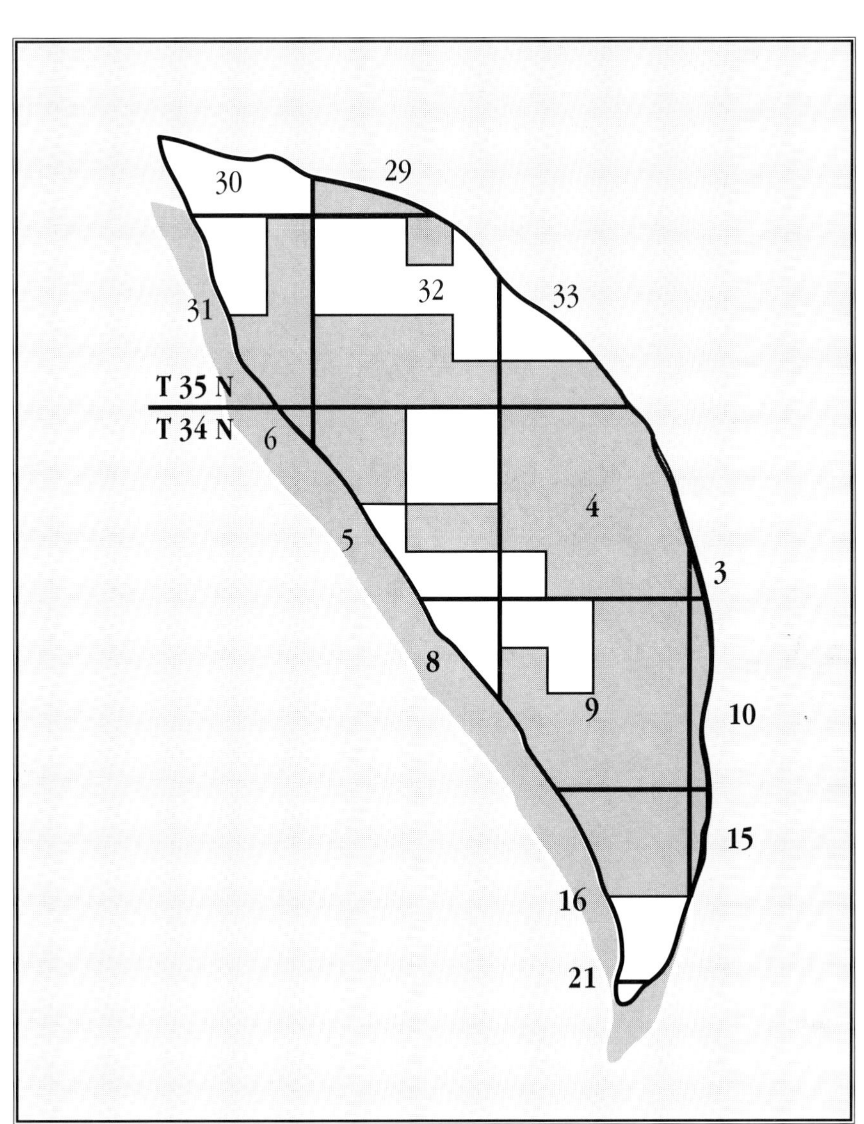

South Fox Island

Beginning in 1954, the Nickerson lumber company began purchasing South Fox Island property and, within a few years, owned all the area indicated by shading. This was sold in 1965 to Lynn Dillin. After his death, Dillin's island property was sold, in 1975, to Stanley Riley, Erwin Gale, and Thomas Stevens. The unshaded areas are owned by the State of Michigan.

South Fox Island

Leelanau County, Michigan

Deer Hunting by Permit Only

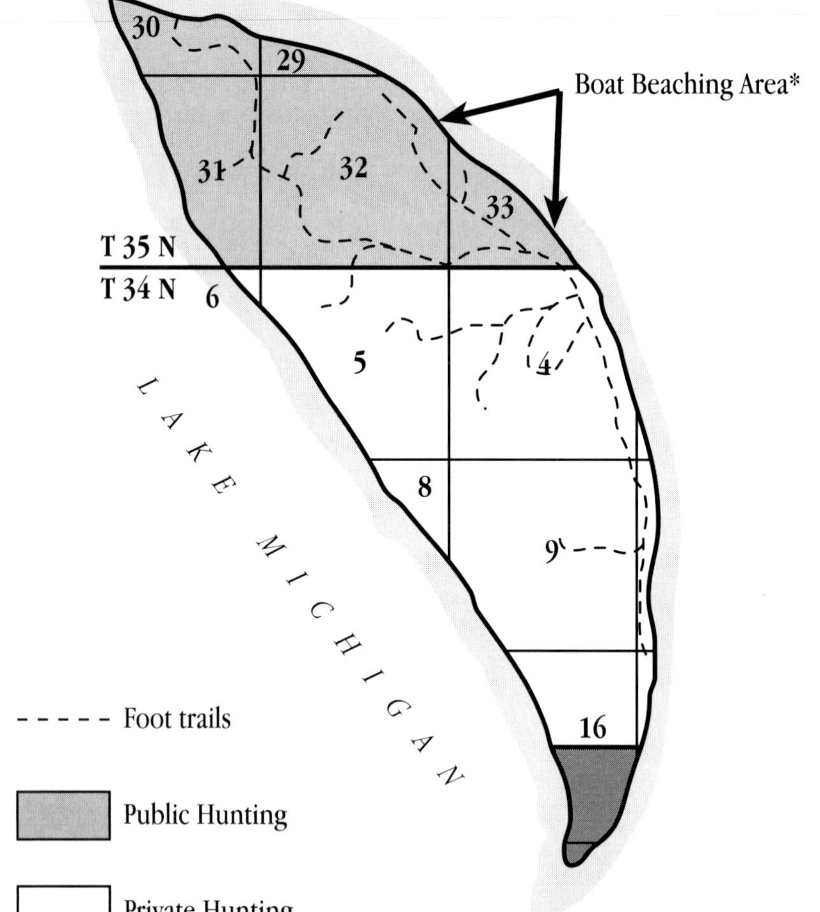

- - - - - Foot trails

Public Hunting

Private Hunting

No Hunting or Camping

R 13 W

* Lake Michigan can be extremely hazardous in November. Boating should be undertaken with great care. There is no sheltered harbor in which to anchor.

PHOTOS BY GORDON CHARLES
Lynn Dillin, left, and his wife Virginia were killed in this plane in 1973 while trying to land on South Fox Island during heavy fog.

The Department of Conservation, renamed the Department of Natural Resources, was anxious to control the deer herd, fearing that the population would destroy the foliage as the herd increased, and that a huge die-off could result. By that time South Fox Island had become famous, having more than 100 whitetails per square mile.[13] The experimental hunting seasons had been taking place as part of the control, but further measures were discussed, including the cutting of portions of timberland each year to maintain new growth. This was begun on a small scale but not completed, and a tragic event left the whole hunting question of South Fox hanging. In June of 1973, Lynn Dillin and his wife Virginia were killed when their small plane crashed while landing on the island during heavy fog. There was no one else on the island at that time, and the wreckage was not found until a week later when it was sighted from the air.[14]

The DNR estimated that there were between 600 and 800 deer on the island at that time, and a decision had to be made before new ownership was settled. The deer were in a precarious situation. Keith Chappel continued as manager of the camp and the Department of Natural Resources authorized a hunt for the 1973 season.

In conclusions reached by Harger and Cook in *The South Fox Island Deer Story*, they stated:

> *Failing either to manage or remove the deer will bring about the inevitable deterioration of the range and the animals. The vegetation of the island will be noticeably altered. A browse line will appear on the palatable trees and larger shrubs; the most preferred species will be eliminated from the flora, e.g. ground hemlock will disappear in a very few years. The understory of tree reproduction and small shrubs will be thinned out and the woods will eventually assume an open parklike*

> *aspect. The deer will become smaller in size, and antlers of yearling bucks will frequently be sub-legal spikes. Reproductive rate will decline, and die-offs will be extensive in particularly severe winters. The island will lose much of its charm and become a piece of landscape not much different from most of the deer-disturbed northern Michigan mainland.*[15]

PHOTO BY GORDON CHARLES
In 1973 the DNR predicted there were 600-800 deer on South Fox Island, urging that the deer herd be reduced or eliminated.

Hunters and conservationists wondered what would become of the hunting camp now that Dillin was gone. He had been falling behind on his payments to the Nickersons for the purchase of the island property, and after his death, a foreclosure was started. In October, 1975, this was averted when three men from Hart, Michigan, purchased it from Dillin's estate for $375,000 and paid off the Nickersons.[16] The new owners, Stanley Riley, Dr. Thomas Stevens and Erwin Gale, bought the island as an investment with the possibility of selling it to the DNR or the federal government as part of the Sleeping Bear National Lakeshore. One year later they offered it for sale for "a figure exceeding one million dollars."[17] In the meantime, Keith Chappel remained as camp manager.

Just before the beginning of the 1978 hunt, a sale did take place for an undisclosed amount. There was much secrecy about the new owners, who had the sellers promise not to reveal their identities, though it was generally concluded they were from the Netherlands or somewhere else in Europe. The mysterious new owners exercised their rights and caused a great disturbance by announcing that there would be no more hunts on their property. Hunters were scheduled to arrive soon, and Keith and Madeline Chappel were kept busy on the telephone, canceling the planned hunt. Then the new owners suddenly reversed their decision after being given "a quick lesson in deer biology," by Dave Jenkins of the DNR.[18]

In 1981 the mystery was solved with the breaking up of an illicit drug trafficking ring of which the new owners were a part. (More about this in another chapter) It was no wonder they had been reluctant to have any visitors on the South Fox property. With this development, the land was reclaimed by Stanley Riley, Erwin Gale and Tom Stevens.

A short time later, Stan Riley, Erwin Gale's brother Gordon, and two other passengers flew from Connecticut, with a planned stop-over at Hart, Michigan, and a destination of South Fox Island. Near Adrian, Michigan, their plane apparently developed engine trouble. The craft tried to make it to the nearby airstrip but struck a power line and landed in a soybean field, killing all four people aboard. Carole Riley, Stan Riley's widow, became the third partner in the Riley, Gale and Stevens ownership of South Fox Island.

The deer camp continued to survive. Hunters arrived in the small planes of George Stevens and Joe McPhillips. Others came by boat with George Grosvenor of Leland, Lloyd Spears of Northport, or in other small vessels.

Those at the South Fox hunting cabins began their days with ham, bacon and eggs, giant flapjacks and steaming coffee prepared by the cooks; George Gee, Chuck Stafford, Irving Hahn, Jim Pence, Fred Hoyt or others. Wearing several layers of warm clothing topped by hunters' orange, the men, and sometimes women, took to the woods. Some were taken by pickup truck to their selected hunting sites, and Keith Chappel transported others in the camp's all terrain vehicle. By supper time they returned with empty stomachs and stories to tell, some managing to bring down their quarry on the first day.

Sterling Nickerson, whose idea it was to put the original deer on South Fox Island, hunted there until his death in 1973. According to Chuck Stafford, Nickerson loved to stay up until all hours playing cards, and Stafford stayed up with him. Though Stafford thought it was great fun, the reckoning came in the morning when he had to get up at 4 a.m. to start breakfast. Nickerson liked to sleep in until noon.

COURTESY ERWIN GALE
Deer hunters take time out for telling deer stories, during a game of cards.

In the evening the deer were inspected as they hung from the buck pole outside the cook shanty. Although, for some, the terrain and tangled vegetation of South Fox proved to be too much, numerous hunters returned season after season. Some of these hunters were "honored" by having dirt trails named after them. Big John's Lookout, Gene's Drive and Paul's Loop were a few of these trails marked by casually painted markers. "Big John" Godbey, a pipeline electrician working in Fairbanks, Alaska, began many years of hunting on South Fox Island with the very first organized hunt. Other familiar faces were Louis Reno and Jim Pence of Kingsley; Marty Helm, publisher of the *Tri-City Times* in Imlay City; Gordon Charles, outdoor

PHOTO BY GORDON CHARLES
Writer Gordon Charles with a fine 12-point buck he shot on South Fox Island in 1980–the biggest trophy of his many years as a deer hunter.

writer for the *Traverse City Record-Eagle*; Charles Easterly of Grayling; and Bill Hubbell of Milford, who dressed in clothes of the voyageur era and shot with a black powder .54 caliber muzzleloader.

Sitting around the cook shanty, sportsmen proudly boasted about the trophies they had hanging outside on the buck pole. If a hunter admitted to "the one that got away," he was soon reprimanded by one of the cooks or the manager who came at him with a meat cleaver. To the new hunter, this could be a frightening experience, until he realized that only a piece of his shirt was being cut from him to be nailed from the rafters as a tribute to his folly. This bit of "horseplay" came to a stop when the rafters were covered with plasterboard in a move for modernization.

Two additions were also put on the cook shanty by the Riley, Gale and Stevens families. During the summer seasons, when there were no deer hunts, the three families entertained many friends at the camp. Their more comfortable eating quarters were destroyed in a fire, however, only three days after the closing of one of the November hunts. Three loggers narrowly escaped the burning building. Another loss to the hunting camp was the death of long-time island caretaker and camp manger, Keith Chappel, in May, 1988. The cook shanty was much easier to replace than the familiar caretaker who had managed the hunts most years since 1965. George Gee from Kingsley accepted the challenge.

In the spring of 1989, the owners sold their South Fox Island property to David V. Johnson, a businessman from Southfield, Michigan. Public access to the private lands was limited during that fall's hunting season, as Johnson made an assessment of the safety of the grassy airstrip and of how the hunts would be handled on his newly acquired land. In addition to the friends and family who hunted at Johnson's private camp that year, several hunters came by boat and pitched tents on the northern end of the island, designated for public hunting. Eighty-eight deer were taken from the entire island.

When the 1990 season began, improvements had been made to the old airstrip, and David Johnson allowed more reservations to be taken for the extended hunting period, the entire month of November. Continuing the arrangement first made with the Department of Natural Resources in 1971, a seasonal "swap" of hunting rights allowed for all public hunting to be done on approximately the northern third of the island, with private hunting extending to the south, almost to the government lighthouse property. The deer kill increased to 166 that year.

By the end of the 1991 season, thirty years of deer statistics had been kept on the South Fox Island whitetail herd. As reported by long-time hunter, Gordon Charles, in the

Record-Eagle, from the 1961 release of the original fifteen deer until the end of 1991, hunters had taken 2,644 deer.[19]

Deer on any island are always a concern for deer biologists. The borders are too limiting, the vegetation too vulnerable. The 1986 logging operations on South Fox created new development of undergrowth and nourishment for the whitetails. Only continued timber management will allow for natural reproduction of suitable browse. Although island owner David Johnson is not a hunter himself, he agrees with the DNR that the herd needs to be controlled to prevent a die-off. Some control comes by increasing the bag limit to three deer per hunter and by lengthening the hunting season beyond what is allowed on the mainland. Johnson and his employees on the island also give supplemental feedings to the deer. Imperial White Tail Clover, named for the Imperial White Tail Institute in Nebraska, was planted in 1991, along with three other varieties of clover. The deer also eat thimble berries, apples, morels and strawberries from the island's woods and clearings. Mineral supplements were initiated, by way of salt blocks, and by the 1992 hunt, the results of the supplements began to appear in increased antler growth.

COURTESY GORDON CHARLES
Mark Moore examines a 10-point buck mount, from a deer shot in 1992 by Gordon Charles.

With the goal of having fewer deer but of better quality, David Johnson worked with the Department of Natural Resources, District Six, and, in 1993, hired Michigan State University graduate student, Mark Moore, to live-trap and tag deer on South Fox so that a reliable census could be obtained. The work was directed by Dr. Harry Jacobson, Professor of Wildlife Management in the Department of Wildlife and Fisheries at Mississippi State University; and by Michigan State University Professor, Scott Winterstein, of that institution's Fisheries and Wildlife department. Dr. Jacobson had gained national renown for his whitetail deer research.

Moore set up several bait sites on the island. With drop nets placed over piles of corn, the whitetails were captured, ear-tagged and then released. Twenty camera sites were also set up around the island and the locations baited with corn. Two infrared sensors activated the cameras — one for motion and one for heat. The resulting photographs showed which deer had tags and which didn't and whether some deer showed up for retakes. One little buck, liking this easily found meal, was photographed 42 times. Johnson decided to continue the survey, and the same procedures were carried out in 1994. When the study was completed, the entire population of the deer herd could be determined.

Moore estimated from his camera census that there were 225-250 deer on South Fox before the 1994 spring fawns were born. DNR Biologists working on the pellet surveys were delighted when their results and Moore's were amazingly close.

The work of Mark Moore on South Fox Island was hoped by the DNR to be replicated on other islands and on the mainland. David Johnson was pleased with the work of Moore and, seeing the desirability of on-going research, hired Moore as a full-time employee. Moore's Master's Degree in Fisheries and Wildlife became an asset for further investigations on the deer, as well as in horse breeding research and other studies concerning the island.

In 1993, for the first time, the number of hunting permits was limited, and no buck with less than six antler points could be legally taken. This was initiated to see whether the number of trophy bucks could be increased. With bucks usually reaching their peak at about six years old, eliminating the hunting of small-antlered deer would allow for bucks to reach greater maturity. Two-thirds of the limited permits were granted to Johnson's private camp, since two-thirds of the property was his. This requirement for antler size held down the kill that year, and only sixteen bucks were taken, along with seventy antlerless deer. Each hunter was allowed three deer, but only one could be antlerless. A decision was made to continue this experiment for several seasons, in hopes of having fewer deer eating the limited foliage, as well as having larger, healthier deer for the hunters. David Johnson, with the advice of Scott Winterstein and the DNR, determined that a deer population of about 100 would be best for South Fox Island.

Charlie Blacker, manager of Johnson's development companies, also assumed management of the South Fox Island deer hunts when Johnson became owner of the island. As coordinator of all building projects on South Fox, Blacker's efforts were appreciated by hunters using the updated cabins, bathhouse, and hot and cold running water. Blacker worked closely with Rod and Gary Hayward, who added their muscle and talents to these hunting camp projects. Gary was given the nickname "gutpile" because of "special services" performed at the hunting sites. Gary also began field testing on South Fox Island for C. J. Buck, owner of Buck Knives, the largest producer of knives of all kinds in the United States.

Present-day deer hunters on South Fox Island's private camp lack little. Safe transportation is a priority, along with modern communications equipment. More comfortable sleeping quarters make visits more enjoyable, as hunters rest up for the next morning's hunt. Transportation to a hunter's favorite outpost is available by pickup truck, and deer are brought back to the buck pole in the same way. A day in the woods is topped off by irresistible aromas and tasty meals of prime rib and roast turkey, prepared by Steve Romanick, in the ranch house. And hunters still enjoy their evenings of sitting around the table, telling their tales of adventures in the wild.

Just as in the earlier days, some hunters return to hunt on South Fox year after year. Brian Berlenbach, Jamie Gibbs and Mark Hubbard, Dave Johnson's friends and associates, join the others in telling tales of their eight- and ten-point bucks. Cameron Piggott, Donn Vidosh and David Dettloff are other repeat hunters.

How has the deer herd fared? In some years, mild winters have kept the deer so healthy that many does have produced twin and triplet fawns. But, overbrowsing or a chain of severe winters could still cause a die-off of the herd. So far, the deer have survived beyond the DNR predictions. But the habitat has been affected. The once-lush ground hemlock has been nearly destroyed, although, by 1995, Mark Moore had enclosed some remaining patches. Cedar trees now carry a definite browse line. When a coyote was

MIRADA RANCH PHOTO
Brian Berlenbach and Mirada Ranch owner, David Johnson, in front of the buck pole, 1994.

sighted on South Fox during a 1978 deer hunt, some speculated that the DNR had planted coyotes there to wipe out the deer herd. The DNR denied that rumor, and it is likely that this and other coyotes wandered across the winter ice and have since reproduced. Coyotes have managed to get their photographs taken at deer baiting sites, with the electronic camera flash. They do not appear to be a serious threat to the deer herd.

According to Gordon Charles, in his "Outdoor" column of the *Traverse City Record-Eagle*, the hunting on South Fox Island is "just the way it used to be all over Michigan in the 'good old days' when it was hunter vs. deer. There are no bait piles (during the hunting season)... and you won't hear any kind of traffic noises in the distance, barking dogs or other distractions."[20]

No matter what past events have happened on the Fox Islands, sportsmen remember North and South Fox for their fantastic deer herds. While a future deer herd on North Fox seems unlikely, in 1995 David Johnson was issued a game breeder permit for the island, since it remains part of the Beaver Island Wildlife Research Area. This is a perpetual permit which would transfer to any future owner of North Fox. And surrounded by the waters of Lake Michigan, South Fox Island continues to provide trophy bucks for eager hunters.

A Report of South Fox Deer Harvests by Years

Year	Total	Notes
1965	1	
1966	6	
1967	15	
1968	28	
1969	188	
1970	382	probably heaviest whitetail harvest per acre in the world
1971	119	311 hunters
1972	24	
1973	53	91 hunters
1974	169	238 hunters
1975	140	132 firearm hunters, 155 bow hunters
1976	135	
1977	155	107 on private land, 48 on public
1978	70	164 hunters
1979	44	78 hunters
1980	73	83 hunters
1981	125	182 hunters (includes 8 by bow hunters)
1982	76	8 by bow hunters
1983	88	9 by bow hunters
1984	58	
1985	70	3 by bow hunters
1986	64	
1987	68	
1988	84	
1989	88	
1990	166	76 hunters on private land, 90 on public
1991	152	106 deer from private land (including 4 by bow hunters), 46 deer from public land
1992	114	73 on private land, 41 on public
1993	86	54 on private land, 22 on public
1994	66	38 on private land, 28 on public
1995	91	54 deer from private land, 37 from public land

These figures were recorded by and used with permission of Gordon Charles.

[1] Donald Y. McBeath, Letter to Francis D. Shelden, October 20, 1972.

[2] Robert Huff, Letter to Francis D. Shelden, June 25, 1974.

[3] Francis D. Shelden, facsimile to author, June 13, 1995.

[4] Robert Huff, Letter to Francis D. Shelden, February 7, 1975.

[5] F. Glenn Goff and Phyllis J. Higman, *North Fox Island Development, Environmental Impact Report* (Vital Resources Consulting; Sept. 1990), p. ES-4.

[6] Robert Hatt, *Island Life* In Lake Michigan (Bloomfield Hills: Cranbrook Institute of Science, 1948), pp. 48, 136.

[7] Ray Voss, "Extended Deer Hunting Season on South Fox Island No Setup," *Flint Journal* 20 Sept., 1969, p. 19.

[8] Jerry Chaipetta, "Ease Limits on Doe?" *Detroit Free Press* 1966.

[9] Elsworth M. Harger and Jack L. Cook, *The South Fox Island Deer Story*, Michigan Dept. of Natural Resources, Research and Development Report No. 164, April, 1972, p. 4.

[10] Ibid, p. 1.

[11] Ibid, p. 5.

[12] Mark Dilts, "Another season of hunter controversy on South Fox," *North Woods Call* 22 Dec., 1971.

[13] Gordon Charles, "South Fox Island could have 800 deer on five square miles," *Traverse City Record-Eagle* 23 Oct., 1973.

[14] *Leelanau Enterprise* 14 June, 1973.

[15] Harger and Cook, p. 20.

[16] Charles, "South Fox Island area sold for $375,000 to 3 men," *Traverse City Record-Eagle* 26 Nov., 1975, p. 3.

[17] Charles, "South Fox Island is Sold," *Traverse City Record-Eagle* 7 Nov., 1978.

[18] Charles, "Dutch trio who purchased island change mind on hunt," *Traverse City Record-Eagle* Nov., 1978.

[19] Charles "Hunters took 2,644 deer from release of only 15," *Traverse City Record-Eagle* 5 March, 1992, p. 5B.

[20] Charles "Weather hurt island deer hunts," *Traverse City Record-Eagle* 21 Jan, 1993, p. 4B.

CRIME AND PUNISHMENT

It's easy to think of islands as places unaffected by modern life. Some have tried to capitalize on the remoteness of the Fox Islands, believing that their distance from the mainland offers protection from state and federal laws.

The mysterious purchasers of South Fox Island, who bought it from Riley, Gale and Stevens late in 1978, wanted to keep their indentities and details of the purchase a secret. Three years later their reasons for secrecy were unraveled in the breaking of a drug-smuggling ring. The buyers had fallen behind on their payments for the property, and it was being reclaimed by the former owners when the mystery group was indicted by a federal grand jury in Detroit.

The ringleaders had bought the property with the help of a Birmingham, Michigan, lawyer, who was told not to complete the sale unless there was an agreement that neither the purchasers' names nor the price be made known. Investigators later revealed that the purchase price had been $950,000, with about $250,000 having been paid before the ring was broken. After the drug operation was discovered, five residents from the Flint, Michigan, area and several others, including the lawyer, were tried on varying charges of drug conspiracy, income tax evasion and operation of a continuing criminal enterprise. The purchase of South Fox Island was one of several efforts arranged to "launder" profits from the sale of drugs. Other cover-ups were businesses, homes, motor homes, yachts, diamonds and real estate. A group of interlocking trusts was set up to conceal the ownership of the island and other purchases. One of these was the Sagitta Corporation, based in Netherlands Antilles, West Indies. Sagitta was controlled by a trust fund on Guernsey Island in the English Channel. A beneficiary of that trust was a firm in the Cayman Islands in the Caribbean, which was in turn, controlled by another company in Liechtenstein.

Such complicated arrangements were made to foil investigators, but an 18-month investigation by the Internal Revenue Service and the Drug Enforcement Administration linked the South Fox Island owners to the other foreign corporations. Throughout the 1970's, the dope-smuggling ring allegedly brought tons of marijuana from Latin America to the Great Lakes area. Several persons were found guilty of the various charges early in 1982.

Late in 1976, North Fox Island also gained notoriety when its owners were charged with operating a pornography enterprise. The most prominent figure in this alleged crime fled to Europe, and at this writing, no prosecution has taken place. Leelanau County District Court file number 2233 may forever remain an open case, since many overseas countries will not extradite on these charges.

Other offenses have occurred regarding the natural resources of the islands. In 1986 a company of loggers was charged with the removal of over 700,000 board feet of timber from 130 acres of state forest property on South Fox Island. The loggers had a timber contract with the Riley, Gale and Stevens families, owners of the two-thirds private land on South Fox. The hired caretaker of the private property noticed the illegal logging and reported it to the Michigan Department of Natural Resources, which quickly launched an investigation. DNR forestry experts at first placed a value of up to $155,000 on the timber. The patchwork mix of state and private acres was cited as the cause of the loggers' intrusion into state forests. Whether or not the harvest of state timber was intentional, an agreement was reached whereby the offenders paid restitution of $28,000 to the state, an amount believed to reflect more accurately the timber's value.

The logging company had also sought to destroy a barge they had used as a docking and loading platform, by setting off charges of dynamite inside the barge. Shreds of steel and large pieces of yellow-orange Styrofoam were blown into the water and along the beach. As barrels and Styrofoam began to appear on mainland shores, an investigation traced the litter to South Fox Island. Although foam bits could be found for several years after, the logging company paid no extra fines but did clean up some of the debris.

It would be nice to think of North and South Fox only in positive terms, but evidence shows that even these beautiful islands have been touched by the negative side of humanity.

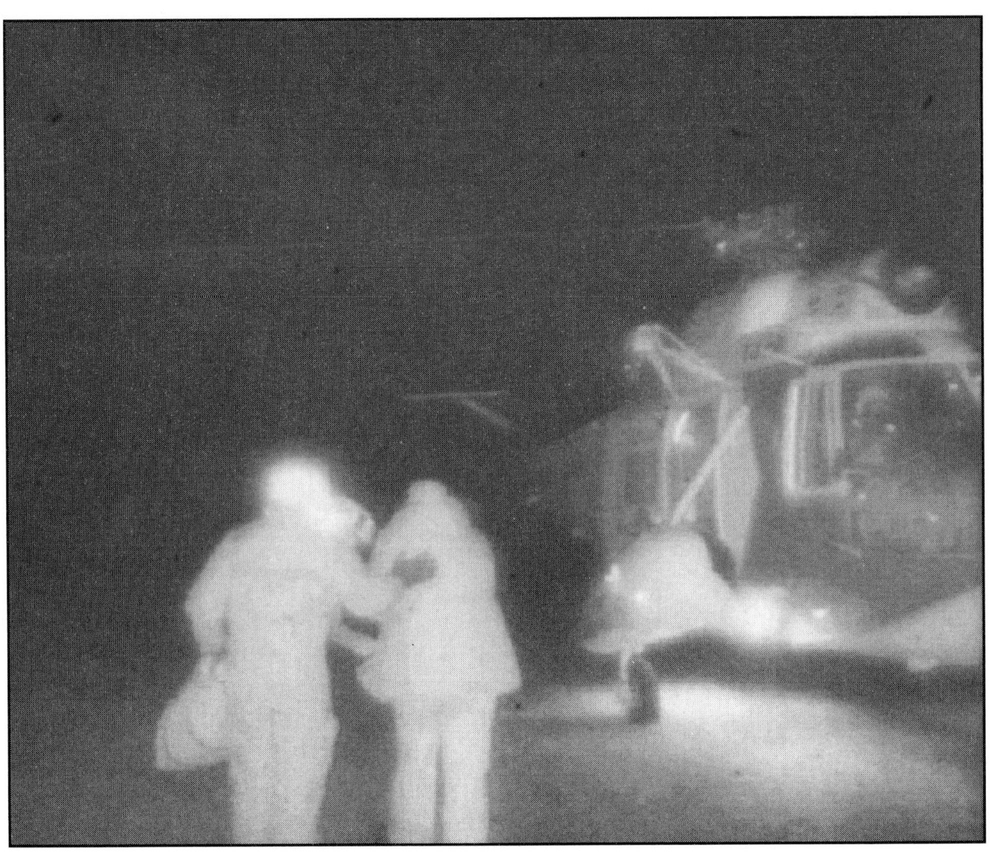

PHOTO BY GORDON CHARLES
A 1984 hunter prepares to board the Coast Guard helicopter, to be transported from South Fox to the mainland, for treatment of injuries.

EMERGENCY! FOX ISLAND CALLING!

Modern communications have made island occupants less vulnerable to tragedy than in years past. The remoteness of the Fox Islands makes any life-threatening emergency all the more serious, but through the years, health and safety measures have improved with time and technology.

Anna Palmer gathered ginseng from South Fox in the 1870's to make medicine. Her partial Native American ancestry bequeathed to her some knowledge of medicinal plants. The Raphaels and other Native Americans also harvested ginseng from the island woodlands. There were no modern remedies.

The Leo family had to make do with what was available at the South Fox lumber camp in the 1920's when little Willard climbed up to the high shelves and turned his tongue blue with a poisonous liquid. A mill worker made a fast sprint to the Ance farm to get milk, the only antidote available. Fortunately, the boy survived.

About 1930 Katherine Green, wife of South Fox Lighthouse Keeper William Green, fell down the stairs one night and broke her wrist. Without a modern hospital emergency room on the island, the assistant keeper's wife, Sadie Bourisseau, bound the wrist in bandages and it healed, although with a little bend.

Little Douglas McCormick was injured when, as a child living at the South Fox Light, his hand was trapped and scraped between the metal pier and the keepers launch, as the launch approached. His mother washed the cut, took her sewing needle and stitched the wound closed.

When Dick Boston, one of the Leo employees, was cut badly with a saw, he was transported out to the boatline, the common route for vessels, and taken to the mainland. Nels Ask was likewise fortunate when fisherman George Abbott went to Northport in his fish tug to bring Dr. Robert E. Flood to South Fox. Arriving back in Northport early the next morning, Ask's appendix was removed, and he recovered and later returned to the island to work. Irving Carlson injured his hand in a stone crusher, while working at the lighthouse in the 1920's. He was taken in the lighthouse boat to Northport, where the hand was stitched together by the doctor.[1]

In the 1950's a Coast Guard helicopter landing site was marked on the flat, sandy area just north of the lighthouse. The large criss-crossed lines graded on the "flat" is still visible from the air. Emergency helicopter landings were also made on the grassy airstrip to the north.

Archie Miller and Sam Brown were injured while working for John Ingwersen, and they were flown from South Fox to Charlevoix and taken to the hospital. Nelson Holton of Northport was removed from the island by a helicopter from the Coast Guard Air Station in Traverse City, when he was struck in the head by a logging chain in 1957.

On North Fox, Moses Carter accidentally chopped his foot while using an ax in the clearing of the airstrip. Frank Kalchik, who had been contracted by island owner Francis Shelden to clear the strip, took Carter to Northport aboard the tug *Ace*, and the injury was treated.

A Coast Guard helicopter rescued the elderly Sterling Nickerson when, during a 1960's hunting trip to South Fox, the weather prevented the hunting party from taking other transportation, and his insulin supply and all the food had nearly run out. Six other men and Nickerson's wife Eva were rescued at that time, after trying to depart from South Fox for nearly a week. The heavy winds and high snow drifts had caused one of the party's planes to overturn during an attempted take-off, and finally the Coast Guard was called.

In another emergency Orville McQueen, a deer hunter from Chicago, nearly had two fingers severed when the wind smashed a heavy, steel door against his hand during a 1984 hunt. By radio phone the emergency was called in to the air station, and a helicopter arrived through the night darkness to take the injured man to the mainland. But some emergency situations have not turned out so well.

When Martin Hansen was crushed between logs during loading operations on South Fox in 1924, there was nothing anyone could do; he died instantly.[2]

Kenneth Stauffer went from Kingsley to South Fox Island to work in the Nickerson mill in 1955, and he died there when a dead tree top fell on him that spring. The mail boat operator, George Grosvenor, transported Stauffer's body to Leland the following day.

During a heavy fog in June, 1973, Lynn Dillin's plane missed the South Fox runway, and he and his wife Virginia died on the island they loved. Their bodies were discovered in their plane a week later.[3]

Elmer Bergeron, the elderly caretaker for the closed-down Nickerson mill, died of natural causes while he was alone on South Fox. His death was suspected when he failed to answer the daily short-wave radio call.

On July 9, 1983, a U.S. Army Chinook helicopter crashed on South Fox Island. Six men from the 101st Airborne Division* died in the crash when their helicopter burst into flames as it slammed into a steep, wooded hillside, at a speed of about 115 miles per hour. The helicopter had been practicing over-water flight navigation when the crash took place,

PHOTO BY TED McCUTCHEON Elmer Bergeron, from Canada, cooked at the Nickerson lumber camp and continued on with the deer camp in the 1960's. He died of natural causes while alone on South Fox.

*Newspaper accounts reported "101st Airborn Division," but William Harrelson, a civilian spokesman at Fort Campbell, referenced the unit's "correct name" as the 160th Aviation Battalion.

just before midnight, on the southeastern side of the island. Killed in the crash were Chief Warrant Officer 4C Larry Jones of Redding, California; Chief Warrant Officer 3C Thomas Crossan II, of Falls Church, Virginia; Chief Warrant Officer 2C James Jansen of Newark, Ohio; Staff Sergeant Luis Sanchez of Vega Alta, Puerto Rico; Staff Sergeant Mark Cornwell of Colorado Springs, Colorado; and Sergeant Mark Reilly of Oceanside, California.

COURTESY TRAVERSE CITY RECORD-EAGLE U. S. Army officials examine the wreckage of a Chinook Army helicopter which crashed on South Fox in 1983.

Though Hansen, Stauffer, the Dillins, Bergeron, and the six men aboard the helicopter all died on South Fox, their bodies were taken for burial to other places. Some of the earlier residents are buried on the island that was their home.

The South Fox lighthouse workers made several daring rescues through the years, but the fourth keeper, William Lewis, met his fate when he died in June of 1885 from injuries received in a bad fall. There were no doctors or fast transportation. Lewis is believed to be buried in the unmarked grave on the little knoll behind the South Fox lighthouse.

In 1888, at age 46, Christopher Widerman (Wyderman) died of tuberculosis on South Fox.[4] His body may be buried there, but no confirmation has been found.

Although there was no traffic for the early children to fear, there was always the danger of the water. While the Robert Roe family was visiting the Manitou Islands in July of 1878, little Sarah, who was just over three years old, drowned after falling from the dock where a group of children were roughhousing.[5] Sarah was taken back to South Fox and buried near the family farmhouse. For many years a small fence protected the grave and a lilac bush bloomed in her honor. The Johnson horse corral fence now passes beside the little girl's grave.

Ivan Miller, a Peshawbestown resident who worked at the Nickerson sawmill in the 1950's, cleared brush and decaying leaves from the small cemetery in the area of the Native American allotments, near the center of the island. Some of the graves had small headstones, and Miller constructed white crosses for the others. There were no names on the markers, but it is known that Benjamin Ance, who died in February 1906 after being hit by a falling tree, is buried at this site. Benjamin and Jeanette Ance had previously lost an infant son, Oliver Ance, and he is probably buried near his father. Four-year-old Benjamin Raphael, son of Peter and Hattie Pewash Raphael, died on South Fox the summer of 1913. The cause of death was listed as "gastritis," and he is buried on the island.[6] Through the years the cemetery has again been taken over by Mother Nature and the wooden crosses destroyed.

When David V. Johnson bought the private holdings on South Fox Island in 1989, his first project was to insure maximum safety. A general clean-up was undertaken, including moving to one location the unsightly machine trash which was scattered everywhere and had resulted from earlier lumbering and hunting camp operations.

On the advice of his attorneys, use of the grassy airstrip by visitors was quickly discouraged, even to the point of limiting access during the usual deer hunting season. Listing safety as top priority, this airstrip was soon improved for temporary use, by wider mowing and improvement of the turf. A new runway was completed on South Fox Island during the summer of 1991, and lengthened in 1995. Industrial equipment was brought by barge from Ironton, on Lake Charlevoix, to construct the new strip. The old runway had been known for its downdrafts, lying on a low strip of field and next to the woods. The newer runway, with four wind socks, was designed to meet all FAA standards, is flat, straight and double the width, as well as twenty feet higher than the original landing strip. About 1,500 feet longer than the old runway, it measures 5,000 feet in length and is 120 feet wide. A 62-foot mono-pole beacon was installed in 1995 for nighttime approach. Johnson's twin engine Navajo Chieftain made its first landing on the new strip on Johnson's birthday, August 10, 1991. Johnson soon hired experienced pilot, Kenneth Chio, and purchased a King Air B-200, with state-of-the-art electronics. With his own private flying service, Johnson can be flown from Pontiac to South Fox in about one hour.

Inside Johnson's ranch house, the dining house, a digital weather station was installed, as well as an aircraft ground station for communicating with the aircraft. Johnson's first communication equipment consisted of only a ship-to-shore radio, which soon was accompanied by cellular and mobile telephones, citizen's band radio and a fax machine.

Because the old lumber dock had long since been broken up by the winter's ice, mooring buoys are used on the east side of South Fox Island, in order for watercraft to be held securely.

To promote health and safety, as well as comfort and self-sufficiency, a new septic system was installed near the buildings. Instead of the old boat-turned-reservoir that had sat among the tree limbs, a water-well distribution system was put underground, as were all of the electrical systems. Six generators were installed to supply the electricity.

One of the most difficult emergencies to handle on an isolated island is that of fire. In 1985 the 68-foot cook house burned when either the stove-pipe was knocked ajar or the fire was allowed to get too hot by careless loggers. Some of the men were burned on their arms and hands, but since the radio communications had also burned, there was no way to call for help. The fire occurred on Sunday, and the plane that was expected to arrive on Monday was grounded due to bad weather. The First Aid kit had also burned, so the injured had few resources to treat themselves. Finally, four days later, two of the loggers took the 16-foot boat and an extra motor out into the frigid waves and made it to land five miles south of Charlevoix. The injured men on South Fox were soon reached by a Charlevoix aircraft and taken to the mainland for treatment. Workers from the same logging camp were rescued on two more occasions – once when an all-terrain vehicle went end-for-end over a sand bank, and again when the cook broke her leg during a Fourth of July party at the South Fox dune. According to Erwin Gale, who had contracted the logging firm, "If it weren't for bad luck, the loggers would have had no luck at all!"

COURTESY ERWIN GALE
Keith Chappel examines the ruins of the new South Fox Island cookhouse, after it burned in 1985.

The farmhouse built by Robert Roe in 1859 and later owned by John Oliver Plank and then the Nickerson lumber camp, was struck by lightening and destroyed by fire in 1991 when owned by David Johnson. Johnson's Mirada Ranch workers battled a forest fire near the lighthouse, when hunters spotted the blaze during the 1991 hunting season. The workers could only fight that fire with shovels. Since there are no fire departments on South Fox Island, at the site of Mirada Ranch, two miles of underground sprinkler system can be tapped to pump 800 gallons of water per minute.

Present communications and better facilities on South Fox offer a much safer environment than in the past, and that adds to the peace and tranquility of this island in the waters of Lake Michigan.

As the future of North Fox Island is determined, the dangers of island isolation must also be considered in planning for residents and visitors.

[1] Bette McCormick Olli, The Way It Was, Memories of My Childhood at Grand Traverse Light (Northport, Mich.: Bette McCormick Olli, 1990), p. 3.

[2] Wisconsin Man Killed Loading South Fox Logs" in Traverse City Record-Eagle 16 July, 1924, p. 1. microfilm.

[3] "Bodies of 2 Found in Crashed Plane" in Leelanau Enterprise 14 June, 1973, p. 1.

[4] Leelanau County Death Records, Liber 1 & 2, p. 67.

[5] Manitou County Death Records p. 3, at Michigan State Archives, Lansing.

[6] Leelanau County Death Records.

COURTESY STANLEY DEFORGE
Milton and Zella Green spent much of their childhood at the South Fox Lighthouse.

CHILDREN OF THE FOX ISLANDS

When we think of the lives of people who have gone before us, it is common to picture adults only and ignore what it must have been like to be a pioneer child or a Native American child. As their parents set out for new territories and new frontiers, children had little or no say in decisions that affected their lives and sometimes their very existence. What was it like to be a Native American youngster, moving from camp to camp as parents searched for fish and game, walking north and south as the seasons changed? What was it like to be a European child on a sailing vessel, moving with the wind across the Atlantic Ocean to a land far away?

It is not known if any Native American children lived on the Fox Islands before the 1890's. The first white children found to have lived on South Fox Island arrived there about 1846. When Samuel Rice's wife died in Wisconsin, he was left with five small daughters. He took up fishing and built a home on Mackinac Island where he could base his operation. Like many fishermen, he sailed between the islands, and the summer of 1846 brought him to South Fox. Mrs. Snell, whose husband John was working on the surveying of the island, took Martha, Melissa, Emma and Anna Rice and their other sister (name unknown) into her home while the girls' father built a little house for them. From that time until the present, children, though not shaping the island's history, have witnessed it and lived it in their own special way. The Rice family left island living when their father married a woman from Beaver Island and they all lived for a time in Northport. By 1863 the Rice sisters were young women and attending school in the first schoolhouse in Traverse City.

In the struggle between Mormons and "gentiles," the children of the Fox Islands must have been bewildered at suddenly having to leave their homes. Although King Strang reported in 1851 that there were seven Mormon children living on South Fox with their families, we do not know how many there were at the time of Strang's assassination and the subsequent uprooting of the Mormons in 1856.[1]

In 1860 the U. S. Census recorded three children living on North Fox Island. Henry Roe and Laura Roe, ages ten and eight, lived on the island with their parents, Rushand and Harriet. Henry should not be confused with Henry Roe, child of Robert and Catherine Roe, nor with Henry Roe, the first lighthouse keeper of South Fox. Apparently, Henry was a popular name at that time, and there were at least three Henry Roes living on the Fox Islands in the 1800's. Ten-year-old Henry Roe and his younger sister Laura were both born in Illinois, and their parents may have moved to North Fox as part of James Strang's Mormon kingdom; however that has not been proven.

Another North Fox family in 1860 was John and Catherine Subnow and their one-year-old daughter Edell. The baby was born in Wisconsin and the family must have come to North Fox when she was only a few months old. It is hard for us to imagine anyone moving to an isolated and nearly deserted island and bringing a small baby along. But at that time, nearly all of the Great Lakes area was still wilderness, and living in remote places was the way of life.

The Subnow family was living on North Fox with 23-year-old Robert Boyd in 1860. Also living with Boyd was little John Fitz, just four years old. Until other proof is made, one can only speculate that Boyd took in an orphan boy or that John Fitz was Boyd's nephew or other relative.

North Fox Island property records indicate one child who received property on that island. Some Bounty Lands awarded to men who served in the Civil War were located on islands. Sarah E. Aydelott, young daughter of Private Joseph Aydelott was awarded 160 acres of some of the most beautiful property on North Fox Island, the eastern sandy shoreline and the dune. It is doubtful that she ever set foot on the island, and the land was later transferred by the government to real estate speculator Reuben Goodrich.

There are many unanswered questions concerning the North Fox Island children and their families. Why did they come to the island? Why did they leave and where did they go? There was no one at all, adult or child, recorded as living on North Fox Island on the 1870 and 1880 Censuses. On South Fox it was just the opposite. In 1860 no people were recorded on South Fox, but in 1870 and 1880 there were several.

Charles Roe was three months old in 1859 when his parents, Robert and Catherine, moved to South Fox Island to operate a wooding business, even though they were apparently away from the island the day the census was taken. Three sisters, Mary, Helen and Abigail, were born on South Fox, and then brother Henry arrived. After that, Katherine, Sarah and James were born. Some of the older children were sent to Buffalo, New York, for a time to receive an education. In 1867 the State of Michigan had deeded to the United States lots 3 and 4 near the South Fox lighthouse as "primary school lands," but there is no evidence of a school having been established. Charles Roe, being the oldest son of Robert and Catherine Roe, was the most assured to learn his father's trade. Passing steamers stopped to pick up cordwood; and extra hands, even young ones, were needed to load the wood into smaller boats to be taken out to the steamers. When the Roe family moved to Harbor Springs in 1881, Charles was a good enough lumberjack to operate the South Fox Island shingle mill his father had built. Fishing experience also made him an excellent fisherman.

Little Cora McFall was living in one of the Roe households in 1870, when she was eight years old. It is not known how she came to be there, nor any other details of her life. Florence and Mabel Roe were probably cousins of the other Roe children. Their father Henry J. Roe was the South Fox Light's first keeper and stayed on the island from September, 1867, to the middle of 1871. Florence was born in Illinois and came with her parents to the island when she was just a few months old. Mable was born about two years later, possibly on the island.

Mary Olson may also have been born on South Fox Island. Her parents had come from Norway and, by 1870, were living on South Fox, when Mary was just a year old.

Mary Garthe was 17 that year and had come to Michigan with her father and two older brothers just two years earlier. Her mother had died in Norway when Mary was just twelve years old. Mary and her brother Steiner stayed on South Fox with Ole Goodmanson while Steiner worked as a woodcutter, probably at the Robert Roe mill. Mary's father died four years after their arrival in Michigan, and so, this nineteen-year-old girl found herself without parents and living just four years in America. Her brothers, Steiner and Isaac, no doubt, looked out for her and they all settled in Leelanau County.

Other children living on South Fox in 1870 were Henry and George Williams, ages

14 and 12. They lived with their father (or uncle) Joseph, who had come from Ohio.

Anna Palmer, a widow, was living on South Fox Island in 1870 with her seven children: Mary, Julia, Edward, Lincoln, Augusta, Sarah and Jeremiah. Two other children, one two years old and the other six months, also lived with them. Their first names were Eddie and Edwin but the last names are unknown. Jeremiah Palmer was born on South Fox a short time after his father was lost on Lake Michigan. Anna and her children helped to support themselves by gathering ginseng and selling it to passing steamer crews for medicinal tea.

Other children born on South Fox during the 1870's were Elizabeth, Joseph, Clara and Grace Widerman, children of Christopher and Julia. By 1880 other Widerman children; Mary, William, Evaline and Elnora were living on the island with their parents, William and Elizabeth. William and Elizabeth had a least two other children, born in Northport in 1872 and in 1884, and it is nearly certain that little Jennie and Gertrude were also with their family on South Fox.

Mary Palmer Williams, daughter of Anna Palmer, was a young woman who was either widowed or abandoned by her first husband, Otto Williams. She wed John Floyd after he came to South Fox as a woodcutter. Most of their children were born on the island. Edward, Johnny, Mary, Anna, Agnes, Joseph, Elizabeth, Catherine, James and Frederick added to the busy household where Mary's older sons, George and Frank, already lived. Feeding a family this large was quite a task, and the older children were often asked to help by picking wild berries. Frank wasn't fond of this chore, however, and had a habit of putting small stones with the fruit in his pail, just to prove what a bad berry picker he was. The oldest child, Edward, is listed on a Beaver Island plaque "In Memory of Beaver Islanders Who Died on the Great Lakes," with his date of death being November 26, 1915.

Willis and Sarah Warner came to the South Fox Lighthouse in 1876. Sons George and William were already 18 and 16 when the family arrived, old enough to be of help to their parents, while Lillian and Clarence were only five and two. Another child of Willis and Sarah Warner was nearly born on the island, but his father managed to get the family to Northport in early December, 1881, just a week before the baby's birth.

These children lived the same pioneer lives their parents lived — a mixture of adventure, hardship, tragedy and joy. Somewhere in the stillness of the island's present are echoes of the voices of many nineteenth century children; though, surely, some of their names have been lost.

Probably the only family of these children who did not have others to pay with were the Rice girls, but their summer was not without adventure. This tale is recorded in *Island Stories* by Marion Morse Davis.[2] Besides exploring South Fox, the family spent time sailing to North Fox in their fishing boat, *Sea Gull*. One day Melissa and Martha decided to row the *Sea Gull* over to North Fox by themselves. Young and inexperienced, they soon lost the oars and then the rudder. North Fox was ahead of them and South Fox behind. To the northwest was only the vast expanse of water, and a southeast wind could take them out of sight of any land. Stranded and helpless, they were fortunate that a friendly wind began pushing them in the right direction, back toward South Fox. Their father sighted them, and as he came near in another boat, he threw them a rope. Frightened and glad to be towed ashore, the girls promised never to go off on such a venture again.

The Big Lake was sometimes friend, sometimes foe. While it made possible the transportation of wood products from the Roe mill, it also brought Robert Roe and his other children scrambling out of bed in the middle of the night at the sound of a gale. The sons knew it was their job to help take their boat to the other side of the island, where it would be sheltered from the battering wind and waves.

COURTESY JAMES & HARRIET ROE Catherine Fenton Roe

Robert and Kate Roe looked out for the safety of their children on occasions such as this. Kate also cared for the well-being of the sons of families she knew back on Beaver Island. When a Civil War recruiter stayed with the Roe family while on his way to Beaver to recruit young men for the war, Kate had a plan for protecting those she knew. She gave the recruiter enough liquor to make him pass out, found his recruitment roster and removed the names of those men and boys she wanted to protect.

But all adventures were not so dangerous. The Roe family history notes the visits by two well-known people. Chief Andrew Blackbird of Harbor Springs brought his bride to the island for their honeymoon, and the newlyweds stayed in the Roe home. According to notations left by Catherine Roe, one day a passing steamer lay over at South Fox. Among its passengers was Mrs. Abraham Lincoln, who was soon a guest of the Roe family. Imagine the children's glances, knowing that the well-dressed lady at their table was the president's wife!

Nathan DeGrolier was fourteen in 1880 and his sister Ida a young lady of 21, living with their father and mother as their father was stationed at the South Fox light. It has not been determined when the family first arrived at South Fox, but they moved to Northport in the fall of 1880.

The 20th Century found other children living on South Fox. The Bourisseau children were some of the first of these. Frank was the youngest child of Lewis and Susan Bourisseau. He and his brothers, Louis, William, and James, and their sisters, Philaman, Josephine and Gertie lived at the lighthouse where their father worked. Frank watched his father and the assistants clean and light the lamp which glowed from the tower. He counted the 48 metal steps which circled to the top of the building, probably never dreaming that when he was grown, he would climb those steps as an assistant keeper of the South Fox Island light. His childhood experience at South Fox was good training when,

COURTESY LAVERNE SWENSON
Dale and Keith Bourisseau sitting on the roof of the storage building near the lighthouse, about 1924, when their father, Frank Bourisseau, was an assistant keeper. Grandfather Lewis Bourisseau was a keeper at South Fox, beginning 1891.

as a man, it became his turn to light the lamp.

The Indian settlement, near the middle of the island and extending to the north, brought several more children to South Fox.

When Louis and Margaret Ance arrived on the island in 1903, they brought their grown, married children and their son Ben and daughter Abbie. When Ben finished attending school on the mainland, he married Jeanette Oliver from High Island; and they lived on South Fox, where their son Julius was born. Julius Benjamin Ance was named after his father and his Uncle Julius, who had died just before the Ance family moved to the island. Before little Julius really had time to get to know his father, Ben was killed in a logging accident on South Fox. It was a sad time for the family and doubly sad when Julius' mother decided to return to her people on High Island, just west of Beaver Island. Knowing that some months later she would give birth to another child, and following the Native American custom of dividing the children when a family separates, Jeanette left three-year-old Julius in the care of his grandparents, Louis and Margaret Ance.

COURTESY DOROTHY WEBB
Julius Benjamin Ance continued to live on South Fox with his grandparents, after his father died in 1906 and his mother returned to High Island. This photo was taken on High Island while Julius was visiting his mother.

A bed was made for him in the storeroom, and Grandma Ance took good care of him. He liked to see the apples drying from the kitchen ceiling and to taste the maple sugar. He enjoyed playing with his cousins; but when he was alone, he found chasing the chickens to be good sport. Or he could comfort the little ox named Washington. Born on George Washington's birthday, the ox had later had its ears frozen off by the cold. Grandpa Ance built Julius a little sled, which the ox pulled while Julius rode. Between his playing and visiting his cousins and Aunt Lizzie, it was Julius' chore to haul water from the well nearly a mile away. Sometimes he visited his father's grave near the Ance homestead, and occasionally he was taken to High Island to see his mother and sister Emaline. Julius left South Fox forever when he was eight years old. The Mount Pleasant Indian School became his new home. When he finished there, he attended Haskell Institute and then went into federal service at Crownpoint, New Mexico.

It was a case of a brother and sister marrying a sister and brother. After Ben Ance had married Jeanette, Ben's sister Abbie married Jeanette's half-brother, John Andrews. Abbie Ance was only ten years old when her parents moved to South Fox Island, and about nine years later she and John married. Their two oldest children, Henry and Raymond, were born on the island. As with all of the other island births, there were no doctors — only women assisting each other in their deliveries. Sometimes there were problems and the babies didn't survive. When they made it safely to toddler years, parents had to keep a close watch — it was so easy for a child to get lost in the dense woods; and, of course, there was always the danger of the surrounding water. After one frantic search for little Henry, his parents were happy to find him wandering among the trees, carrying a sap bucket. At least Henry knew where to find food. The Andrews family left the island in about 1916 when it was time for Henry to attend school.

There were several other Ance children on South Fox at that time. August and Christine Ance lived in their log cabin with their first four children: Fred, Mable, Luke and Francis. Lizzie Ance Chippewa and her husband Enos were the parents of John, Dorothy and Josephine. Marceline Ance married William Pabo, and he had a daughter Clara from a previous marriage.

COURTESY DOROTHY WEBB
Raymond and Henry Andrews left South Fox Island with their parents in 1916 so that Henry, on the right, could attend school in Northport.

Alex Cornstalk gained his Indian allotment when he was just a child living in Northport. His family moved to the island, near the Ance lands. Alex lived long enough to become the person who owned South Fox Island property for the greatest length of time — about 52 years. He lived his adult life on the Beaver Islands but sometimes came to the Fox Islands to fish.

Peter and Hattie (Pewash) Raphael had a little son named Benjamin. Near the northern end of South Fox, Benjamin lived with his parents. But when he was about four years old, he died of gastritis and was buried on the island in June, 1913.

Joseph D. Raphael was born June 1, 1916, near the South Fox Island dunes. His parents were Peter and Rose. When Joe was only about three years old, his mother died, and he and his father had to go it alone. They lived in a small, frame house on the island off and on for about six years, with travels to the mainland to wherever his father could find work. At South Fox, Mr. Raphael took care of the Zapf Fruit Packaging Company's horse teams. The Zapf Company had two kitchens on the island, and one of young Joe's greatest delights was to go between kitchens sampling the pumpkin and mincemeat pies.

Most island families had gardens to tend, and some had cows, chickens and pigs. There were summer weeds to pull, barns to clean, eggs to gather. One rewarding chore was that of picking wild strawberries and thimbleberries. The Raphaels and other Native American families also made maple syrup and maple sugar.

Joe Raphael had no other children to play with until the lighthouse keeper's children would arrive for the summer. Then he and his dad would sometimes borrow a horse from Zapf and ride to the tip of the island to visit the McCormicks and Bourisseaus.

Sometimes Joe and his father would walk around the island gathering floats which had come loose from fishermen's nets and washed ashore. The Raphaels would then go to the mainland in the lighthouse boat, or on Captain Anderson's barge, and take the floats to mainland Omena and sell them. Wooden floats sold for a penny each, and aluminum ones brought five cents. Joe got a new suit of clothes from the sale of one of the batches.

Joe went to school in Harbor Springs and then in Peshawbestown, where he was expelled for skipping too much. When he was 14, he went to Traverse City and worked in the Zapf factory there. He settled in Peshawbestown in later years.

John Oliver Plank came to the island with his dream of a resort in the late 1800's. In 1899 he invited his friends from Chicago, Frederick and Ruth Kilbourn, to spend the summer with his family in their big house on the island. The Kilbourn children, also named Frederick and Ruth, came with their parents. By the next summer, the Kilbourn family had their own house on the island and spent several summers there.

The children took many pleasant and some not so pleasant trips by boat from their Chicago home to Northport. In Northport they boarded a car ferry, which took them close to the South Fox shoreline, and then a lifeboat took them to their property along the beach. Their parents had bought the land and buildings from fisherman John Nelson. Nelson had built a small house, a fish storage shed, a building for skinning the fish and one for stringing nets. The Kilbourns used these as a divided house, with separate quarters for eating and for sleeping.

Young Ruth and Frederick were acquainted with the fishermen on the island and would sometimes go for a ride with Louis Ance on his sailboat. They also enjoyed watching Mr. Schrader tighten his purse net, trapping the fish inside. Such enjoyable hours were interrupted at mealtime when the maid, whom their parents had brought from Chicago, would clang the iron dinner hoop hanging outside the kitchen building.

In November of 1905, during a violent storm, the steamer *Vega* sank with a load of iron ore off South Fox. Indian families helped to rescue the crew, but the vessel sank to the bottom. As Frederick and Ruth later rowed their little boat around the wreck, they felt a part of a "spooky" adventure, seeing the vessel through the water, which distorted its image below.

Bernice and Hildegarde Leo, children of William and Anna, watched the *Vega* being salvaged one summer by men wearing rubber suits and using air pumps. The sisters and their younger brother, Willard, shared many memories of their childhood years on the island, from 1904 to 1921. Willard was honored by their father when the family boat was named *Willard L.*

COURTESY BERNICE LEO
Taken about 1914, this photo shows Mrs. Frank (Gertie) Stafford, left, and Mrs. William Leo in front of the Leo brothers' cook shack. Children are, left to right: Willard "Red" Leo, Marcella Leo, Hildegarde Leo and Dorothy Stafford.

Bernice, Hildegarde and Marcella Leo worked along with Willard to tie shingles into bundles as the product came from their father's mill. Their family's house sat on a little hill not far from the mill and was sided with some of the shingles the mill had produced. In

COURTESY HILDEGARDE LEO MCDONALD *Little Hildegarde Leo stands in the foreground of the Leo mill on South Fox. She and her sister and brother helped to bundle shingles, as shown by the mill, when they were old enough.*

addition to their chores, the Leo children found plenty of time for play. One of their friends was Christine Raphael, whose mother cooked for a time for the mill hands. Dorothy and Wilbur Stafford were other playmates when their parents also cooked at the mill. Sometimes the Leos would walk to the other end of the island with their mother or Aunt Cora to get the mail, which came in every two weeks at the lighthouse. That was a pleasant chore, for there they could play with the lighthouse children.

Sometimes more than one family of children lived at the lighthouse. The keeper's family and the assistants' families shared the property, and their times of service overlapped. The Bourisseaus knew the Greens, the Greens knew the Wilsons and Dames and McCormicks, and so it continued. The children often attended school together in Northport. During the summer months the school-age children would join their parents and younger brothers and sisters on the island.

William and Mary Wilson arrived at the lighthouse in 1898 with their teenagers, Mary and Ella, 10-year-old Ethel, and toddlers, William Edwin, and Douglas. Wilson served at the light during two different periods, for a total of six years. During the school months, his older children lived in Northport at the Porter House Hotel with their grandparents.

Zella Green came to the lighthouse with her parents, Will and Kate, in December, 1907, when she was three years old. Her brother Milton was born about two years later, and these two children spent many seasons at the island. Zella found island living to be rather lonely, seldom having a girl her own age to play with. For a time Annabel Comfort was there when her father came from Charlevoix, with a work party, to build the new assistants' quarters. And Jeanette Plank, daughter of John Plank, Jr., spent some time on the island.

Milton sometimes played with Dale Fick, son of farmer Adolph Fick. And Assistant Buttars children, Margaret and George, were closer in age to Milton, than to Zella.

COURTESY LUJEAN BAKER
William and Mary Wilson and their children spent six years at South Fox Island lighthouse at the turn of the century. This photo, taken soon after the family left the island, shows (left to right) sons, William Edwin and Douglas, and daughters, Mary "Belle", Ella, and Ethel.

Occasionally Zella would go by rowboat for a visit to the Leo mill with some of the lighthouse workers. She visited with Bernice and Hildegarde there, and sometimes played with Josephine Chippewa. Whenever the assistants from the lighthouse went off on a little adventure, they took Zella along. Besides rowing to other parts of the island, they sometimes took her away from shore to watch the fishermen lift their nets. On the lighthouse grounds bricks and sand were arranged to make miniature villages for Zella; and the men named them Zellaville and Greenville. Sometimes Zella would pretend that a clump of birch trees near the lighthouse was her little home. One summer there was a litter of puppies born in the old boat house by the fishermen's flat. Assistant Vannetter owned the mother dog, but Zella selected the smallest pup to be her own and named it Teddy. The playful puppies helped relieve Zella's lonliness that summer.

Zella and Milton's years at the lighthouse were a combination of happy days and lonely ones, and the foggy nights were frightful. The loud and mournful warning of the foghorn kept them awake and made them afraid, but it wasn't quite so bad after their father took them into the signal house one night and let them see how the horn worked. Will Green took his children past the men who were shoveling coal to feed the steam

COURTESY SALLY GREENE *Everyone enjoyed a visit with the lighthouse families. At left are Mr. and Mrs. William Leo and baby Marcella. Hildegarde Leo, Zella Green, Bernice Leo, and Milton Green are standing. Susan Bourisseau, Gertie Stafford, and Kate Green are seated at right. Wilbur and Dorothy Stafford are the children in front, in this 1914 photo.*

boiler and up the stairs to the horn. Though the sound was nearly deafening, they were somewhat relieved to find that it was only a bit of machinery and not some horrible monster. A sound Zella and Milton didn't mind was that of firecrackers brought by their father, for the Fourth of July.

On quieter days there was the dog to play with, a whittling spot beside the assistants, overlooking the great expanse of water, or the wonderful, big basement where the children could roller-skate. Zella loved the big, brick house and spent many hours playing with paper dolls in the nearly empty rooms, cutting the figures from the *Ladies' Home Journal.*

COURTESY BERNICE LEO *William and Anna Leo and their children lived in this cottage near the Leo mill on South Fox Island. Some of them slept in the tent shown in the background at the left. This home and other buildings at the Leo mill site were later moved by the Wells-Higman camp, to the northwest shore of the island.*

Because of Zella's loneliness for other children, her parents arranged for her to spend one summer in Northport with her Uncle Howard and Aunt Laura Green. It seemed a fine plan, except that Zella missed her family so much, she caught the first lighthouse boat headed back to South Fox. Zella didn't like boat rides because she always became seasick from the motion and the smell of the gasoline engine. When her father was piloting, he tied a rope around Zella and set her on the top in the fresh air. When she was lying on the floor sick, Zella was always happy to hear her father's words, "Slack her down!" and then "Shut her off!" That meant they were coming to the dock and the voyage was almost over.

Sometimes the island families were transported to South Fox by large ferries that carried railroad cars between Northport and Wisconsin. That was always a smoother ride than on the smaller boats.

When Will Green was keeper, the lighthouse property was sometimes shared for a few weeks in the summer with The Reverend Allington's Northport Boy Scout troop. About 15 boys sailed to the island on the lighthouse boat and then pitched their tents on the well-kept grounds. From there they explored the island wilderness, beaches and dunes.

When James McCormick served at the light, from about 1915 until 1924, his apartment in the assistant's quarters was a busy place. He and his wife Mary had ten children. Violet, James, Justine, Margaret, Don, Douglas and Leon arrived at South Fox Island with their parents; and Bette, Janet and Grace were born in Northport during McCormick's duty at the island.

The lightkeepers' children would have the normal tasks any mainland child would have, but mainland houses were not subject to unannounced inspection at any moment by the federal government. Though these children surely visited the beacon tower with their fathers, fingerprints on the brass could not be tolerated. When Mrs. McCormick saw the inspector pulling into the boatway, her many children had to disappear so that they could not leave anything out of place.

It was a good time to go to the Plank farm where their sister Violet worked, and where their family had a garden of strawberries and vegetables. But if they saw Plank's wild horse coming toward them, they dropped everything and ran the opposite direction. Sometimes they would stop by the Leo Brothers' lumber camp and be invited in for a meal with the mill hands. That was always a treat because the cooks served such delicious food. At other times, they picked ginseng for their parents to sell.

One day Margaret found some discarded cans of paint, used by the keepers, and painted her younger brother Don. Most of his bare skin was painted green, but he had red buttons down his belly. When he was a little older and wiser, Don sometimes made boats from the cork floats of fishing nets. Even while living later at the Grand Traverse Light at Cathead Point, the McCormick children were reminded of "Old 63," the South Fox lighthouse keepers boat, since brother Don's cork float boats were modeled after it. Two of the McCormick children carried on the maritime tradition; Don became a sailor on the Great Lakes ore carriers, and Douglas served over 30 years in the Coast Guard before becoming a resident guide and caretaker of the historic Grand Traverse Light.

Though South Fox Island's population was never very large, there were still occasions for romance. When James McCormick's son James was old enough, he married Mabel Ance, the daughter of August and Christine Ance. Another match was made when McCormick's daughter Violet married Assistant Keeper Irving Carlson, from Leland. Their children, Irving, Jr., Darrell and Rosalie soon took their places among South Fox Island's youngsters.

COURTESY DOUGLAS McCORMICK
Rosalie Carlson, daughter of Irving Carlson and Violet McCormick Carlson.

Fred Leslie, Jr., went to the lighthouse when he was six years old and lived between there and Northport most of his life. He died in 1939, at age 19, in Northport while his father was still stationed at South Fox. Another lighthouse youngster who died early was Vivian Dame, adopted daughter of Oscar and Ella Dame. She died in Northport in 1928 when she was 15. Lighthouse children who were more fortunate were Dale, Keith and Zane Bourisseau, sons of Frank and Sadie Bourisseau.

Certainly, there were other children throughout the years, who lived with their families at the lighthouse. For some it was for only a few months, while their Coastguardsmen fathers spent a summer season there.

Another visitor to South Fox, whom the Leo children enjoyed, was John Oliver Plank. He would come sailing in on his yacht to spend time at his big house, the house built by the Roe family. Bernice Leo recalled that Plank was not a very large man. The children would measure their feet next to his while he told them they would be grown up when their feet were as big as his.

The Leo sisters often played with the Ance and Raphael girls. One day they were walking along one of the dirt roads and, rounding a bend, came face to face with the cows of Paul Thomas. Frightened, the girls scattered quickly, and while the others climbed a tree, Bernice ran the opposite direction. Mr. Thomas was close by and chased the cows away from the base of the tree where they were pawing with their hoofs. The other children scampered down the tree, but Bernice was not found for several hours. She had taken refuge in the upstairs of an abandoned building on the Ance farm and was afraid to come down. Huddled in the attic, she was fully convinced the unfriendly cows might even climb the stairs to get her.

One special adventure the Leo children and their friends enjoyed on the island was looking for the buried treasure. The different versions of treasure legends of North and South Fox Island are covered elsewhere in this book. The Leo children sought a valuable treasure, which was supposedly buried next to a tree with a nail in the bark. Whenever they and their friends walked in the woods, they kept an eye out for such a tree. Maybe someday they would get lucky and go back to the mainland with their riches.

There was no church on South Fox Island, but Mrs. Leo always made her girls get dressed up on Sunday. Abbie Ance had a sewing machine on the island, and being a good seamstress, was hired by Mrs. Leo to make dresses for the girls. Some traditions just couldn't be broken, even on an isolated island. Another of those was the raising of the American flag. Every day their father William and Uncle Herman raised the Red, White and Blue.

About 1934 Jim Goudreau arrived on South Fox with his mother and his father, as his father became third assistant keeper. In *Living At A Lighthouse*, published by the Great Lakes Lighthouse Keepers Association, Jim recalls doing chores around the South Fox Light grounds. He would mow grass, help unload supplies from the barges, and roll the fifty-five gallon drums of oil up the hill. During the winter months Jim and his mother would live at Seul Choix Point, where he could attend school.

One thing that couldn't be accomplished on the island was schooling, though King Strang made reference to a township meeting to be held on South Fox Island at the district schoolhouse. Apparently, the Mormons did have a school of some type. Some of the earlier children on the island just didn't attend school, and therefore didn't learn to read or write. But most of them spent the school year on the mainland, some in Harbor Springs and many in Northport. The Leo children lived in Suttons Bay in the winter.

Cheryl Davis lived at the lighthouse with her grandparents, Al and Anna Cain, during most of her first five years. By that time, in the late 1940's, there were no other children on the island. According to her grandmother, Cheryl had no time to get lonesome, though, being the apple of everyone's eye among the lighthouse employees. Cheryl, too, had to go to the mainland when she was of school age, but returned to spend the summers with her grandparents.

Other summer children were Rose and Dan Leemaster, whose mother cooked for John Ingwersen's logging crew in the early 1950's. When fall came, they had to return to the

COURTESY ANNA CAIN
Cheryl Davis spent her preschool years, in the late 1940's, at the South Fox Island lighthouse with her grandparents, Allen and Anna Cain. She had no other children to play with, but is shown here with her kitten, a curious red fox, and the fish she helped catch.

PHOTO BY CHARLES STAFFORD
The abandoned assistant keepers' quarters on South Fox Island sits in silence, since the departure of the many lively children and their families, who lived in the big, brick house.

COURTESY REGINA LAWSON
Rose and Dan Leemaster, in 1952, play with their dog near a pile of John Ingwersen's logs.

mainland, as other children had done.

This lack of a school was nearly challenged in the 1950's. When George Grosvenor came in his mail boat from Leland with government orders that the island would be assessed higher school taxes, the Nickersons at the lumber camp didn't like the notice they saw posted on a tree. Why should school taxes be paid, but no school provided for the residents?

NICKERSON FAMILY PHOTO
Since they had to pay school taxes, the Nickersons considered requesting that a school be built on South Fox Island for their children. Right, clockwise are Max and Donaldine Nickerson's children: Patricia, Max, Jr., Janice, Pamela, Steven and Greg.

NICKERSON FAMILY PHOTO,
In 1958 Evelyn Nickerson accompanied her father, Sterling Nickerson, Jr., on the Mackinac Straits ferry to inspect the Bridgebuilder *at St. Ignace.*

NICKERSON FAMILY PHOTOS
These 1955 photos show John, Kathy and Nancy Nickerson, children of Sterling, Jr., and Bernice Nickerson. The Miss Manistee *is tied to the dock, after bringing the children to South Fox for their first visit. They soon found their way to the large sawdust pile, between the sawmill and the water.*

The lumber mill was a year-round operation, but the wives and children lived on the mainland and only visited occasionally. If Max and Sterling Nickerson, Jr., moved their wives and children to the island, 11 children would need an education. There were other men working at the camp whose families could move there also. This thought was tossed around, but in the end, it was decided not to be worth it. In the 1800's it had not been such an inconvenience for settlers to live on an isolated island, because the sparsely populated mainland was not much different. Now the mainland offered more than schools. There were doctors and stores and washing machines, summer activities for the children and employment for the women back in their hometown of Kingsley. To move to the island just to prove a point to the government seemed to be a step backward, and the idea was dismissed. The Nickerson children did spend many happy summer days on the island, however. Sterling III and Max, Jr., often traveled on the lumber boats and helped to load and unload the lumber.

(TOP) PHOTO BY NANCY NICKERSON (BOTTOM) PHOTO BY MARIE GALE Grandchildren of South Fox Island owners have also enjoyed their days of exploring. Above, Bradley Craker, son of Kathleen Firestone and grandson of Sterling Nickerson II, in 1982. Left, in 1988, Sarah Mull rides the three-wheeler behind her grandfather, Erwin Gale. Sarah's mother, Susan Mull rides in the wagon.

The Erwin and Marie Gale family included twelve grandchildren, when the Gales owned South Fox in partnership with the Riley and Stevens families in the 1970's and 80's. The grandchildren often visited the island during the summer and explored the same fields, woodlands, dunes and beaches that other children had done for at least 100 years.

MIRADA RANCH PHOTO
Samara Danielle Johnson enjoys her island paradise.

Samara Danielle Johnson made her first visit to South Fox Island when she was just two years old. Her parents, David and Lesli Johnson, liked what they saw when they inspected South Fox and bought it in 1989. Samara was just a baby then, but when she was two, she flew aboard Island Air, from Charlevoix to her new island playground. By 1993, at four years old, she was learning to ride the horses at Mirada Ranch, and Bandit became her favorite. The family also brought to the island a six-month-old black labrador pup, Mirada's Moon Shadow. Shadow has become a willing playmate for Samara.

As with most island children, playing on the beach and collecting rocks has captured Samara's interest. Bugs and snakes hold no fear. Growing up around horses, both at Mirada Ranch and at her home on the mainland, Samara, at age six, has announced her wish to become a veterinarian when she grows up.

Samara loves riding on the ranch's four-wheelers. She and her father take the trail to their "secret spot" on South Fox Island, where she can talk with him about anything she likes. What a fortunate child she is —having a secret place on a very special island!

South Fox Island has always been an adventureland for children. There have been problems, of course, for the island's children through the years. In the early 1900's when school in Suttons Bay closed for the summer and her classmates were discussing all the things they were going to be doing in the months ahead, Bernice Leo began to cry. When asked why she was crying, she replied, "Because I have to go to the island." She knew she

PHOTO BY CHARLES MUELLER
Samara and her mother, Lesli Johnson, saddle up for an afternoon ride at Mirada Ranch, 1995.

would miss her friends and could not be a part of their plans. But in their older years, Bernice and her sister Hildegarde said, "We often thank God we had the experience of spending our summers there."[3]

Even Zella Green's loneliness as a South Fox child was tempered by good memories of the peacefulness. "It was beautiful sometimes, coming home from the other end," she said as an adult. "A beautiful day — the sun shining; beautiful water — it's getting sunset — and going up when Father would be on watch, to light up at night. Go up with him and you could look all over the island!"[4]

Treasured days. Treasured memories. Treasured islands.

[1] James J. Strang, *Northern Islander* (St. James, Mich.: printed by Strang, May 31, 1855), Section 5.

[2] George N. Fuller, ed. *Island Stories* (Lansing: State Printers, 1947), pp. 60, 61;
collections of Marion M. Davis articles from *Michigan History Magazine.*

[3] Bernice Leo and Hildegarde Leo McDonald in interview with author, 1982.

[4] Stanley DeForge, typed manuscript of interview with Zella Green DeForge, 1983 p. 129.

PHOTOS BY K. FIRESTONE
Scenes of North Fox Island

DEVELOPMENT DREAMS AND DILEMMAS

It's nearly impossible to visit an isolated island without getting visions of a cozy, cottage retreat. Dreams of a slow-paced life with quiet morning walks and lazy afternoons wander through the visitor's mind. For some, the dreams are more sophisticated and take the form of resort lodges, golf courses and modern marinas.

In early America, dreams were plentiful, and who can say which men or women first thought of turning the Fox Islands into Lake Michigan retreats? King Strang had hoped in the early 1850's that the islands would offer some peace and prosperity for some of his disciples from Beaver Island. Strang had plans for pottery and brick-making operations on South Fox Island and wrote in his *Ancient and Modern Michilimackinac* the following:

> *"The bluffs of Patmos (as he called South Fox) are immense piles of clay. The quality is suitable for pottery. For brick it is equal to the Milwaukee. Sand and clay can be obtained in the same yard, the wood cut within a quarter of a mile, and the brick shipped from the kiln over the gangway plank. The want of capital has prevented the business being undertaken."* [1]

Such a business would have helped support the island settlers; but before this came to be, the Mormon farmers and fishermen left the Fox Islands after Strang was assassinated on Beaver Island in 1856.

Clay bluffs and sand dunes highlight the beauty of South Fox Island.
GALE FAMILY PHOTO

EARLY DREAMS OF SOUTH FOX

It is not known whether Susan Zeller ever set foot on South Fox, but she realized an opportunity when she saw it. When the Mormon settlement disappeared from the island, Zeller bought the cleared fields and homesites the people had abandoned. She began buying tax deeds as early as 1885 and by the turn of the century owned several parcels. This former Mormon property sat along the southeastern shore and reached as far as the western dune, with scattered acreage stretching north and south. It also surrounded the wooding station, home, and mill site of Robert and Catherine Roe. Susan Zeller's investments paid off when she sold her holdings in 1898 to hotel architect and engineer, John Oliver Plank.

COURTESY GRAND HOTEL, MACKINAC ISLAND
John Oliver Plank

Plank was born in Planktown, Ohio, in 1856. Perhaps his family was accustomed to having places named after them, hence, when he was asked to manage the newly opened Grand Hotel on Mackinac Island in 1887, he convinced the owners that, as long as he managed it, the place would be called "Plank's Grand Hotel."[2] John Oliver Plank had operated three hotels in New England and a large summer hotel on the Thousand Islands in the St. Lawrence River before going to Mackinac Island. At Mackinac he helped in the planning and construction of the Grand Hotel. In 1890, after managing it for three years, he resigned from his post and departed not much richer but with lots of resort hotel experience and a new dream.

Plank bought property from Susan Zeller and others, both on North and South Fox Islands. Being the resort man that he was, he had big plans for his island property—plans that never became a reality. He did visit the islands often, however, arriving in his yacht, and on South Fox, tying up at his new dock. His second wife Alma spent several summers on South Fox, where she and Mr. Plank had a prosperous farm.

Though his plans never materialized for a big resort community, Plank did convince his friends from Chicago, Frederick and Ruth Kilbourn, to buy property and spend summers on South Fox. The Kilbourn house was not a typical resort cottage — in that the quarters for living, sleeping and eating were made of separate small buildings left behind by fisherman John Nelson, but the residents did bring along a maid.

Frederick and Effie Burdick also came from Chicago, in 1905, and homesteaded a piece along the shore. Plank served as trustee for other shore property owned by Jennie Horton and also handled business for property owner James Scott.

Though Plank's dream for a resort brought in only a few friends, he did leave his mark. The house, which was built by Robert Roe about 1860 and later bought by Plank, was known as the Plank house until it burned in 1991.

On Beaver Island, construction of the Wildwood Inn was begun in 1916 but halted three years later because of financial problems. *The Journal of Beaver Island History, Volume One*, states that the designer of this would-be luxurious hotel was also the architect of Mackinac Island's Grand Hotel.[3] Plank was the Grand Hotel's architect. It appears that John Oliver Plank had an attraction to islands, especially those where he thought resort dreams might be fulfilled. But his dreams for the various islands brought little financial profit to him.

John and Lillian McElwee also had resort plans for South Fox when they purchased the land where Magnus Fredrickson and Nels Nelson had raised cattle in the 1920's. The McElwees also purchased the property of Howard and Beatrice Sweet and some from the government. These parcels were inland from the southwestern dunes and were mostly hills and dune slopes. A view of the water was not visible from some of these pieces, but 80 acres reaching nearly from shore to shore, across the bluff near the lighthouse, would have made excellent resort property. Mr. and Mrs. McElwee bought real estate in many locations besides South Fox Island. They were people with dreams. Before these dreams were realized, however, John McElwee passed away.

COURTESY ALICE STEVENS LIPE
Charles Stevens cleared the first airstrip on South Fox.

Another man whose dreams never materialized, but who also left a mark on the island, was Charles A. Stevens. A native of Northport, he had moved to Wayne, Michigan, but began his dream for an island resort when this father, Alva Stevens, was helping to bring cattle off the island from the Plank farm. In October of 1948 Charles Stevens set to work on making his dream happen. With an ax, a shovel and a scythe he began clearing land for an airstrip on the long piece of property he planned to buy from John Oliver Plank's widow, Alma. In seven days he would clear the growth from a 100 foot-wide, 3,000-foot-long stretch of abandoned farm fields where young trees and bushes had taken over. While he chopped and shoveled and smoothed, he dreamed of cozy log cabins where visitors would come to vacation at his modern dude ranch. Stevens had spent a lot of time around horses and had recently given riding lessons to the wealthy people of the Northport Point resort near his hometown. Dreams of hangars, beacons, night lights and plane-service facilities kept him working for seven days and danced in his head as he climbed into his sleeping bag each night. The first part of his dream came true. After seven days, Charles Stevens watched the first civilian plane touch down on South Fox Island as his friend Rafael Suarez landed on the newly cleared airstrip.

The next step was an even more difficult one, that of raising money to erect the buildings. It was during this stage of the dream that Stevens began working with John Ingwersen in his logging operation, helping on the tug *Major*. Ingwersen had his own dreams for the island and thought that, by logging off some of the property, he could raise the funds needed to get a resort underway. As was related in an earlier chapter, the dream disintegrated when timber losses on rough seas took away all the profits. And though Stevens never saw his dude ranch become a reality, the airstrip served as the main landing field until 1991.

PAST ENTREPRENEURS OF NORTH FOX

Although smaller in size, North Fox Island has also had its share of enterprising dreams. As on South Fox, land speculators bought property on North Fox, because it was either free or the price was right and the prospects of reselling at a profit were good. Thomas Bates, 27-year-old entrepreneur and newspaperman of Traverse City's *Grand Traverse Herald*, bought the center of the island and extending to the western shore from J. Haines Emery in 1868. Three years later, in 1871, he opened a real estate office in Traverse City, and that same year transferred his North Fox property to his father-in-law, Jesse Cram, also of Traverse City. Cram was owner for only a year or less, since there was apparently some question of Bate's rightful title. In 1872 the U. S. Government granted the property to Reuben Goodrich.

From 1872 to 1898 Reuben Goodrich, a land baron and real estate agent in Northwestern Lower Michigan, gained almost all of North Fox Island. In 1898 Goodrich sold his property to William B. McCreery, a real estate partner. McCreery's heirs, living in Flint, Michigan, sold the North Fox property to John Oliver Plank twenty years later, in 1898.

After buying most of North Fox from McCreery, the rest was gradually acquired by Plank and his wife from other property owners or by tax sale. By 1950 all of North Fox Island was owned by Plank's widow, Alma Plank. Mr. Plank had begun his North Fox purchases at the same time he bought on South Fox, with plans for a big resort.

Elija and Julia Harpold, in business with the Garden City Sand Company of Chicago, purchased Lots 1, 2 and 3 of Section 13, North Fox Island, in 1890. This was land not owned by Goodrich nor subsequently by McCreery. Harpold's property was part of the wide, heavily graveled shoreline on the eastern side of the island. Volume 2 of the *History of the Great Lakes* records that also in 1890, the Garden City Sand Company purchased the tug *A. C. Van Raalte* from Captain Albert Majo of Muskegon.[4] The *Van Raalte* may have been used to transport gravel from North Fox Island. According to George N. Fuller, Editor of Marion Morse Davis' *Island Stories*, the business' name was the Fox Island Gravel Company.[5] Records for 1890 show that Harpold also bought property on Whiskey Island and the Manitous, along with the right to build docks for vessels used in the hauling away of gravel. In addition, he had property on Beaver Island.

PHOTO BY K. FIRESTONE
The east side of North Fox is a heavy gravel beach.

At this time, Chicago was experiencing a construction boom, due to the great fire and also encouraged in part by the coming 1893 World's Fair. The islands from South Manitou on up the Beaver Island chain were convenient sources for wood products, sand and gravel. According to Robert H. Ruchhoft's

1991 publication, *Exploring North Manitou, South Manitou, High and Garden Islands Of The Lake Michigan Archipelago*, the Garden City Sand Company operated dredges just off much of the South Manitou Island shoreline and that "a whole series of lake boats and barges loaded their holds with thousands of tons of nearby lake bottom, and hauled them off....[6] Whether the same was done off other islands in the archipelago has yet to be determined. But ownership of properties on North Fox, Beaver and Whiskey Islands must lead us to wonder.

Harpold borrowed $2,500 from William Penhallow of Chicago and put his North Fox property up as security. After just two months he paid Penhallow off, with money borrowed from The Midland Company, also of Chicago. The Garden City Sand Company owned much of South Manitou, including a good deal of land at the eastern harbor and some at the southern end of the island, where resorts were platted. It is possible that a resort was also planned for North Fox Island; however, the gravely section the company owned on the island's eastern side seems a less likely place for a resort than on the sandy southwestern side. In the end, no Garden City resorts were established on the Manitous nor on the Fox Islands. The North Fox Island property was abandoned and went up for tax sale.

John Oliver Plank paid the taxes on it, and in 1889 the Garden City Sand Company's North Fox property was transferred to Plank, who by that time already owned most of the rest of North Fox, as well as much of South Fox. Jennie Horton, of Ohio, also bought tax sale lands on both islands about 1905, and Plank served as trustee for her in making business deals, such as timber contracts.

Several entrepreneurial woodcutting and logging operations took place on North Fox Island throughout the years and are covered in another chapter of this book.

In 1937 Dr. Robert Hatt and a party of scientists from Cranbrook Institute of Science examined the island, and during their survey found an old, abandoned cabin at the edge of the woods in the area where the Garden City Sand Company had owned property fifty years earlier. Among decaying boards and rotted tin cans, old wagon tracks still traced from the cabin down to the shoreline. Another attempted enterprise on North Fox cited in Hatt's book, *Island Life in Lake Michigan*, was a 1922 skunk ranch. That endeavor was short lived and "had little effect on the island's history."[7]

LARGER PARCELS, BIGGER DREAMS

By the end of the 1950's all of North Fox Island had only one owner — Alma Plank; and all of South Fox Island, except for one third owned by the government, was owned by the Nickerson lumber company. This made it possible for a single owner of either island to have a huge effect. Indeed, when the Michigan Department of Natural Resources realized that South Fox parcels were being bought up by the lumber company, the DNR stepped in and made purchases of its own, in order to preserve lands for the public. Both Alma Plank and the Nickersons sought buyers for their property on the two islands.

In August, 1959, Detroit area businessman, Francis D. Shelden, and his brother Alger Shelden bought North Fox Island from Alma Plank; and in 1965 Lynn Dillin purchased the Nickerson property on South Fox. The Sheldens also owned a piece of property on Leelanau County's mainland, in Solon Township.

Francis (Frank) Shelden had done a geological study on Canada's Manitoulin Island as part of his master's degree thesis. According to him, "I was a pilot and plane-owner, and flying to and fro to the island I had often wondered about the ownership of the various other islands in Lake Michigan and Lake Huron — especially the American islands, since reaching them wouldn't involve border-crossing and all the hassles of customs and immigration I had to go through every time I touched down at Gore Bay on Manitoulin and then again returning to Detroit."[8] Soon after, when he learned that North Fox Island was for sale, he flew over it in his Beachcraft Bonanza, contacted Alma Plank and settled on a purchase price.

The Sheldens announced plans for a vacation destination for aircraft owners. Over the next two years contractor Frank Kalchik from the mainland area of Omena had a crew of about fifteen men on North Fox, clearing and grading the landing area into a 3,300-foot-long by 250-foot-

COURTESY FRANK KALCHIK
Standing, L-R: Ralph Kalchik, Frank Kalchik, Jerry Kalchik, Darwin Holton. In front (L-R) Frank Shelden, Alger Shelden. The Shelden aircraft is shown after the first landing on North Fox Island, 1962. A "fly-in" was held a short time later.

wide strip. According to Kalchik, the area was partly a mud hole, which Kalchik filled with sand from the dune on the southern end of the island. While the landing strip was being constructed, Francis Shelden landed at the South Fox airstrip and boarded a boat which he kept beached near the Nickersons' lumber dock. From there he traveled across the water to North Fox. He made the first aircraft landing on North Fox Island on June 23, 1962, with his Beechcraft Bonanza. That same summer Shelden hosted a "fly-in" at North Fox and served cubed stake and corn-on-the-cob to several pilots who arrived to view the proposed resort destination.

COURTESY FRANK KALCHIK
Frank Kalchik's work crew in front of the tents where they made camp on North Fox Island beach. Standing behind: LeRoy Shocko: In row, L-R: Moses Carter, Alvin Ance, unknown, Ivan Cobb, Louis Koon, Clayton Thomas, Ron Kalchik, Unknown; In front;unknown and Klinton (Skip) Kellogg.

Frank Kalchik also constructed a supply dock on the east side of North Fox, built over two miles of road and cleared a site for the proposed community center. Pete Jurica of the Leland area hauled the construction machinery aboard a barge to North Fox Island. The well rig was taken on Kalchik's tug *Ace*, and according to Kalchik, "displaced a lot of water." A citizen's band radio tower was erected on the North Fox beach; and with Kalchik's radios on his vessels *Ace* and *Betty K* and at his mainland home, communication was made possible. Workers were usually transported on the boats, but sometimes also used Phillips Flying Service out of Charlevoix. Kalchik sometimes rode alone with Frank Shelden in Shelden's aircraft.

COURTESY FRANK KALCHIK
A stone-filled crib was constructed on North Fox's eastern side, where the Kalchik's Ace *and* Betty K *and supply barges could unload.*

COURTESY FRANK KALCHIK
Frank Kalchik vibrates cement forms to settle the foundation of the main house.

PHOTO BY K. FIRESTONE
A cottage sits amid the North Fox greenery.

Sheldens' North Fox Island Company also had a small house and guest cottage built, along with a few outbuildings. After purchasing the island for about $2,000, the Shelden brothers invested approximately $100,000 in the improvements. Ten lots were platted for sale along the western shore and dedicated as "North Fox Island Subdivision." There were plans for future plats along the other shores.

The Sheldens introduced whitetail deer to North Fox. It was hoped that the beauty and solitude of the island, along with plenty of hunting and fishing opportunities for sportsmen, would attract outdoorsmen with small airplanes. A brochure was printed and mailed to aircraft owners, but Frank Shelden recalled, "We had no takers, and, to be honest, I don't think we were very good promoters."[9] Frank Shelden had made many friends on the Leelanau county mainland and allowed them to visit the island whenever they liked. He later bought his brother Alger's interest in North Fox. Frank Shelden was described as a "millionaire, pilot, graduate geologist, amateur botanist, part-time university professor, land developer, oil consultant and market investor." [10] But, whatever plans he had for North Fox Island were suddenly interrupted in December, 1976, when a warrant on criminal charges was issued for his arrest. He fled the country, leaving his Northern Michigan friends with confusion and unanswered questions.

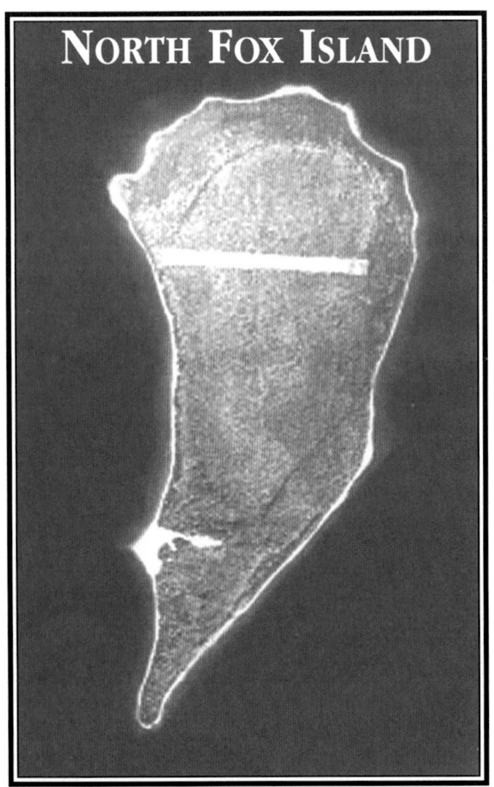

Ownership of North Fox was transferred to a trust company until being sold in 1986 to William and Susan Walter of Frankfort, Michigan, at a price of $587,000.

William Walter had always wanted to own his own island and said he only bought it for a retreat and had no plans for further development.

Meanwhile, the two-thirds private lands on South Fox Island were sold by the Nickersons to Lynn Dillin in 1965. Dillin planned to keep the island in its natural state and used it only as a get-away and a deer hunting camp until his death on the island in 1973. An unidentified land developer with big dreams sought to buy the island and build a deer hunting lodge, a number of cabins, a stone breakwater, and a marina. But the purchase fell through and the dream did not materialize.

Stanley Riley, Erwin Gale and Tom Stevens bought South Fox Island on speculation in 1975 and soon put it up for resale. However, they admitted to occasional dreams of a man-made inlet for boats, a religious retreat or small clusters of cottages. Both North and South Fox Islands were nominated for Michigan Natural Resources Trust Fund acquisition but were turned down several times, including in 1986. During that same period, a study completed by the National Parks and Conservation Association recommended that an islands unit, including North and South Fox Islands and Beaver Island be added to the Sleeping Bears Dunes National Lakeshore, which would have agreed with former South Fox owner, Lynn Dillin. In 1973 Dillin had even offered his South Fox Island holdings to the national park at a reduced price, in order that the island would be preserved. But Dillin died and never saw the plan materialize.

GALE FAMILY PHOTOS July, 1977: Carole Riley, part owner of South Fox, leads hikers Susan Mull, Carolyn and Dave Johnson, Stanley Riley and Erwin Gale.

Erwin Gale (shown) and his partners had this cook-house constructed on South Fox after the earlier building burned in 1985.

It appeared that there would be a sale of South Fox Island when Farhad Vladi, a citizen of Canada with offices there and in West Germany, posed for a photograph showing South Fox's western side in the background. The photo's caption read, "This will be our surprise for 1988!" Vladi published the photo and announcement in his newsletter, *Vladi Private Islands*, which was circulated to the rich and famous around the world.[11] Vladi changed his mind about buying the island and reselling it on the international market, and so his announcement developed into nothing more.

In the spring of 1989 Riley, Gale and Stevens sold their South Fox property to David V. Johnson, a developer from Southfield, Michigan. Mineral rights, which had been retained by the Nickerson lumbermen heirs, were also sold to Johnson.

Since the new owner of South Fox was the developer of luxury homes and a major office building site in Southeastern Michigan, mainlanders cautiously waited for announcement of development plans. Instead, large-scale development was announced for North Fox Island by a Beaver Island resident, who had a purchase option for North Fox. Real estate agent and developer Mark Conner had previously done rehabilitation and restoration of inner-city neighborhoods in the St. Louis, Missouri, area. His Beaver Island home was eight miles north of the shores of North Fox Island.

North Fox development plans included 612 residents, an 18-hole championship golf course, two marinas, and an enlarged airport. Mainland environmentalists wasted no time in opposing the development efforts, citing their feared destruction of the natural character of the isolated island. Mr. Conner and Dr. F. Glenn Goff presented lengthy, detailed plans, which promised to protect and enhance the island's natural features. In addition to buildings and recreation areas, their plans called for creation of the "North Fox Island Institute," to provide for an "environmental research and education center."[12] After five years of public meetings, presentations, threatened lawsuits and much expense, Conner's North Fox Island Enterprises, in the face of continued and organized opposition, retreated and dropped the plans for an island development. In spite of the outcome, the controversy did bring before the public opposite, but valid, arguments from both sides of the debate—arguments which could be applied to other island and mainland development issues. Some of those arguments, taken from various presentations and reports, are as follows:

In favor of island development

A large percentage of island property in Lake Michigan is already in public trust.

The North Fox development, as proposed, would represent "harmony between humans and the environment," and would be "the most environmentally sensitive development anywhere."

The island would become accessible to more people.

Island residents could enjoy a "world-class facility" with golf, tennis, fishing, sailing, cultural events and nature activities.

The development would provide jobs in maintaining roads, the sewage system and the man-made harbor; in construction; in emergency fire and medical services on the island.

The development would provide increased business activities on the mainland.

Opposed to island development

Mainland Michigan is being developed too fast, without regard to the environment. Let's not do the same with islands.

Character of the island will be lost as population density increases.

The relatively unchanged, pristine, natural environment may be irreversibly altered.

Development would be a threat to several plant species and migratory birds.

North Fox contains rare forest habitats which should be protected.

Plants which are insect-pollinated would be hurt by golf course insecticides.

Paving and widening the airstrip will increase water run-off and affect the water table.

Township and county tax base would increase.

The island could become a wilderness preserve, in perpetuity.

The man-made harbor would be a harbor of refuge along the major pleasure boat routes.

The project's benefits outweigh the need to preserve the island in its present state.

Plant life is renewable and animal life recoverable.

To disallow development on a privately owned island amounts to government confiscation.

The State of Michigan passed up the chance to buy North Fox Island, on more than one occasion.

Land owners should be able to do anything they wish with their property.

The many residents and visitors would have a negative impact on the water quality surrounding the island.

Habitat fragmentation would occur — the inside of the forest would change as forest edges are developed.

The island itself is an endangered species, worthy of protection.

If the project went bankrupt while not completed, the island character could be completely destroyed.

Zoning laws should not be changed just to accommodate developers.

Jano Yockey, in a letter to the *Traverse City Record-Eagle*, summed up the sentiments of those opposed to island development. "Hotel here, golf course there — we will lose forever something that has taken nature millions of years to develop."[13]

In June, 1994, South Fox Island owner, David V. Johnson, also purchased North Fox Island. Although he had not taken part in the North Fox development controversy, he had feared that the great increase of visitors and inhabitants of a nearby island development would have a negative effect on the tranquillity of his South Fox Island get-away. He had signed a purchase agreement with William Walter in January of that year, when the North Fox Island Enterprises' option expired. At the time of purchase of North Fox, Johnson quickly announced that he had no interest in owning two islands; his purchase of the smaller island had been only to prevent some other developer from coming along with large-scale plans. Being a developer himself, Johnson admitted that he would consider a much smaller development of North Fox, but that his preference was for a trade with the Michigan Department of Natural Resources. With the DNR still owning one-third of South Fox Island, Johnson felt that trading his ownership of all of North Fox Island to the DNR for its one-third of South Fox would be in the best interest of all. The public would gain North Fox Island, certainly pleasing the development opponents; and Johnson would own all of South Fox Island. The DNR had turned down a property trade in 1989, when real estate agent David J. Lue proposed to trade some Lake Superior shoreline for DNR holdings on South Fox. However, David Johnson's offer, five years later, was island-for-island property. As the developer of mainland Petoskey's Bay Harbor development, Johnson told the *Traverse City Record-Eagle,* "We have worked very hard in Bay Harbor to be the good guy. We would like to think there could be some way to be the good guy in this."[14] Johnson continued to assure the public that he had no plans to develop South Fox Island. In the spring of 1995, North Fox Island was again nominated for acquisition through the Michigan Natural Resources Trust Fund, and again rejected. Unless ownership of North Fox is acquired by the public, there will always be the possibility of timber harvesting, re-introduction of deer, or resort development.

PHOTO BY K. FIRESTONE Mark Hubbard, personal friend and corporate attorney, with David V. Johnson on South Fox Island

PHOTO BY K. FIRESTONE Riding his four-wheeler, David Johnson pauses on the South Fox shoreline, as development controversy rages over the island in the background — North Fox.

Flying overhead or passing by in a pleasure boat, one might think that a comfortable motel, with its cedar exterior and dormer windows, awaits on South Fox Island. But there is no resort lodging, and only David Johnson's horses stay in the large 142 by 42 foot, two-story building which overlooks the waters of Lake Michigan. Mirada Ranch, a working ranch, is the only development on South Fox Island.

David Victor Johnson, a Personal Profile

David Victor Johnson

David Victor Johnson purchased South Fox Island in 1989 and North Fox Island in 1994. The solitude of these islands is in sharp contrast to the fast pace of Johnson's business endeavors throughout the years.

Born in Michigan in 1949 to Swedish immigrant parents, David Johnson adopted his father's practice of "If you pay for it, they can never take it away." Since graduating from Michigan State University with a Bachelor of Science degree, centered on packaging engineering, this pay-as-you-go approach has paid off in Johnson's myriad of real estate and development projects. His first business endeavor was in the ownership and management of seven gasoline service stations in the Lansing area, during 1971 and 1972. Then, after serving in 1973 and 1974 as president of Howard T. Keating Company, a residential real estate building firm, Johnson formed his own brokerage business, Maple Associates, Inc. It soon became one of the top five real estate firms of Southeastern Michigan's Birmingham/Bloomfield Board of Realtors.

Abbey Development Company, a sole proprietorship, was founded by Johnson in 1979, for the development of luxury residential communities and the creation of unique commercial projects. In 1984, the numerous and varied real estate activities were incorporated as Victor International Corporation, with David Johnson as president and chairman of the board.

Victor Center, a luxury office facility in Southfield, Michigan, is a joint venture between Victor International and Plante & Moran, CPA's, and both house their corporate offices there. Victor Corporate Park in nearby Livonia, is a major office complex which includes Embassy Suites Hotel, luxury office buildings, separate restaurants, and retail areas.

To David Johnson's credit, Southeastern Michigan displays several of the Midwest's finest residential projects: Heron Bay, Heron Pointe, Heron Ridge, Heron Woods, Echo Park, Lakes of Echo Park, Chestnut Hills — all in Bloomfield Township — and WindRidge in Northville Township.

In 1996 the 500-million-dollar development in progress is Bay Harbor, Michigan, along five miles of Lake Michigan shoreline near the resort community of Petoskey. The acreage will include 750 homesites, 500 boat slips, a world-class marina and yacht club, and an accompanying 27-hole golf course, all set on the reclamation site of an old cement factory. Johnson and his Bay Harbor project received the State of Michigan's 1995 Environmental Excellence Award, as recognition for turning a Lake Michigan eye-sore into an environmentally sound resort development.

With all real estate projects, Johnson draws upon the expertise of in-house legal counsel, as well as from attorney Cameron Piggott of the Dykema Gossett law firm. Johnson also works with selected professional architects, land planners, engineers and general contractors. Quality performance is key to the success of Victor International Corporation's team operations.

David Johnson established the Victor Foundation in 1988, a foundation which grants funds to various children's causes. In 1990, Mr. Johnson was awarded the Detroit Metro Youth for Christ "Service to Youth Award." Johnson became a member of the Young Presidents' Organization in 1989 and continues to be involved in a number of professional and social organizations. His philosophy of "Be Creative, Be Aggressive, Be Professional" is presented as he lectures to many local and national real estate organizations.

The "What to do with islands" question is as local as Leelanau Township's (of which the Fox Islands are a part) 1990 adopted Islands Conservation District; as regional as the State of Michigan's 1991 proposed greenbelt recreation loop, which included the Fox, Beaver, Power and Gull (Bellows) Islands; and as national as U. S. House of Representatives 1989 oversight hearing titled "America's Islands: Open Space at Risk." From owners of complete islands, to parcel owners on various islands, to island visitors and to those who will never set foot on an island but can only view from mainland shores, islands are part of America's national treasures. How the future of these islands is directed should be of importance to us all.

[1] James J. Strang, *Ancient and Modern Michilimackinac* (1854; reprint, Mackinac Island: W. Stewart Woodfill, 1959), p. 47.

[2] W. Stewart Woodfill, *Grand Hotel, The Story of an Institution* (Princeton: The Newcomen Society, 1969), p. ll.

[3] "Names and Places of Beaver Island," in *The Journal of Beaver Island History, Volume One*, (St. James, Mich,: Beaver Island Historical Society, 1976), p. 211.

[4] *History of the Great Lakes*, Vol. 2 (1899, reprint, Cleveland, Ohio: Freshwater Press, Inc., 1972), p.136.

[5] George N. Fuller, ed., *Island Stories* (Lansing: State Printers, 1947), p. 363; collection of Marion Morse Davis articles from *Michigan History Magazine.*

[6] Robert H. Ruchhoft, *Exploring North Manitou, South Manitou, High and Garden Islands Of The Lake Michigan Archipelago* (Cincinnati: The Pucelle Press, 1991), p. 87.

[7] Robert Hatt, *Island Life in Lake Michigan* (Bloomfield Hills, Mich.: Cranbrook Institute of Science, 1948), P. 42.

[8] Letter to author from Francis Shelden, 7 Nov., 1992.

[9] Ibid.

[10] Marilyn Wright, "Millionaire sought by police has rich, prominent background," *Traverse City Record-Eagle*, 22 Dec., 1976, p. 3.

[11] Farhad Vladi, *Vladi Private Islands* Hamburg, Germany and Halifax, Nova Scotia, 1987, p. 4.

[12] F. Glenn Goff and Phyllis J. Higman, *North Fox Island Development, Environmental Impact Report* (Vital Resources Consulting; Sept. 1990), p. 6-98.

[13] Jano Yockey in "Letters" (to the Editor), *Traverse City Record-Eagle* 18 Dec., 1991, p. 6A.

[14] Diane Conners, "N. Fox Island sale ends plan for project," *Traverse City Record-Eagle* 15 June, 1994.

PHOTO BY K. FIRESTONE
Solitude of a quiet walk on South Fox shores.

MYSTERY, FANTASY, POETRY

Every island seems to have its share of legends, intrigue and buried treasure. The mere sight of an island raises visions in our minds of things hidden, things unknown, things awaiting discovery. And what cannot be found or explained or discovered is often invented.

Upon studying island histories, one has to wonder if there is a single island anywhere that doesn't have a hidden treasure. North and South Fox Island are included in this list of "treasure islands."

South Fox lightkeeper, Willis Warner, who began island service in 1876, handed down to his descendants an account of buried treasure on South Fox Island. It seems that a man who had been hired to murder someone was sailing for parts unknown with his pay-off money. His ship was wrecked off South Fox Island, where the murderer made his way to shore and hid the money somewhere on the island. The version that Joe Raphael heard as a child on the island, about 1920, stated that the $35,000 was buried in large dishpans. The Leo children had heard this story, or some version of it, with the addition of the clue that the treasure was buried by a tree with a nail pounded in it. Whenever they and their island friends would be walking through the woods, they would keep an eye out for the tree with the tell-tale nail. Maybe someday they would get lucky and go back to the mainland with their riches.

The North Fox treasure was reported in the Traverse City *Evening Record* in 1905.[1] For forty years the story had been told around mainland Northport that North Fox Island held a buried treasure. Some said it was $150,000 in Spanish gold, sealed in fruit jars and buried in an iron chest. Searchers dug holes in the sand at different points around the island but could not uncover the treasure. Others said Beaver Island's King Strang had buried the treasure, but no one seemed to know if he had dug it up again before his assassination.

The version told by the *Evening Record* that day, in the fall of 1905, was written when two Northport residents, Joe Gagnon and Jay Spangle, followed two mysterious strangers to North Fox Island, after the strangers had arrived by train into Northport and then hired a local launch to take them to the island. Gagnon and Spangle followed in their own boat and, hiding from the strangers, watched their every move. All they saw were some trees being blazed by the two strangers, who called each other "Cap" and "Mate."

Cap and Mate made a second trip to North Fox a few days later, after purchasing tools and supplies. Northport fisherman Gus Petander said the two consulted maps and charts as they were passengers on his fishing boat. After a three-day stay on the island, the two were picked up by Petander and, upon returning to Northport, made a quick departure aboard the train. In their hands they carried a large handbag and a gunnysack. An employee of Petander said the two had found the chest of gold near a tree emblazoned with the date "1870." The story was that $150,000 in gold coin had been stolen in Chicago at the time of the great fire. Two men had made off in the dark, aboard a small craft up the waters of Lake Michigan. After burying the loot on North Fox, the two sailed for Canada, one dying there in prison and the other telling his wife of the treasure while on his death bed. Several years later, when the two mysterious strangers made their visits to North Fox Island, Northporters believed the buried treasure had been found, fueled by the reports of Gagnon and Spangle. But some believed the strangers were merely land speculators looking for resort property. If so, the treasure was still there for the finding — if there ever really was a treasure.

PHOTO BY K. FIRESTONE
North Fox Island, sugar sand beach near the southwest end.

So much for treasures. Gaining just as much space in the newspapers, but a lot less believable, was the 1992 report in the tabloid *Weekly World News* of the capture of a large sea monster between North and South Fox Islands.[2] The November 17 cover story was headlined with "U. S. Navy Captures Monster in Lake Michigan." The 140-foot monster was reportedly captured alive by Navy divers and put in an underwater cage off South Fox. The report and accompanying "photo" of the 35-ton monster brought conversation to the coffee shops and lighthearted citizen quotes in the "real" newspapers. From school superintendent William Crandell's "It's been eating salmon off my (fishing) lines for the past 20 years,"[3] to proposed North Fox developer Mark Conner's reply that it may be "a bloated environmentalist,"[4] the news story brought a little laughter into the gray-skyed days of November. Even if one believed in the sea monster, the land shown in the background of the monster photo did not resemble South Fox Island in the least!

Under the mysterious, and the serious, is the unanswered question of why a U. S. Army Chinook helicopter was making a night flight over the Fox Islands on July 9, 1983. Six men from the 101st Airborne Division died when their helicopter burst into flames as it slammed into a steep, wooded South Fox hillside, at a speed of about 115 miles per hour.

PHOTO BY JIM NIESSINK
As viewed from North Fox Island, skim-ice reaches from island to island and reflects South Fox in the distance.

Newspaper reports said that the helicopter had been practicing over-water flight navigation when the crash took place, just before midnight, near the southern tip of the island. An unconfirmed admission by a high military official, several years later, was that the airmen were practicing for the eventual U. S. invasion of the island of Grenada, which took place in October, 1983, just three months after the crash on South Fox Island.

Other lingering mysteries regard some of the previous owners and residents of the islands. While research can uncover much information, some questions remain. This author still searches for clues and answers about the following individuals and families:

J. Wilder or J. Wilbur; James Douglass; John and Minerva Pappenaw; Daniel Falkerson; James C. Scott; Robert Boyd; John Fitz; John, Catherine and Edell Subnow; Rushand, Hariett, Henry and Laura Roe; the babies, Edwin and Eddie who lived with the Palmer family on South Fox in 1870; Cora McFall, who lived with one of the Roe families on South Fox in 1860; J. Haines Emery and wife Ann W. Emery; Richard and Mariett Cooper, the George and Elizabeth Roe family; the Henry and Marie Roe family; George, William, Florence and Mabel Roe; Christian and Ingra Olson and their children, Mary and

John; Joseph, Mary, Henry, George and Charles Williams; Ole Goodmanson; Nelson Willard; Otto Williams; Jerry Williams; Susan Zeller; Jenny M. Horton; Frederick Monroe Burdick and Effie Leone Burdick; John Oliver Plank, Jr.; Howard J. Sweet and Beatrice Sweet; Henry Shoor; and Charles Leiter.

There will always be some mysteries left unsolved, but the question of why islands attract us needs little research. A first walk around an island usually provides all the answers needed. The beauty, solitude and events of happiness and sadness have inspired writers, painters, songwriters and poets.

Though John Ingwersen tried logging South Fox Island, he felt some remorse for cutting down these sentinels of the past. Some of his sentiments are recorded in a poem, which was first published in *Poetry* in 1967.[5]

MIRADA RANCH PHOTO
Charlie Blacker in front of a giant cedar on South Fox.

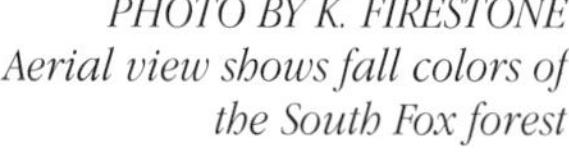

PHOTO BY K. FIRESTONE
Aerial view shows fall colors of the South Fox forest

POEM
"To the North"

by John Ingwersen

To the north,
on the south island
of the fox, I learned devouring:
I and my arm longer
by snarling chain, felled forties
of hard maple and slender ash
through a long spring and a long summer,
and it was fall; and the green leaves
dressed for death.

The great birch stood alone;
seven logs to the first limb
and its girth was four armspans,
and its brazen bark,
lined with black and laced with silver,
was smooth as sapling.

All morning I worked at the notching;
the four cuts meeting true at noon
and the chock dropped soft.

With the day down-going,
there was only the tree and myself
in the grove of my saw's snarling;
force from my earth-braced foot
through locked hip and inching shoulder
into the unseen teeth endless,
cutting the heart deep,
and dust deepening
from cream to crimson,
my cheek pressed close to the trunk
and breath fogging the bark's burnish,
lined with black and laced with silver;
the air now cold with the sun's falling
and the fall leaves staining
the air's red more red.

Then knowing the unfelt quiver,
stopping saw, and silence
bursted the air;
slowly on splintering hinge
the stiffening tree tilted,
grooving the last quadrant,
to my eyes opening
the tower of life
a cleaved pomegranate,
to my ears unfolding
the double sun's
single cymbaling,
the downed limbs rending
in green gust of juniper
in the groves' clanging.

And I splayed spent upon the red stump,
spanning her circles of rain and greening
that gathered all this red.

Never tell me
earth cannot be changed;
I, with this shoulder and this shoulder,
nine hundreds and thirty and one
rings of reigning, circles of silence,
brought loud to earth.

ISLAND SESTINA*

inspired by South Fox Island

by Kathleen Firestone

There's something magical about an island.
No other meets the feeling, quite serene,
of walking on a quiet beach of white sand
and skipping stones across the liquid blue.
The solitude is seen in wandering footprints
and heard in whispering leaves of nearby trees.

The kingbird and the bluebird perched in song trees
bring music to the silence of the island,
and chipmunks on the ground leave tiny footprints.
The flight of gulls above is so serene.
The flowers in the meadow, bells of soft blue,
and daisies spring up sweetly from the sand.

The dune is but a mountain made of beach sand.
Its borders are made green with cedar trees.
The green appears more bright against the sky's blue
to compliment dune's bleakness on the island.
The dune crest, place for resting, so serene,
gives way in gentle servitude to footprints.

A blowout in the dune is crossed by footprints.
One dancing in delight across the sand
falls silently to sand and rests serene
beside decaying trunks of cedar trees
and feels the peace of being on an island,
while gazing up at skies of brilliant blue.

The dune slopes down to meet the water's blue.
The water fills small craters left by footprints.
Footprints trace the border of the island,
leaving peaceful stride marks in the sand;
and inland from the beach, the whispering trees
still sing a soothing melody, serene.

Is there a place on earth that's more serene?
A place where there's no cause for feeling blue?
If they could speak, these solid, stately trees,
of past explorers who have left their footprints,
what messages would they write in the sand,
of solitude discovered on an island?

The mood of peace serene is left by footprints.
The water, tranquil blue, caresses sand,
as songs from whispering trees praise such an island.

*A sestina is a form of poetry with very strict rules. There are six stanzas, each with six lines. Each line ends with one of six selected words; these words are repeated at the end of the other sentences and must be placed in a particular order. The finale is three lines, repeating the six words, and the six words must appear in designated order. Island Sestina was written in 1988 and copyrighted in 1991 by Kathleen Firestone.

MIRADA RANCH PHOTO
On South Fox Island, wildflowers, warm sands, and an expanse of blue inspired "Island Sestina" *in 1988.*

Perhaps one day a poet will write of the Lake Michigan mirages. It's very common to look from the mainland toward islands such as North and South Fox and to see them in distorted form. Often they appear to be rising out of the water on some high, undercut bank. Or they may seem to be floating in the air just above the water. This phenomena is known as "cold-air lensing." It happens when light passes through layers of different temperatures and various densities of air. The light rays bend as they shoot through these layers, distorting the island images. On rare occasions, one can see from Michigan to Wisconsin, or from Wisconsin to Michigan, with light bending over the edge of the horizon as far as seventy miles away. Distant waves can also appear as Christmas trees on the horizon, with the illusion of standing nearly vertical. The phenomena is also known as "Arctic mirage," or "The Hillingar effect."

There is at least one Indian legend concerning the Fox Islands. In this legend, retold in John and Ann Mahan's *Wild Lake Michigan*,[6] Manabozho and a wolf set out in a race from the tip of the Leelanau Peninsula to Harbor Springs. In order to win the race, Manabozho threw large chunks of earth and clumps of trees into Lake Michigan to use as stepping stones. Thus, the beautiful Fox Islands were created, and Manabozho defeated the wolf.

Whether by legend, mystery or artistic expression, the lore and lure of the islands of Lake Michigan hover in the mist and stir our imaginations.

[1] "Hidden Wealth Wasn't Found," *The Evening Record* 9 Sept, 1905, p. 1, microfilm.

[2] "U. S. Navy Captures Monster In Lake Michigan," *Weekly World News* 17 Nov., 1992., p. 1.

[3] Amy Hubbell, "Loch Mich. 'monster' captured!," *The Leelanau Enterprise* 12 Nov., 1992, p. 1.

[4] Karen Emerson, "Monster myth?" The *Traverse City Record-Eagle* 11 Nov., 1992, p. 1.

[5] John Ingwersen, POEM, "*To the North*," in *Poetry*, March 1967, pp. 378, 379.

[6] John and Ann Mahan, *Wild Lake Michigan* (Stillwater, Maine: Voyageur Press, Inc., 1991), p. 58.

Sharing memories of childhood days on South Fox Island:
(Top) Douglas McCormick, Hildegarde Leo McDonald, Bernice Leo;
(Middle), Julius Benjamin Ance, Zella Green DeForge.

Epilogue

TRAVELING BACK IN TIME AND PLACE
OUR PERSONAL JOURNEYS

My first visit to any island was in 1955, when I was ten years old, and that island was South Fox. My father piloted the *Miss Manistee* between Northport and South Fox Island, as a partner of the Nickerson lumber business. Later, he let my brothers and sisters and me take our turns at maneuvering the ship's wheel on the lumber carriers *Tramp* and *Bridgebuilder* and showed us how to use a marine compass.

On the island, we explored the woods, dunes and tumbling farmhouses and speared suckers from the big dock. There were also occasional chores for us girls of helping wash the enameled plates and tin cups in the cookhouse, and my older brother often loaded lumber onto the boats. There are many happy memories of those days, but our family also experienced tragedy when my father disappeared on the Big Lake in 1959.

Twenty years later I began to write a family history of our involvement with South Fox — a history which turned into a much larger project — that of the island's history rather than just my own family's. My first book, *They Came To South Fox Island,* was published in 1983. As it became time to update that publication, research was done on North Fox Island, and now both islands are included under the new title, *The Fox Islands, North and South.*

These histories came from no other historical compilations, since only brief sentences referring to the Fox Islands could be found. Research has led me to many interviews and new friendships with the owners and descendants of former residents of North and South Fox Islands. The most rewarding part of this venture has been the knowledge that the almost hidden and unrecorded facts and memories of these families will not be forever lost. A most enjoyable event for me was seeing the happiness on the face of Joe Raphael, who was born on South Fox in 1916, when I presented him with a wedding photograph of his parents. Since his mother had died when Joe was only three, and all of Joe's photos had been destroyed in a fire, he cherished this wedding photo and kept it on the nightstand beside his bed, until he died in 1988. Dorothy Webb, daughter of Julius Ance who was born on South Fox in 1903, related that her father kept his copy of *They Came To South Fox Island* beside his favorite chair and that it was "the most dog-eared book he owned." Like many others who were interviewed during the research, Julius has also passed away, but his memories have been preserved.

Memories of island days are difficult to explain, because it is not so easy to go back to the old homestead or to take our descendants there. Some remembrances we can only hold in our hearts. I have come to love all islands, as my travels and research have included many in the Great Lakes; but South Fox Island will always be a significant place for me, because it is on that island where I feel closest to my father and his last two years with us. Walking up the sandy bank from the location of the former lumber dock, I can almost

Family descendants of Ance, Cobb and Chippewa visit South Fox Island.

Arriving at South Fox to visit the Kilbourn cabins.

Archie Miller and George Yannett returned to logging sites; some located Ance family cabins.

Rose Leemaster Pridemore came to show her childhood playground to daughter Gwen.

Mrs. Louis (Edith) Ance & family, descendants of August & Christine Ance and Louis & Maggie Ance.

South Fox Island
1983 Memory Trip

PHOTOS BY K. FIRESTONE

Family of Max & Donaldine Nickerson, during 1983 reunion.

John Nickerson on the South Fox dock, and Kathy & Nancy Nickerson with South Fox in the background – children of Sterling (II) and Bernice Nickerson.

PHOTOS BY K. FIRESTONE (Top) Jim Niessink, former North Fox caretaker, standing on the North Fox dune. (Middle) James and Harriet Roe in Harbor Springs, and Stan Floyd in Charlevoix shared stories told to them by their island ancestors. (Bottom) South Fox owners, Erwin Gale (middle) & Carole Riley (left) with Carole's daughter, Susan, and son-in-law, Eric Meier. Marie and Erwin Gale shared photos and memories with author, Kathleen Firestone.

believe that the old sawmill, cook shanty and bunk house are still there. The "office," like all the buildings, had the aroma of freshly cut lumber, and I can still see the wool, patchwork quilts that my grandma made, on the bunks.

PHOTO BY GRACE DICKINSON
In 1983 the Leo sisters returned to the site of their family's mill.

Because my own Fox Island memories are important to me, it was with special joy that I was able to arrange two separate boat trips and reunions for some of South Fox's former families and those families' descendants. One of the trips was a foggy journey. When we broke into clear air, the island was suddenly visible and appeared as a dream coming true to some who had spent long-ago childhood days on the island. The Leo sisters, Bernice and Hildegarde, had not returned since the days of their father's shingle operation from 1904 to 1921, not until the 1983 reunion. They visited the site of their childhood summer cabin and saw the remains of the shingle mill. Many descendants of the Native American families also came to see the cabins where the Ance, Raphael and other of their ancestors had lived. We explored together old homesites, the lighthouse grounds, and locations of earlier businesses. When Edith Kilbourn visited the site of the Kilbourn 1900 vacation cabins, she said, "I feel as though I've stepped back in time." Indeed, the journey was a step back in time for all of us.

Although I had seen North Fox Island many times from the shores of South Fox, I did not have an opportunity to walk its woodlands and beaches until 1993. The early settlers of this island have disappeared even further into obscurity that those on South Fox. But recent owners of and visitors to North Fox also have their treasured memories of walking the beaches, fishing off the shoals, and watching the sunset from the southern dune.

It's a rare person who can spend time on an isolated island and not have the urge to return. Somewhere in Lake Michigan's mist, a voice seems to echo, "Come back, come back, come back." Those of us who have had the opportunity to do so, are forever blessed and grateful.

Kathleen Firestone

VASCULAR PLANTS OF THE FOX ISLANDS

Adapted from compilations made by Brian T. Hazlett, Ph.D.

The latest comprehensive studies were completed in 1987 by Hazlett, who incorporated earlier findings of Frederick Test, Larry Wolf and E. U. Clover. The later additions of Glenn F. Goff and Phyllis J. Higman have been included by the author, in addition to one entry by Dennis A. Albert and Gary Reese for Michigan Natural Features Inventory. The collectors are noted by their last initials; (T), (W), (C), (G) Goff and Higman, and (A) Albert and Reese.

* designated "endangered," "threatened," or "rare" by Michigan Natural Features Inventory, 1993

N. Fox = N S. Fox = S

(Unless otherwise noted, listed are also found on the Manitou Islands)

Clubmoss Family		
Stiff Clubmoss	(H)	S
Round-Branch Ground-Pine	(H)	S
Shining Clubmoss	(T) (H)	N/S
Tree Clubmoss	(H)	N/S
Selaginella Family		
Field Horsetail	(H) (C)	N/S
Clute	(H)	S
Water Horsetail	(H)	N
Scouring-Rush	(H) (T)	N/S
Dwarf Scouring-Rush	(H) (C)	N/S
Woodland Horsetail	(H)	N
Equisetum x variegatum	(H)	N/S
Adder's Tongue Family		
*Sleeping Bear Dunewort (rare on S.Fox also)	(H)	S
Daisy-Leaved Moonwort	(H)	N/S
Botrychium minganense Vict.	(H)	S
Leathery Grape Fern	(H)	N/S
Least Moonwort	(H)	S
Rattlesnake Fern	(H)	N/S
Adder's Tongue	(H)	N
Royal Fern Family		
Cinnamon Fern	(H)	N
Royal Fern	(H)	N
Fern Family		
Maidenhair Fern	(H) (C)	N/S
*Green Spleenwort	(T)	S
Lady Fern	(H) (C)	N/S
Bulblet Fern	(T) (C)	N/S
Fragile Fern	(H)	S
Crested Shield Fern	(H) (C)	N/S
Evergreen Wood Fern	(H)	N/S
Marginal Wood Fern	(T) (H)	N/S
Spinulose Wood Fern	(T) (H)	N/S
Wherry	(H)	N/S
Oak Fern	(H)	N/S
Ostrich Fern	(H) (C)	N/S
Sensitive Fern	(T) (H)	N/S
Common Polypody	(H) (C,W)	N/S
Christmas Fern	(T) (C,T)	N/S
Braun's Holly Fern	(H)	S
Northern Holly Fern	(H)	S
Bracken Fern	(H)	N/S
Marsh Fern	(H)	N
Northern Beech Fern	(H)	N/S
Cypress Family		
Common Juniper	(H)	N/S
Creeping Juniper	(H) (C)	N/S
Juniperus virginiana L. (rare on N. Fox & not found on S. Fox nor N & S Manitou)	(H)	N
White Cedar	(H)	N/S
Pine Family		
Balsam Fir	(H) (T)	N/S
Larch	(H)	N
White Spruce	(H)	S
White Pine (rare)	(H)	N/S
Yew Family		
Yew	(H) (C,W)	N/S
Arum Family		
Jack-In-The-Pulpit	(T) (C,W)	N/S
Skunk-Cabbage (not on N/S Manitou)	(H)	N/S
Spiderwort Family		
Tradescantia virginiana L. (not found on N Fox nor N/S Manitou)	(H)	S
Sedge Family		
Carex aquatilis	(H)	N
Carex arctata	(H) (W)	N/S
Carex aurea	(H)	N/S
Carex bebbii	(H)	N/S
Carex brunnescens	(H)	N
Carex canescens	(H)	N

Carex cephaloidea	(H)	S
(not found on N Fox nor on N/S Manitou)		
Carex communis	(H)	N
Carex convoluta	(H) (C)	N/S
Carex deweyana	(H) (C)	N/S
Carex eburnea	(H)	N/S
Carex garberi	(H)	N
Carex gracillima	(H) (C)	N/S
(not on N/S Manitou)		
Carex houghtoniana	(H)	S
(not found on N Fox nor N/S Manitou)		
Carex hystericina	(H)	N
Carex intumescens	(H)	N/S
Carex lanuginosa	(H)	S
Carex leptonervia	(H)	S
Carex lupulina	(H)	N/S
(not on N/S Manitou)		
Carex pedunculata	(G)	N
Carex plantaginea	(T) (H)	N/S
Carex praegracilis	(H)	N
(not found on S Fox nor N/S Manitou)		
Carex prasina	(H)	S
(not found on N Fox nor N/S Manitou)		
Carex projecta	(H)	S
Carex retrorsa	(T)	N
Carex rosea	(H)	N
Carex sprengelii	(H)	N/S
(not on N/S Manitou)		
Carex stipata	(H)	S
Carex tuckermanii	(H)	N/S
Carex umbellata	(H)	S
(not found on N Fox nor N/S Manitou)		
Carex vesicaria L.	(H)	N
(not found on S Fox nor N/S Manitou)		
Carex viridula	(T) (H)	N/S
Carex vulpinoidea	(H)	N/S
Eleocharis elliptica	(H)	N
Eleocharis olivacea	(H)	N
(not found on S Fox nor N/S Manitou)		
Eleocharis pauciflora	(H)	S
(not found on N Fox nor N/S Manitou)		
Scirpus atrovirens	(H)	S
Scirpus cyperinus	(H)	N/S
Scirpus pendulus	(H)	N
Scirpus validus	(H)	N

Grass Family

Agropyron dasystachyum	(T) (H)	N/S
Quackgrass	(H)	N/S
Redtop	(H)	S
Agrostis stolonifera	(H)	S
(not found on N Fox nor N/S Manitou)		
Beach Grass	(H)	N/S
Little Bluestem	(H)	S
Smooth Brome	(H) (C)	S
*Pumpelly's Bromegrass	(H)	N/S
Blue-Joint	(H)	N
Calamovilfa longifolia	(H)	N/S
Orchard Grass	(H)	N/S
Elymus canadensis L.	(T) (C)	N/S
Nodding Fescue	(H) (C)	N/S
Festuca occidentalis	(H)	N/S
Restuca rubra L.	(T) (H)	N/S
Festuca saximontana	(H)	S
Fowl Manna Grass	(H)	N/S
Bottlebrush Grass	(H)	N/S
June Grass	(H)	S
Melica smithii	(H)	N/S
Millium effusum L	(H).	N/S
Oryzopsis asperifolia	(C)	S
Panicum implicatum	(H)	N/S
Proso	(H)	S
(not found on N Fox nor N/S Manitou)		
Reed Canary Grass	(H)	N
(not found on S Fox nor N/S Manitou)		
Timothy	(T) (H)	N/S
Poa alsodes	(H)	N
Canada Bluegrass	(T) (H)	N/S
Poa nemoralis L.	(H)	N/S
Fowl Meadow Grass	(T)	N
Poa pratensis L.	(H)	N/S
False Melic	(H)	N/S

Iris Family

Iris pallida	(H)	S
(not found on N Fox nor N/S Manitou)		
Wild Blue Flag	(H)	N
Southern Blue Flag	(H)	N
Blue-Eyed-Grass	(H)	N

Rush Family

Juncus alpinus	(T) (H)	N/S
Juncus balticus	(T) (H)	N/S
Juncus brachycephalus	(H)	N
(not found on S Fox nor N/S Manitou)		
Juncus nodosus L.	(H)	N
(not found on S. Fox nor N/S Manitou)		
Juncus tenuis	(T) (C)	N/S

Arrow-Grass Family

Triglochin maritumum L.	(H)	S
(not found on N Fox nor N/S Manitou)		

Duckweed Family

Duckweed	(H)	N

Lily Family

Wild Leeks	(T)(C,W)	N/S
Garden Asparagus	(H)	S
Corn-Lily	(H)	N/S
Lily-Of-The-Valley	(H)	S
Adder's-Tongue	(H)	N/S
Wood Lily	(H)	N/S
Canada Mayflower	(H)(C,W)	N/S
Hairy Solomon's Seal	(H)(C.W)	N/S
False Spikenard	(H) (C)	N/S
Starry False Solomon's Seal	(T) (C)	N/S
Rose Mandarin	(H) (W)	N/S
Nodding Trillium	(H)	N/S
(not on N/S Manitou)		

Stinking Benjamin	(T) (H)	N/S
Trillium flexipes	(H)	N/S
Common Trillium	(H) (W)	N/S
White Camas	(H)(C.W)	N/S

Orchid Family

*Calypso or Fairy Slipper	(H)	N
Spotted Coral-Root	(C)	S
Striped Coral-Root	(H)	N/S
Early Coral-Root	(H)	N
Yellow Lady-Slipper	(W)	S
Helleborine	(H)	S
Giant Rattlesnake-Plantain	(H) (W)	N/S
Goodyera repens		
var. ophiodes	(G)	N
Dwarf Rattlesnake-Plantain	(G) (W)	N/S
Checkered Rattlesnake-Pltn.	(H)	N
Club-Spur Orchid	(H)	N
Habenaria dilatata	(H)	N
(not found on S Fox nor N/S Manitou)		
Tall Northern Bog Orchid	(H)	N/S
Round-Leaved Orchid	(H) (W)	N/S
Bracted Orchid	(H) (W)	N/S
Fen Orchid	(H)	S
Broad-Leaved Twayblade	(H)	N
Malaxis monophylla	(H)	N
Spiranthes romanzoffiana	(H)	N

Pondweed Family

Potamogeton gramineus L.	(H)	N/S

Bur-Reed Family

Sparganium angustifolium	(T)	N
(not found on S Fox nor N/S Manitou)		

Cat-Tail Family

Common Cat-Tail	(H)	N/S

Maple Family

Box Elder	(H)	S
(not found on N Fox nor N/S Manitou)		
Striped Maple	(H)	N
Red Maple	(H)	N/S
(rare on S)		
Sugar Maple	(H)	N/S
Mountain Maple	(T)(C,W)	N/S

Amaranthus Family

Tumbleweed	(H)	S
Amaranthus blitoides	(H)	S
(not found on N Fox nor on N/S Manitou)		
Rhus x pulvinata	(C)	S
(not found on N Fox nor on N/S Manitou)		
Rhus radicans	(G)	N
Staghorn Sumac	(H)	S
Poison-Ivy	(H) (C)	N/S

Dogbane Family

Spreading Dogbane	(H)	N/S

Holly Family

Michigan Holly	(T)	N

Ginseng Family

Bristly Sarsaparilla	(H) (C)	N/S
Wild Sarsaparilla	(H) (C)	N/S
Spikenard	(T)(C,W)	N/S
*Ginseng	(C)	S

Milkweed Family

Common Milkweed	(H)	N/S
Green Milkweed	(H)	S

Touch-Me-Not Family

Spotted Touch-Me-Not	(H)	N/S

Barberry Family

Blue Cohosh	(T) (H)	N/S

Birch Family

Yellow Birch	(H)	N/S
White Birch	(T) (H)	N/S
Beaked Hazelnut	(T) (H)	N/S
(not on N/S Manitou)		
Ironwood	(H)	N/S

Forget-Me-Not Family

Northern Wild Comfrey	(H)	S
(not found on N Fox nor N/S Manitou)		
Common Hound's-Tongue	(H) (T)	S
Hackelia americana	(H)	S
Puccoon	(T)(C,W)	N/S
Myosotis scorpioides L.	(T)	S
(not found on N Fox nor N/S Manitou)		

Boxwood Family

Pachysandra terminalis	(H)	S
(extirpated on S Fox, not found on N. Fox nor N/S Manitou)		

Harebell Family

Harebell	(H) (W)	N/S
Campanula trachelium L.	(H)	S
(not found on N Fox nor N/S Manitou)		

Honeysuckle Family

Bush Honeysuckle	(W)	N/S
Twinflower	(H) (W)	N/S
Wild Honeysuckle	(H) (W)	N/S
Hairy Honeysuckle	(H) (C)	N/S
Sambucus pubens	(H)(C,W)	N/S
Snowberry	(H)	N/S
Maple-Leaved Viburnum	(C)	S
Highbush Cranberry	(T)	N/S

Pink Family

Thyme-Leaved Sandwort	(H)	N/S
Rock Sandwort	(H)	N/S
Common Mouse-Eared Chickweed	(T) (W)	N/S
Deptford Pink	(H)	S
Sweet William	(H)	S
Bouncing Bet	(H)	S
Sleepy Catchfly	(H)	S
Night-Flowering Catchfly	(C)	S
(not found on N Fox nor N/S Manitou)		

White Campion (rare on N)	(H)	N/S
Bladder Campion	(T) (H)	N/S
Northern Starwort (not found on S Fox nor N/S Manitou)	(H)	N
Common Stichwort	(H)	N/S
Common Chickweed	(H)	S

Staff-Tree Family

Bittersweet	(H)	N/S

Goosefoot Family

Lambs-Quarters	(H)	S
Strawberry Blite	(T) (W)	N/S
Chenopodium hybridum L. (not found on N Fox nor N/S Manitou)	(H)	S
Bugseed	(H)	N/S

Rockrose Family

Beach Heath	(H)	S

Composite Family

Common Yarrow	(T) (H)	N/S
Common Ragweed	(H)	N
Ambrosia psilostachya	(H)	S
Pearly Everlasting	(H)	N/S
Field Pussytoes	(H)	N/S
Antennaria plantaginifolia L.	(H)	S
Common Burdock	(H) (W)	N/S
Artemisia biennis (not found on N Fox nor N/S Manitou)	(H)	S
Tall Wormwood	(T) (C)	N/S
Aster laevis L.	(H)	S
Aster sagittifolia (not found on S Fox nor N/S Manitou)	(G)	N
Aster lateriflorus L.	(H)	N/S
Large Leaved Aster	(T) (C)	N/S
Panicled Aster	(H)	N/S
Spotted Knapweed	(H)	N/S
Ox-Eyed Daisy	(H)	S
Canada Thistle	(H)	N/S
*Pitcher's Thistle	(T)(C,W)	N/S
Bull Thistle	(H)	N/S
Hog Weed	(H)	N/S
Lance-Leaved Coreopsis	(N) (C)	N/S
Erigeron annuus L.	(H)	N/S
Erigeron philadelphicus L.	(H)	N/S
Erigeron strigosus	(H)	S
Joe-Pie Weed (not found on S Fox nor N/S Manitou)	(H)	N
Orange Hawkweed	(H)	N/S
Hieracium canadense (not found on N Fox nor N/S Manitou)	(H)	S
Hieracium pretinse (not found on S Fox nor N/S Manitou)	(G)	N
King Devil	(H)	N/S
Lactuca canadensis L.	(H)	N/S
White Lettuce	(C) (W)	S
Black-Eyed Susan	(H)	S
Balsam Ragwort	(H)	S
Canada Goldenrod	(H)	N/S
Zig-Zag Goldenrod	(H) (W)	N/S
Solidago gigantea	(H)	N/S
Grass-Leaved Goldenrod	(H)	N
Solidago gentsen (not found on S Fox nor N/S Manitou)	(G)	N
Solidago juncea	(H)	S
Solidago petiuolaris (not found on S Fox nor N/S Manitou)	(G)	N
Gray Goldenrod (not found on N Fox nor N/S Manitou)	(H)	S
Solidago ohioensis (not found on S Fox nor N/S Manitou)	(H)	N
Solidago spathulata	(H)	N/S
Sonchus arvensis L. (not found on S Fox nor N/S Manitou)	(H)	N
Sonchus uliginosus	(H)	N
*Huron Tansy (not on Manitous)	(T) (H)	N/S
Dandelion	(H)	N/S
Tragopogon dubius	(T) (H)	N/S
Sweet Colt's Foot	(G)	N

Dogwood Family

Pagoda Dogwood	(H) (C)	N/S
Bunchberry	(H)	N
Round-Leaved Dogwood	(T) (C,W)	N/S
Red-Osier	(T) (W)	N/S

Orpine Family

Mossy Stonecrop (not found on N Fox nor N/S Manitou)	(H)	S
Live-Forever	(H)	S

Mustard Family

Arabis drumondii	(H)	N
Arabis hirsuta (not found on N Fox nor N/S Manitou)	(W)	S
Draba verna (not found on S Fox nor N/S Manitou)	(G)	N
Sand Cress	(T) (H)	N/S
Yellow Rocket	(H)	S
Hoary Alyssum	(T)	S
Sea-Rocket	(T) (H)	N/S
Camelina microcarpa	(W)	S
Shepherd's Purse	(H) (W)	N/S
Cardamine pensylvanica	(H)	N/S
Cuckoo-Flower	(H)	S
Two-Leaved Toothwort	(H)	N/S
Cut-Leaved Toothwort	(H)	N/S
Lepidium campestre	(H)	S
Lepidium densiflorum	(W)	S
Watercress (not found on N Fox nor N/S Manitou)	(H)	S
Field Mustard	(H)	S
Hedge Mustard (*altissimum*)	(W)	S
Hedge Mustard (*officinale*) (not found on N Fox nor N/S Manitou)	(H)	S

Oleaster Family

Buffaloberry	(T) (H)	N/S

Heath Family

Bearberry	(T) (H)	N/S
Pine Sap	(H) (W)	N/S
Indian Pipe	(H)	N
Pyrola chlorantha	(H)	S
Shinleaf	(H)	N/S
One-Sided Pyrola	(H) (W)	N/S
Velvet-Leaf Blueberry (rare on N. Fox)	(H)	N

Spurge Family

Flowering Spurge (not found on N Fox nor N/S Manitou)	(H)	S

Beech Family

Beech	(H)	N/S
Red Oak	(H) (C)	N/S

Fumitory Family

**Adlumia fungosa*	(A)	N
Golden Corydalis (not on Manitous)	(T) (H)	N/S
Squirrel-Corn	(H)	N/S
Dutchman's-Breeches	(H)	N/S

Gentian Family

Buckbean	(H)	N

Geranium Family

Geranium maculatum L. (rare on S Fox, not found on N Fox nor N/S Manitou)	(H)	S
Geranium pusillum	(H)	S
Herb-Robert	(H) (T)	N/S

Gooseberry Family

Wild Black Currant	(H)	N
Wild Gooseberry	(H) (C)	N/S
Ribes lacustre (not found on S Fox nor N/S Manitou)	(G)	N
Ribes triste (not found on N Fox nor N/S Manitou)	(H)	S

St. John's-Wort Family

Kalm's St. John's-Wort	(H)	N
Common St. John's-Wort	(H) (T)	N/S

Mint Family

Common Motherwort	(H)(C,W)	S
Water Horehound	(T) (H)	N/S
Lycopus asper (not found on S Fox nor N/S Manitou)	(G)	N
Lycopus uniflorus	(H)	N/S
Mentha arvensis L.	(H)	N/S
Catnip	(W)	S
Self-Heal	(H) (W)	N/S
Basil	(W)	S
Common Skullcap	(H)	N
Mad Dog Skullcap	(H)	N

Bean Family

Beach Pea	(T) (C)	N/S
Everlasting Pea	(H)	S
Lathyrus palustris L. (not on S Fox nor N/S Manitou)	(H)	N
Black Medic	(H)	S
Alfalfa	(H)	S
White Sweet Clover	(H)	S
Hop Clover	(H)	N
Trifolium dubium (not found on N Fox nor N/S Manitou)	(H)	S
Trifolium hybridum L. (not found on S Fox nor N/S Manitou)	(H)	N
Red Clover	(H)	N
White Clover	(H)	N/S
Hairy Vetch	(H)	S

Lobelia Family

Kalm's Lobelia	(H)	N

Mallow Family

Common Mallow	(H)	S

Mulberry Family

Hops	(H)	S

Olive Family

White Ash	(H)	N/S
Black Ash	(H)	N/S
Red Ash (not on Manitous)	(H) (W)	N/S
Lilac (rare on N Fox)	(H)	N/S

Evening Primrose Family

Dwarf Enchanter's Nightshade	(H)	N/S
Circaea lutetiana L. (not on Manitous)	(H)	N/S
Fireweed	(H)	N
Epilobium ciliatum	(H)	N/S
Epilobium leptophyllum	(H)	N
Oenothera oakesiana	(H) (C)	N/S

***Broom-Rape Family**

Beech-Drops	(H)	N/S
One-Flowered Cancer-Root	(H)	N/S

Wood-Sorrel Family

Oxalis acetosella L. (not on S Fox nor N/S Manitou)	(H)	N
Oxalis fontana	(H)	S
Oxalis stricta L.	(H)	S

Poppy Family

Bloodroot	(T) (H)	N/S

Plantain Family

English Plantain	(H)	N/S
Plantago major L.	(H)	N
Pale Plantain	(H)	S

Milkwort Family
Flowering Wintergreen (H) N/S

Smartweed Family
Jointweed (H) N
(not found on S Fox nor N/S Manitou)
Knotweed (H) S
Fringed False Buckwheat (H) (W) N/S
Black-Bindweed (H) S
Mild Water-Pepper (W) S
(not found on N Fox nor N/S Manitou)
Willow-Weed (T) N
(not found on S Fox nor N/S Manitou)
Lady's-Thumb (H) S
Sheep Sorrel (H) (C) N/S
Sour Dock (H) N/S
Bitter Dock (T) (W) N/S

Purslane Family
Carolina Spring Beauty (H) N/S
Common Purslane (H) S
Tufted Loosestrife (H) N
Star Flower (H) N

Buttercup Family
White Baneberry (H) (W) N/S
Red Baneberry (H) N/S
Thimbleweed (H)(C,W) N/S
Red Anemone (H) S
Wood Anemone (H) N/S
Anemone virginiana L. (H) N
(not found on S Fox nor N/S Manitou)
Wild Columbine (H) (C) N/S
Marsh Marigold (H) N/S
Goldthread (H) N
Sharp-Leaved Hepatica (T) (H) N/S
Small-Flowered Buttercup (H) N/S
Common Buttercup (H) N/S
Swamp Buttercup (H) N
(not on S Fox nor N/S Manitou)
Hooked Crowfoot (H) N/S
Thalictrum dasycarpum (H) N
(not found on S Fox nor N/S Manitou)
Early Meadowrue (H) (C) N/S

Rose Family
Agrimonia gryposepala (H) (W) N/S
Amelanchier arborea (H) N
Amelanchier interior (H) (C) N/S
Amelanchier laevis (H) N/S
Amelanchier sanguinea (H) N/S
Amelanchier spicata (H) (C) N/S
(not on Manitous)
Woodland Strawberry (H) N/S
Wild Strawberry (H) N/S
Geum aleppicum (H) (C) N/S
Geum canadense (H) (W) N/S
Apple (H) N/S
Nine-Bark (T) N
(not found on S Fox nor on N/S Manitou)
Silverweed (T) (H) N/S
Silvery Cinquefoil (H) (W) N/S
Rough Cinquefoil (T) (H) N/S
Sulfur Cinquefoil (W) S
Sweet Cherry (H) S
Pin Cherry (H) (C) N/S
Sand Cherry (T) (C) N/S
Choke Cherry (T)(C,W) N/S
Rosa blanda (H) (C) N/S
Rosa multiflora (G) N
(not found on S Fox nor on N/S Manitou)
Sweetbriar (H) N/S
Swamp Rose (H) N
Thimbleberry (H) (C) N/S
Dwarf Raspberry (H) N
Wild Red Raspberry (H) (C) N/S
Mountain Ash (H) (C,W) N/S
Bridal-Wreath (H) S

Madder Family
Cleavers (H) N/S
Galium boreale L. (H) S
Sweet Scented Bedstraw (T) (W) N/S
Partridgeberry (T) (C) N/S

Willow Family
Balsam Poplar (H) N/S
Big-Tooth Aspen (H) N/S
Quaking Aspen (H) (C) N/S
Beaked Willow (H) N
Salix glaucaphylloides (G) N
(not found on S Fox nor N/S Manitou)
Sand-Dune Willow (H) N/S
Pussy Willow (H) N
(not found on S Fox nor N/S Manitou)
Sandbar Willow (H) N/S
Shining Willow (H) N
Slender Willow (G) N

Sandalwood Family
Bastard Toadflax (H) S

Saxifrage Family
Bishop's Cap (H) S
Naked Miterwort (H) N/S
Philadelphus coronarius L. (H) S

Figwort Family
Purple Gerardia (H) N
Cow Wheat (T) N
Wood Betony (H) S
Common Mullein (H) N/S
American Brooklime (H) S
Common Speedwell (H) S
Veronica serpyllifolia L. (W) S

Nightshade Family
Clammy Groundcherry (C,W) S
Horse Nettle (H) S
Nightshade (H) N
Solanum nigrum L. (W) S

Basswood Family

Basswood	(H) (C)	N/S

Elm Family

American Elm	(H)	N

Parsley Family

Wild Carrot	(H)	N/S
Cow-Parship	(T) (W)	N/S
Osmorhiza chilensis	(H)	N/S
Osmorhiza claytonii	(T) (C,W)	N/S
Osmorhiza longistylis	(H)	N/S
(not on Manitous)		
Wild Parsnip	(H	S
(not found on N Fox nor N/S Manitou)		
Sanicula marilandica L.	(T)	N/S
Sanicula trifoliata	(C)	S
Sium suave	(H)	N
(not found on S Fox nor N/S Manitou)		

Vervain Family

Verbena simplex	(H)	S
(not found on N Fox nor N/S Manitou)		

Violet Family

Viola adunca	(H)	S
Sweet White Violet	(H)	N/S
Canada Violet	(H)(T,W)	N/S
Dog Violet	(H)	N/S
Marsh Violet	(H)	N/S
Viola nephrophylla	(H)	N
(not found on S Fox nor N/S Manitou)		
Yellow Violet	(H)	N/S
Viola renifolia	(H)	N
(not found on S Fox nor N/S Manitou)		
Great-Spurred Violet	(H)	N/S

Grape Family

River-Bank Grape	(H)	S

COURTESY CRANBROOK INSTITUTE OF SCIENCE
Part of the Cranbrook Institute of Science team which visited several Lake Michigan Islands in the 1930's. Shown on North Fox are (L-R) William Jewell, Clifford Pope, Robert Hatt and George Stanley. Van Tyne, Staebler and Case are not shown.

COURTESY BRIAN T. HAZLETT
(L-R) Brian T. Hazlett, Paul Thompson and Susan P. Hendricks collecting specimens on South Fox Island, 1984. Hazlett's studies included the Manitou Islands and both North and South Fox.

Additional Plant Studies

BIRD SIGHTINGS ON THE FOX ISLANDS

North Fox = N South Fox = S	Van Tyne, Staebler, Case, and Hatt, 1937-39	William Scharf, 1972-73 & 1987	G. Dulin & P. Higman, Aug., 1990
Brewers Blackbird		S	
Red Winged Blackbird		S	N
Eastern Bluebird	S	S	
Northern Blue Jay	N/S	S	N
Bobolink	S	S	
Indigo Bunting	S	S	
Cat Bird		S	N
Black Capped Chickadee	N		
Eastern Cowbird	S	S	
Eastern Crow	N/S	S	N
Black Billed Cuckoo	S	S	
Yellow Billed Cuckoo	S		
Mourning Dove	S	S	
Mallard Duck			N
Northern Bald Eagle	N/S	S	
Eastern Goldfinch	N/S	S	
Canada Goose		S	
Grackle	S	N	
Eastern Purple Finch	S	S	
Northern Flicker	N/S	S	N
Least Flycatcher		S	
Northern Crested Flycatcher	N/S	S	
Canada Goose	N		
Eastern Goshawk	N/S		
Rose Breasted Grosbeak		S	N
Herring Gull	N/S	S	N
Ring Billed Gull		S	N
Duck Hawk	S		
Eastern Nighthawk	S	S	
Red Tailed Hawk	S	S	N
Sharp Shinned Hawk		S	
Great Blue Heron	S	S	N
Ruby Throated Hummingbird	N/S	S	
Killdeer	N/S	S	
Eastern Kingbird	N/S	S	
Kingfisher		S	
Loon	N/S	S	N
Purple Martin	S		
Eastern Meadowlark	S	S	
Mockingbird		S	
American Merganser	N/S	S	N
Red Breasted Merganser	S		
Red Breasted Nuthatch		S	N
White Breasted Nuthatch		S	N
Baltimore Oriole	S	S	
Oven Bird	N/S	S	
Eastern Wood Pewee	N/S	S	N

North Fox = N South Fox = S	Van Tyne, Staebler, Case, and Hatt, 1937-39	William Scharf, 1972-73 & 1987	G. Dulin & P. Higman, Aug., 1990
Eastern Phoebe	S	S	
Belted Piping Plover	S		
American Redstart	N/S	S	N
Eastern Robin	S	S	N
Spotted Sandpiper	N/S	S	N
Yellow Bellied Sapsucker		S	
Clay Colored Sparrow	S	S	
Eastern Chipping Sparrow	N/S	S	N
Eastern Field Sparrow	S	S	
Eastern Grasshopper Sparrow	N/S	S	
Eastern Vesper Sparrow	N/S	S	
Mississippi Song Sparrow	N/S	S	N
Starling	N/S	S	N
Barn Swallow	S	S	
Bank Swallow	S	S	
Rough Winged Swallow	S		
Tree Swallow	N/S	S	
Chimney Swift	S	S	
Scarlet Tanager	S	S	
Caspian Tern	N/S		N
Red Eyed Towhee	N/S		
Rufous Sided Towhee		S	
Brown Thrasher	S	S	
Willow Thrush	N/S		
Veery		S	
Red Eyed Vireo	N/S	S	N
Turkey Vulture			N
Black Throated Blue Warbler	N/S		N
Black and White Warbler		S	N
Black Throated Green Warbler	N/S	S	
Canada Warbler		S	
Chestnut Sided Warbler	S	S	N
Golden Winged Warbler		S	
Magnolia Warbler		S	
Yellow Warbler		S	
Cedar Waxwing	N/S	S	N
Eastern Whippoorwill	S	S	
American Woodcock	S	S	N
Eastern Hairy Woodpecker	S		N
Northern Downy Woodpecker	S	S	
Red Headed Woodpecker		S	
Eastern House Wren	N/S	S	
Sedge Wren			N
Short Billed Marsh Wren	N		
Western House Wren	S		

Other individuals have also sighted the Snowy Owl on South Fox. All of the birds on Scharf's list were also banded. Although Scharf did not conduct a comprehensive survey of North Fox, he stated that it, like other islands in the area, is undoubtedly "a magnet" for migrating birds.

EMPLOYEE LIST

The following is a list of persons employed by Sterling Nickerson & Sons lumber company on South Fox Island between 1954 and 1964. The author regrets employees whose names may be misspelled or missing from this list taken from payroll records. Most records were available, but a few were missing. Unless found elsewhere in this book, these names are not included in the index. Some of these people worked for many years on the island, others for only a few days. Some did not stay at the island but traveled on the boats and helped with loading and unloading of lumber.

Addis, Neil
Andrews, Laurence
Anewishki, Charles
Anewishki, William
Antoine, William
Ask, Alvin

Baca, Mike
Bailey, Raymond
Bailey, Rudy
Bancroft, Lloyd
Bancroft, Roy
Baur, Art
Bendickson, Robert
Benninghaus, Carl
Bergeron, Buck
Bergeron, Elmer
Bogart, Garth
Boucher, Vernon
Bowen, Arthur
Bowen, James
Bradley, Ervil
Bradley, Ethel
Bradley, John
Brown, Robert
Brown, Homer

Carlson, Norman
Carter, Moses
Chippewa, Dan
Chippewa, Dan, Jr.
Chippewa, Eliza
Chippewa, Ernest
Chippewa, Gordon
Chippewa, Mabel
Chippewa, Phillip
Chippewa, Ray
Chippewa, Wayne
Church, James
Cobb, Ivan
Cole, Ronald
Conroy, Patrick
Conway, Ronald
Coon, Cecil
Coon, Jennie
Corriveau, Wilbert
Craddock, Huston
Craddock, Leroy
Craker, Clinton
Craycrift, John
Currigan, Bob

Dalzell, Bob
Dalzell, William
Dashner, John
David, Peter
Davis, Silas
Decker, Albert
Demaska, Myrtle
Demaska, William
Deverney, George
Dexter, Hylton
Dickson, Floyd
Dix, Charles
Donochil, David
Dunlap, Francis

Earl, Charles
Eckert, Charles
Edgerton, Hugh
Erickson, Ralph
Evans, Sam

Farber, Jack
Feigel, Herbert
Ferrin, Larry
Fischer, Edward
Fischer, Eugene
Franks, Harold

Geller, Roman
Gibson, Norman
Gildwisky, Joseph
Gingway, Edwin
Gingway, Nick
Golden, Gary
Gothro, Marshal

Haan, James
Hadley, Elias
Hall, Foster
Hall, Wallace
Hallett, Ed
Hallett, Fred
Hanson , John
Hasler, Clarence
Hautamske, Ray
Henry, Elwood
Henry, Lawrence
Hill, William
Hinman, Clifford
Hoffman, Ted
Holton, Darwin
Holton, Nelson
Hope, Thomas
Horn, Gary
Horn, James
Horton, James
Howard, Garland
Hurt, Mae
Hutchinson, Philip

Isaac, Cecil

Jacobson, Clyde
Jacobus, Louie
Jeska, Joseph
Johnson, David
Joseph, Edna
Joseph, Joe

Kadrovach, Peter
Kagabitang, James
Kalchik, Francis
Keen, Pete
Kellogg, Klinton
Kenoshmeg, Levi
Keshik, John
Kewaygoshkum, Homer
Kewaygoshkum, Jesse
Kewaygoshkum, John
Kewaygoshkum, Leo
Kewaygoshkum, Tom
Kiersey, Gerald
King, Jesse
Kintgen, Robert
Kiogima, Charles
Kirkland, Guston
Klass, James
Klass, Susie
Klass, William
Knutson, Ivor
Kolarik, Gene
Korb, Bob
Kortokrax, August
Kuhle, Anthony

Larson, Charles
Leabo, Mark
Leighton, Clyde
Lewis, Florence
Lindberg, Bruce
Loebich, Ronald
Loomis, Bill
Luna, Ramon
Luna, Rudy

Maginity, Buckley
Magnuson, Arvid
Manitowash, Clarence
Manitowash, Marvin
Marks, Stanley
Marvin, Alvin
McMachen, Larry
McMahon, Ebbie
McMannus, Daryl
McSawby, Alec
McSawby, Homer

Meangwie, Sam
Meyer, Engelbert
Mikowski, James
Miller, Archie
Miller, Glen
Miller, Ivan
Miller, Kenneth
Miller, Ralph
Mitchell, Sam
Mitchell, Wallace
Moore, Bob
Moran, Bill
Morgan, Milton
Murray, Louis

Nickerson, Eva
Nickerson, Eve
Nickerson, Max
Nickerson, Sterling, Sr.
Nickerson, Sterling, Jr.
Nickerson, Sterling, III
Nickerson, E. Quentin
Noah, James
Noah, Joseph

Ockert, Leroy
Ogemaw, Norman

Paton, Pat
Paul, Ambrose
Paul, Bennett
Paul, Clifford
Paul, Ernest
Paul, Kermit
Paul, Norman
Paul, Ramon
Pearl, Bob
Peck, Virgil
Peshaba, Edward
Phillips, Wesley
Pickop, Richard
Prickett, Sam, Jr.
Priest, Ferman
Priest, Robert
Prost, William
Purkiss, Dwain

Quirk, Rolland

Riley, William
Rivera, Victor
Rogers, Allen
Roop, Glen
Rouse, William
Russett, Joseph

Samuels, Julius
Sands, Joseph
Sanzonette, Emanuel
Saunders, William
Saxton, Lee
Scamehorn, Walter
Schwerzler, James
Scott, David B.
Sedlacek, Henry
Sedlacek, Jake
Seese, Robert
Shafley, Rodney
Shawnosky, Frank
Shawnosky, Samuel
Sheahon, Francis
Shelnut, Andrew
Shelnut, James
Shenonaquet, Harry
Shocko, Elmer
Shocko, Leroy
Shomin, Albert
Shomin, Ed
Shomin, Frank
Shomin, Gordo
Souvinouen, Myrna
Souvinouen, Wayne
Sineway, Nick
Sineway, Tony
Skenes, Orville
Smith, Dick
Sowers, Harold
Sprandel, David
Stachnik, Clarence
Stachnik, Isadore
Stage, Hugh
Stauffer, Ken
Sumerix, Frank
Sweet, Leon

Taylor, Cecil
Taylor, Jim
Theodore, Richard
Thomas, Albert
Thomas, Clayton
Thomas, Maurice
Thomas, Warren
Thompson, Clyde
Thompson, Louie
Thompson, Nolan
Tipton, Arvid
Tipton, Bob
Tipton, John
Titus, Gerald
Trager, Ed
Tyler, Ted

Walsh, George
Warner, Ivan
Wasegejib, Lazarre
Watson, Ike
Waukazoo, Steve
Wayashe, Tony
Webb, Edward
Webster, Ralph
Weidner, Edward
Weidner, Dick
Weidner, Marvin
Widdis, Walt
Widenaja, John
Wilcox, Claude
Williams, Orley
Willis, James
Winowiecki, Tony
Wonegeshik, Elijah
Wonegeshik, James
Wonegeshik, Levi

Yagle, James
Yannett, George, Sr.
Yannett, Silas

INFORMATION SOURCES

BOOKS

Bald, Cleaver. *Michigan in Four Centuries*. New York: Harper & Brothers Publishers, 1954.

Beers, J. H. & Company. *History Of The Great Lakes. Volumes I and II*. Chicago, 1899; reprinted by Freshwater Press, Inc., Cleveland, 1972.

Blackbird, Andrew. *History of the Ottawa and Chippewa Indians of Michigan*. Ypsilanti: Ypsilanti Job Printing House, 1887.

Bowen, Dana Thomas. *Memories of the Great Lakes.* Daytona Beach: by author, 1946.

Campbell, Nancy and Judy Ranville. *Memories of Mackinaw*. Petoskey, Mich.: Little Traverse Printing, 1976.

Cashman, William, Project Director. *The Journal of Beaver Island, Vol. I.* Beaver Island Historical Society, 1976. *Vol. II*, 1980. *Vol. III,* 1988.

Craker, Ruth. *First Protestant Mission in the Grand Traverse Region*. 1935; reprint. Mount Pleasant: Rivercrest House, 1979.

Cronyn, Margaret and John Kenny. *Saga of Beaver Island*. Ann Arbor: Braun and Brumfield, Inc., 1958.

Davis, Marion M. *Island Stories*. ed. George N. Fuller. Lansing: State Printers, 1947.

Densmore, Frances. *A Study of Some Michigan Indians.* Ann Arbor: University of Michigan Press, 1949.

Fasquelle, Ethel Rowan. *When Michigan Was Young*. 1950; reprint. Grand Rapids: Avery Color Studios, 1981.

Fuller, George N., ed. *Historic Michigan, Vol. III.* National Historical Association, Inc., undated.

Fitzpatrick, Doyle C. *The King Strang Story*. Lansing: National Heritage, 1970.

Hatcher, Harland and Erick Walter. *A Pictorial History of the Great Lakes.* New York: Bonanza Books, 1970.

Hatt, Robert T., et al. *Island Life In Lake Michigan*. Bloomfield Hills, Mich.: Cranbrook Institute of Science. 1948.

Havighurst, Walter. *Three Flags At The Straits*. Englewood Cliffs, N. J.: Prentice-Hall, 1966.

Hazlett, Brian T. *Factors Influencing Island Floras In Northern Lake Michigan*. Doctoral Dissertation for University of Michigan, 1988.

Kozma, LuAnne Gaykowski, ed. *Living at a Lighthouse, Oral Histories of the Great Lakes.* Detroit: Great Lakes Lighthouse Keepers Association, 1987.

Leach, M. L. *A History: Grand Traverse Region*. Traverse City, Mich., 1883. Reprints from *The Grand Traverse Herald*.

Littell, Edmund M. *100 Years in Leelanau*. Leland, Mich.: The Print Shop, 1965.

Mahan, John and Ann. *Wild Lake Michigan*. Stillwater, Minn.: Voyageur Press, Inc., 1991.

Ohle, William H. *People, Places, Happenings In Northern Michigan*. Collection of articles first published in "The Graphic," by *The Petoskey News-Review.* Collection published in Boyne City, Mich., undated.

Olli, Bette McCormick. *The Way It Was, Memories Of My Childhood At Grand Traverse Lighthouse*. Northport, Mich.: Lighthouse Publications, 1990.

Osborn, Chase S. and Stellanova. *Schoolcraft, Longfellow, Hiawatha*. Lancaster, Penn.: The Jaques Cattell Press, 1942.

Pratt, Julius A. "War of 1812," *World Book Encyclopedia, Vol. 21* Chicago: Field Enterprises Educational Corp., 1975.

Quaife, Milo M. *The Kingdom of Saint James*. New Haven: Yale University Press, 1930.

Ratigan, William. *Great Lakes Shipwrecks & Survivals*. Grand Rapids. Wm. B. Eerdmans Publishing Co., 1960.

Romig, Walter. *Michigan Place Names.* Grosse Pointe, Mich.: Braun & Brumfield, 1976.

Sprague, Elvin L. and Mrs. George N. Smith, *History of Grand Traverse and Leelanaw Counties*. Indianapolis: B. F. Bowen, 1903.

Strang, James J. *Ancient and Modern Michilimackinac*. Beaver Island, 1854; reprint, Mackinac Island, Mich.: W. Stewart Woodfill, 1959.

Strang, *Book of the Law of the Lord*. Beaver Island, 1856, microfilm.

Traverse City and Rural Directory, 1928-29. Lansing: O. L. Bodgett & Co., 1928.

Van Noord, Roger. *King Of Beaver Island*. Chicago: University of Illinois Press, 1988.

Vent, Myron. *South Manitou Island, From Pioneer Community To National Park.* Springfield, VA.: The Goodway Press, Inc., 1973.

Wakefield, Lawrence, ed. *A History of Leelanau Township*. Chelsea, Mich.: Bookcrafters, 1982.

Wakefield, Lawrence and Lucille. *Sail & Rail.* Traverse City: Village Press, 1980.

Weeks, George. *Sleeping Bear, Yesterday and Today*. Franklin, Mich.: Altwerger and Mandel Publishing Company, 1990.

Weeks, Robert P. *King Strang*. Ann Arbor: The Five Wives Press, 1971.

Williams, Elizabeth Whitney. *A Child of the Sea*. 1905 reprint. Beaver Island Historical Society, 1983.

Woodfill, W. Stewart. *Grand Hotel: The Story of an Institution*. Princeton: Princeton University Press, 1969.

NEWSPAPERS

The Detroit Free Press	1966-1976
The Flint Journal	9/20/1969
The Gospel Herald	5/17/1849
The Leelanau Enterprise	1880-1995
The Northern Islander	1847-1855
The Northport Leader	1912-1921
The Traverse City Morning Record	12/10/1889
The Traverse City Evening Record	1905-1910
The Traverse City Record-Eagle	1911-1995
The Weekly World News	11/17/1992

PERIODICALS

Ingwersen, John. "Poem" (To The North) in *Poetry,* Vol. cix. ed. Henry Rago, March, 1967.

Michigan History Magazine, Volumes 1, 22, 29, 56, 65.

Michigan Pioneer and Historical Collections, Volumes 1, 18, 19.

North Woods Call, 2/24/1972 & 11/22/1972.

The Michigan Botanist, Volume 14, 1975; Volume 25, 1986; Volume 32, 1993.

Traverse The Magazine, August, 1985.

PUBLIC RECORDS

Manitou County – Birth Records

Death Records

Book of Deeds, Vol. 1 & 2

Census Records for 1860, 1870, 1880, 1900

Agricultural Census, 1870

Leelanau County – Birth Records

Death Records

Book of Deeds, several

Book of Mortgages, several

Book of Miscellaneous Records, several

Census Records for 1860, 1870, 1880, 1900

U. S. Cong., Senate 15 Feb., 1892, Dec. 38 pp. (52-1) 2892.

U. S. Cong., House of Representatives, *Oversight Hearing, America's Islands: Open Space At Risk?* July 25, 1989.

Light House Establishment *Description of Light-House Tower, Buildings, and Premises at South Fox Island Light Station, Michigan, December 1st, 1907.*

Light House Establishment *Statement of Appropriations, & c.*, 1886.

North Manitou Island Lifesaving Station records.

National Archives Coast Guard Records, register of lighthouse keepers through fiscal year of 1912, RG26.

Survey Notes for North and South Fox Islands.

OTHER PUBLICATIONS

Albert, Dennis A. and Gary A. Reese. *An Overview Of The Plant Community Ecology And Natural Area Significance Of North Fox Island, Leelanau County, Michigan.* report, Jan. 1990.

Brege, Dean A. and Niles R. Kevern. Michigan *Commercial Fishing Regulations: A Summary of Public Acts and Conservation Commission Orders*, 1865 through 1975. report, Nov. 1978.

Burr, D. H. *Map of Michigan & Part of Wisconsin Territory*, U.S. House of Representatives, 1839, at State Library of Michigan, Lansing.

Colton, J. H. *Colton's Trourist Map of the Great Lakes*, New York, 1862, at Clarke Historical Library, Central Michigan University, Mount Pleasant, Michigan.

DeForge, Stanley, *Remembrances of South Fox Island and the South Fox Lighthouse*, TS. S. DeForge transcript of taped interview with Zella Green DeForge, Manhattan, 1983.

Goff, F. Glenn and Phyllis J. Higman. *Environmental Impact Report on the proposed North Fox Island Development*, report, Sept., 1990.

Goff and Higman. *Appendices To North Fox Island Development, Draft, Environmental Impact Report*, Sept., 1990.

Giltner, Charlotte. *Early Settlers of Leelanau County, Mich. by Ethnic Groups.*, compilation of census records from records of the Leelanau Historical Society.

Harger, Elsworth M. and Jack L. Cook. "The South Fox Island Deer Story." *Mich. Dept of Natural Resources. Research and Development Report No. 264*, April, 1972.

Hazlett, Brian T. *Factors Influencing Island Floras In Northern Lake Michigan*, dissertation submitted to The University of Michigan, 1988.

Johnson, David L. *Around Carrying Point*, TS. D. Johnson Private Papers. Manitowoc, Wisconsin.

Leelanau County Element List, Michigan Natural Features Inventory, July, 1990.

McNutt, James Oscar. Diary, 1848-1931 at Clarke Historical Library, Central Michigan University, Mount Pleasant, Michigan.

Payroll Records for Sterling Nickerson & Sons lumber company, 1955, 1956, 1957, 1959, 1960, 1961.

Reidsma, Irene Vander Meulen, *Beaver Island Cemeteries, Charlevoix County Michigan,* compilation of death records and cemetery records, published 1984.

Smith, The Rev. George N., Diary, 1850-79, microfilm owned by Clarence and Avis Wolfe, Northport, Michigan.

Soule, Judith D. *Biodiversity Of Michigan's Great Lakes Islands: Knowledge, Threats and Protection*, report of Michigan Natural Features Inventory, 1993.

Tainter, Suzanne and Ray White. Extension Bulletin E-100, *Seines to Salmon Charters*, May, 1977.

Vladi, Farhad. *Vladi Private Islands*, newsletter, West Germany, 1988.

ORGANIZATIONS AND INSTITUTIONS

Government Offices of Leelanau County, Charlevoix County and Emmet County, Northwestern Michigan College Library, Leelanau Township Library, Leland Township Library, Traverse Area District Library, Joseph Mann Library at Two Rivers, Wisconsin, Milwaukee Public Library, Bentley Historical Library at the University of Michigan, Clarke Historical Library at Central Michigan University, State Library of Michigan, Institute for Great Lakes Research at Bowling Green State University, Detroit Public Library, State Archives of Michigan, Grand Traverse Pioneer and Historical Society and Museum, Beaver Island Historical Society and Museum, Leelanau County Historical Society and Museum, Cranbrook Institute of Science, Manitowoc Maritime Museum, The Grand Hotel, Northport Public Schools, Victor International Corporation.

AUTHOR CONTACTS

(with sincere appreciation)

Personal Interviews: Helen Collar, Pete and Bill Carlson, Stan Floyd, Mary Minor and her mother Elizabeth, Doyle Fitzpatrick, Randa Fredrickson, Stanley DeForge, Zella DeForge, James and Harriet Roe, Mr. and Mrs. Marvin Ance, Edith Ance, Sally Greene, Ivan Cobb, Art Duhamel, Alvina Bailey, Josephine Bailey, John Bailey, Catherine Baldwin, Ester and Louis Koon, Christine Garthe, Dorothy Carlson, Guyles Dame, Elizabeth Seeger, Ford Kellum, Sally Steffens, Georgia Scott, Bernice Leo and Hildegarde McDonald, Archie Miller, Henry Andrews, Joe Raphael, Douglas McCormick, Regina Lawson, Rose Pridemore, Eva, Max, Donaldine, Quentin and Eve Nickerson, Anna Cain, George Grosvenor, George Clark Craker, Keith and Madeline Chappel, Annabel Comfort, David G. Scott, Del Russell, George Stevens, Gordon Charles, Dr. William Scharf, Kathy Hall, Ted McCutcheon, Mike Van Hoey, John and Nancy Nickerson, Mrs. Stanley (Carole) Riley, Erwin and Marie Gale, Dr. Thomas Stevens, Jim Niessink, George and Mike Grosvenor, Gary Reese, F. Glenn Goff, David V. Johnson, Lesli Johnson, and employees of Mirada Ranch.

Telephone Interviews and Letters: Hon. Francis K. Bourisseau, Mrs. Willard (Mary) Leo, Mr. and Mrs. John McElwee, Jr., Mrs. Stevens from Buckley, Mich., Norman Price, Chuck Stafford, Anna Wyman, Dorothy Webb, Mrs. Frederick (Edith) Kilbourn, Jens Thomas, Audrey Thomas, Don Lane, Alice Lipe, Marion Simons, Lucile Warner, Pearl Stark, Don Gilbert, Loujean Baker, Fred Litzner, John Ingwersen, Julius Ance, Fred Leslie, Dr. Robert Hatt, Pipps Hackett of the *Petoskey News Review*, Dr. Paul Thompson, Dr. Brian Hazlett, Francis Shelden, Brenda Williams.

Index

Abbey Development Co. 11, 185
Abbott, George 42, 125, 147
A. C. Van Raalte 176
Ace 127, 179
Adrian, MI 137
Agnes S. 43
Aida 42, 92
Albert, Dennis 25, 27, 123, 202
Algonac, MI 81, 83
Allington, Rev. 163
American Fur Co. 35, 36, 37
American Revolution 49
Ance family 68, 86, 106
Ance, Abbie 69, 71, 72, 75, 157, 164
Angeline 73, 75
August 40, 68, 69, 70, 73, 74, 75, 106, 158, 163, 198
Benjamin 40, 69, 71, 75, 149, 157
Casper 69, 71
Christine 68, 69, 70, 158, 163, 198
Emaline 71, 157
Edith 198
Francis 158
Fred 73, 75, 158
Helen (Blackman) 72
Jeanette 71, 149
Julius 68, 71
Julius Benjamin 69, 71, 157, 196, 197
Lizzie 68-70, 72, 157, 158
Louis I 40, 63, 68-71, 73, 75, 157, 159, 198
Louis II 70, 73, 198
Luke 158
Mabel 158, 163
Maggie 63, 68, 69, 70, 71, 157, 198
Marceline 68, 70, 158
Oliver 71, 75, 149
Simon 73
William 73, 75, 106
Anderson, Albion 44
Caroline 40
Charles, Capt. 112, 158
(fisherman) 44
Harry (Swede) 93
Andrews, Abbie 69, 71
Henry, 71, 157, 158
John 40, 69, 71, 72, 157
Raymond, 71, 157, 158
Ann Arbor No. 5 110, 111
Arrow 113, 114
Ashland, WI 74
Ashton, Samuel 38
Ask, Henry 106, 125
Nels 63, 64, 106, 110, 111, 147
Astor, John Jacob 35
Atkyn, Dr. 53, 54
Atlantic Lumber Co. 121
Aydelotte, Joseph & Sarah 153
Ayers, Ellis 109

Babcock 40
Badger State 95
Baldwin, MI 129
Barnum, William H 78
Barr, Mack 114
Bartlett, Amos 63, 123
Bates, Thomas 176
Baudette, Louis 111
Bay City, MI 82
Bay Harbor, MI 11, 12, 18, 19, 184, 185
Beaver Island 8, 19, 21, 25, 35-37, 39-40, 42-44, 50-55, 60-62, 73, 77, 85,101-103, 105, 113, 153, 155-158, 173, 174, 176, 177, 181, 182, 186, 189
Beaver Island Wildlife Research Area 131, 141
Beckwith, Hiram & Mary 38
Bedford, Thomas 53, 54, 60
Beers, Philo 55
Belfy, William & Erwin 43
Bellows Island 186
Benninghaus, Carl 118
Benton Harbor, MI 112
Benzie County, MI 36, 105
Bergeron, Elmer 115, 122, 148, 149
Berlenbach, Brian 140, 141
Berrien County Package Co. 112, 113, 125
Betty C 43
Big Bay de Noc, WI 113
Bingham, MI 70, 73
Bird, Joseph & Sam 73-75
Birdseye Veneer 114
Birmingham, MI 144, 185
Bissell, Evelyn M 44
Blackbird, Andrew 67, 156
Blacker, Charlie 12, 13, 18, 20, 140, 192
Bloomfield & Bloomfield Hills, MI 185
Boardman, Harry 38
Booth Fishery 42, 43
Borgeson, Oscar 106
Boston, Dick 106, 147
Bourisseau, Dale 76, 156, 164
Frank 68, 93, 156, 164
Gertie 68, 156, 162
James 156
Josephine 68, 156
Josephine Susan 68, 84, 156, 162
Keith 76, 156, 164
Lewis 40, 45, 68, 75, 84-87, 91, 93, 106, 156, 158, 160
Louis 40, 68, 156
Philaman, 68, 156
Sadie 147, 164
William 68, 156
Zane 164
Bowers Harbor, MI 42
Boy Scouts 163
Boyce, Josiah 101
Boyd, Robert 38, 61, 153, 154, 191
Boyle, Francis 101
Bradley, Carl D. 95
Brehmer, Fred 106
Bridgebuilder X 116, 120, 121, 167, 197

Brotherson, _______ 93
Brown, Ada 93
Donald 15
Earl 93
George 88
Martin 109
(Mate) 92
Regina 113, 114
Sam 113, 147
Bruin, William 80
Buck Knives 140
Budd, Capt. 40
Buffalo, NY 53, 82, 154
Bumgartner, Mr. & Mrs. 106
Bunting, Archibald 105
Burdick, Effie & Frederick 174, 192
Bureau of Indian Affairs 115
Burke's Coal Dock 116
Burr, David H. 8
Burroughs, Elvie 113, 114
Buss, Nancy 101
Bussa, Al 114
Buttars, George & Margaret 160
Ray 9

C. A. King 85
Cable, Alva & James 38
Cadillac, MI 128
Cain, Anna & Allen 95, 96, 165
Cal-Cite, MI 95
Canada 61, 67, 68, 122, 128, 148, 178, 181, 190
Caribbean 144
Carl D. Bradley 95
Carlson, Darrel 163
Irving 93, 163
Irving, Jr. 93
Lester (Pete) 43, 44, 112
Rosalie 163, 164
Violet 164
William 43, 44, 95
Carp Lake (Lk. Leelanau) 70, 104, 113
Carter, Moses 147, 179
Cartier, Jacques 49
Case, Leslie 24, 209, 210
Cat Head Light, Point 8, 36, 87, 88, 90, 91, 95, 102
Caymen Islands 144
Chamberlain, George 85
Chambers, William 60, 61
Champlain, Samuel de 49
Champion 82
Caribbean 11
Cartier, Jacques 49
Chappel, Keith 130, 131, 135-138, 151
Madeline 136
Charles, Gordon 28, 129, 137, 139, 151
Charlevoix (explorer) 36
Charlevoix, City & County, MI 12, 42, 43, 51, 52, 55, 61, 71, 79, 88, 91, 92, 102, 107, 115, 121, 128, 150, 160, 170, 179
Charlotte, MI 127
Chase, William 101, 103
Cheboygan, MI 42, 52, 61
Chequamegon 109
Chestnut Hills 185
Chicago (vessel) 83
Chicago, IL 38, 40, 55, 61, 62, 79, 82, 84, 86, 95, 106, 109-111, 148, 174, 176, 177, 189
Chio, Kenneth 12
Chippewa, Angeline, 73, 75
Angeline II 73
Dorothy 71, 158
Enos 40, 63, 69-73, 75, 158
Ernie 113, 114
family 106
Jennie 73, 75
John 70, 72, 158
Josephine 70-72, 75, 158, 161
Lizzie 69-73, 158
Lozrana 73, 75
Lucile (Simon) 73-75
Rose 72
Samuel 73
City of Green Bay 82, 83
Civil War 42, 61, 84, 102, 156
C. J. Buck 140
Clark, Alfred 111
Clark Historical Library 61
Clarkston, MI 14
Cleveland, OH 78, 79, 86
Cleveland District 94
Clover, E. U. 202
Cobb (Cobb-mo-washa), James & Jane 68, 69, 73, 75, 86, 106
John 68, 69, 73
Cole, Galen 61
Colorado Springs, CO 149
Comfort, Annabel 160
Lou 88, 91
Commemorative Bucks of Michigan 128
Conan, William 88
Conestoga 82
Connable, R. & Sons 40
Connecticut 137
Conner, Mark 182, 190
Cook, Jack 130, 135
Marvin 44
Cooper, Carl 109, 111
Marriet & Richard 38, 191
Cornell, Edward & Ulysses 85
Cornstalk (Comstock) Alex 63, 73-75, 158
Daniel 63, 73
Cornwell, Mark 149
Craker, George Clark 25, 93, 94
Alan 188
Bradley 169
Jillene 30
Steve 27
Cram, Jesse 61, 176
Cranbrook Institute of Science, 21, 25, 177
Crandell, William 190
Crescent City 77
Crossan, Thomas 149
Crownpoint, NM 157
Cusino, MI 129
Cutcheon, Byron M. 55

Dakota Territory 39
Dahlmer, A. 40
Dame, Ella 164
Gillman 110
Isa 63
Oscar 85, 88, 90-92, 106, 160, 164
Roland 113
Vivian 164
Davidson, Thomas 39
Davis, Cheryl 96, 165
Marion 37, 176
Day, John 40
DeGrolier (DeGolia, DeGolier), Ida & Nathan 156
Robert 40, 80, 81, 155
Roxena 40
Densmore, Frances 68
Detroit Metro Youth For Christ 185
Detroit, MI 55, 77, 91, 144, 177, 178
Detloff, David 140
Dewey 78
Diamond 43, 44, 80
Diepenbrock, John 106
Dillin, Lynn 122, 130-132, 135, 136, 148, 149, 177, 181
Virginia 135, 148
Dixon, John 52
Dormer 40
Dougherty, Rev. Peter 50
Douglass, James 55, 61, 191
Drug Enforcement Adm. 144
Drummond Township 52
Dulin, Gary 210, 211
Dykema Gossett law firm 185

East Jordan, MI 28
Easterly, Charles 138
Echo Park & Lakes of Echo Park 185
Edgerton, Hugh 118
Elizabeth G 43.
Embarcadero 14
Emery, Ann 191
J. Haines 38, 61, 176. 191
Emmlin Cleveland 38
Emmet County, MI 52, 61
Empire, MI 27
England 39, 61, 101
English Channel, 144
Escanaba 78, 86, 87, 113
Estonia 43
Evelyn M 43, 44

Fairbanks, Alaska 137
Falkerson, Daniel 38
Falls Church, VA 149
Fatseas, Jason 24
*Favorite*102
Fekete, Bernie 18
Fick, Adolph 58, 64, 89, 125, 160
Dale 160
Fillmore, President 50
Finch, Claude 96
Firestone, Kathleen 168, 169, 194, 199, 200
Fitz, John 38, 61, 153, 154, 191
Fitzpatrick, Doyle 53
Flees, Dan 93
Fletcher 82
Flint, MI 144
Flood, Dr. Robert 147
Flora 44
Floyd, Agnes, Anna, Catherine, Edward, Elizabeth, Frank, Frederick, George, James, Johnny & Joseph 155
John 39, 62, 102, 103, 155
Mary 39, 62, 103, 155
Stan 102, 103, 200
Fonntaine, Joseph 84
Fort Wayne, IN 37
Foster, S. H. 78
Fountain City House 38
Fox 40
Fox Island Gravel Company 176
Frank Perew 77
Frankfort, MI 95, 105, 111, 180
Frederick, WI 122
Fredrickson, Magnus 64, 93, 125, 175
France, French 67, 68, 110
French & Indian War 49
Frenchtown 67
Frost, John 114
Fuller, George N. 24, 176

Gagnon, Joseph 42, 189, 190
Gale, Erwin 29, 97, 122, 123, 136-138, 144, 145, 150, 169, 181, 200
Gordon, 137
Marie 169, 200
Gallagher, Owen 88
Garden Island 73, 177
Garden City Sand Company 103, 176, 177
Garthe, Isaac 154
Mary 101, 154
Steiner 102, 154
Garvey, Jack 111
Gee, George 130, 137, 138
Germany 39
Gibbs, Jamie 13, 17, 140
Gilcher, W. A. 84, 85
Gill, William 55
Gills Pier, MI 55
Gladish, David 101
Shirley 61
Glen Haven 79
God 19, 21, 46, 171
Godbey, (Big) John 16, 137
Goff, F. Glenn 182, 202
Golden, Dick 114
Good Harbor Bay 113
Goodmanson, Ole 39, 102, 154, 192
Gore Bay 178
Goudreau, William 93
Goodrich, Reuben 154, 176
Grace 44
Grand Hotel 174, 175
Grand Rapids, MI 106
Grand Traverse County, MI 38, 52
Grand Traverse Light 8, 36, 87, 88, 90, 91, 95, 109, 163
Grant, U.S. 80

Graves, Capt. 82
Edward 89
Mrs. Edward 88
Grayling, MI 138
Great Lakes Consolidated Agency 74
Green, Howard 163
Katherine 72, 88, 147, 160, 162
Laura 163
Milton 152, 160, 162
William 72, 85-88, 91-93, 106, 147, 160, 163
Zella 72, 88, 89, 152, 160, 162, 163, 171, 196
Green Bay, WI 55
Gregg, Phil 43
Greilickville, MI 116
Grenada 171
Griffon 35, 77
Grosvenor, George 44, 137, 148, 166
Guernsey Island 144
Gull Island 186
Guthrie, Percy 44
Guyer, Gordon 17

Hahn, Irving 137
Hall, Wallace 88
Hannah B 44
Hansen, Martin, 112, 148, 149
Harbor Springs, MI 67, 73, 104, 154, 156, 159, 195
Harger, Earl 130, 135
Harpold, Elijah 103, 176, 177
Harris, Bob 96
Hart, MI 122, 136, 137
Haskell Institute 157
Hatt, Robert 21, 24-26, 28, 64, 129, 177, 208, 210, 211
Hayward, Gary 140
Rod 12, 13, 140
Ruby 12
Hazlett, Brian T. 21, 25, 27, 202, 208
Hedges, Bill 18
Helena 79
Helm, Marty 137
Hendricks, Susan 25, 208
Heron Bay, Pointe, Ridge, Woods 185
High Island, 71, 73, 106, 157, 177
Higman, Phyllis 202, 210, 211
Hillingar effect 195
Hollister, David 118
Holton, Darwin 178
Nelson 147
Hopkins, Bill 44
Horn, Edward (McIntosh) 109-111
Horton, Jennie 105, 106, 174, 177, 192
Houghton, MI 129
House of David 106
Hoyt, Fred 137
Hubbard, Mark 18, 140, 184
Hubbell, Bill 138
Hubble 79
Huff, Robert 128
Husted, Robert 111
Hyacinth 89, 92

Ida Keith 102
Illinois (state) 61
Illinois, (vessel) 60
Imlay City, MI 137
Imperial 85
Imperial White Tail Institute 139
Indiana 63
Ingwersen, John 28, 32, 112, 113, 114, 125, 147, 165, 175, 192, 193
Internal Revenue Service 144
Ireland 101
Ironton, MI 12
Ishpeming (vessel) 91
Ishpeming, MI 91
Island Fox 12
Islander 102
Isle Royale Queen II 132
Ithaca, MI 111

Jacobsen, Harry 139
James Platt 82
Jansen, James 149
Jarvis Lord 84
Jenkins, Dave 136
Jewell, William 208
Johnson, "Big John" 113
Carolyn & David 181
David V. 11-19, 64, 65, 138-141, 149, 150, 170, 181, 184, 185
Ed 104
Emil 91
George 40
Lesli 11, 16, 170, 171
Powel 101
Samara 16, 18, 170, 171
Jones, Larry 149
Juliana 38
Jurica, Pete 179
J. W. Timber Company 122, 123
Kalchik, Albert 92, 106, 110
Frank 79, 127, 147, 178-180
Jerry 178
Louis 106
Ralph, 178
Ron, 179
Kaley, Roger 64, 106, 107, 125
Kasson Township 84
Keating, Howard T. 185
Keewaydinoquay 73
Keith, Burton 85
Kelley Lumber Co. 105, 106, 125
Kellogg, Klinton (Skip) 179
Kelly, Walter 105
Kentucky 11
Kerr, Capt. Robt. & family 78
Kewaygoshkim, Homer & Jesse 118
Kiersey, Jerry 118
Kilbourn, Edith 201
Frederick I 109, 125, 159, 174, 198
Frederick II 159, 198
Ruth I 125, 159, 198
Ruth II 159
Kildee, E. A. 105
King, C. A. 85
King, Dr. R. 130
Kingbird, Enos & Tom 72
Kingsley, MI 106, 114, 116, 130, 137, 138, 148

Knight, Mr. 107
Kowieski, Louis 45
Kruell, Mr. & Mrs. 95, 96
Krumlauf, Al 114
Kurtzel, Fred 106

LaFond 43
LaFreniere, Louis 113
Lake Huron 95
Lake Leelanau, MI 70, 113
Lake Nippising 21
Lake Superior 45, 113, 184
Lane, LaVerne 112
Lansing, MI 51, 52
Lapeer County, MI 50
Larsen, Art & Gus 43
La Salle, Robert 35, 77
Latin America 145
Leelanau County 55, 70, 72, 73, 79, 84, 102, 104, 111, 113, 128, 145, 154, 178
Leelanau Peninsula/Township, MI 39, 87, 102, 186, 195
Leemaster, Dan & Rose 165, 166, 198
    Regina 112, 113, 198
Left, Joseph 38, 42
    Frank 42
Leiter, Charles 192
Leland, MI 43, 55, 101, 104, 109, 112, 163, 179
Leo Brothers & Co. 71, 72, 73, 74, 92, 106, 107, 109, 125, 163
Leo, Anna 107, 159, 162
    Bernice 63, 106, 159, 161, 162, 164, 165, 170, 171, 189, 196, 200
    Cora 106, 160
    Herman 106, 164
    Hildegarde 63, 107, 159, 160-162, 164, 165, 171, 189, 196, 200
    Marcella 162
    Willard (Red) 147, 159, 162, 164, 165
    William 106, 107, 159, 162, 164
Leslie, Elizabeth 81
    Fred I 93, 94, 95
    Fred II 163
    Morris 81, 82, 93
Lewis, William 84, 149
Lichtenstein 144
Lincoln, Mrs. Abraham 156
Little Traverse 38
Livingston, Betty & Bill 115
Livonia, MI 185
Loebich, Ronald 96
Longfield, Henry 39, 103
Louis XIII 49
Lue, David 184
Lyons, Capt. Dick 115

Mackinac, Mackinaw 35, 49, 50, 53, 55, 82, 95, 113, 167
Mackinac Bridge 116, 120
    County 50
    Island 37, 39, 42, 50, 54, 61, 62, 174, 175
    Fort 49
Mackinaw boat 26, 67, 77, 101
Maggie 105, 106
Magnet 77
Mahan, John & Ann 195
Maitland, John 54
Majo, Albert 176
Major 44, 113, 175
Malloy, John 103
Malpass, Ted 28
Manabozho, 195
Manigold, Lee 106
Manistee, Miss 115, 168, 197
Manistee, MI 40
Manistique, MI 39, 86, 106
Manistique (vessel) 86
Manitou County 52, 55
Manitou Islands 19, 21, 25, 28, 35, 39, 42, 44, 52, 60, 62, 77, 80, 82, 84, 101, 103, 105, 112, 176, 177, 208
    Logging Co. 112-114
    Passage 35, 77, 101
Manitoulin Island 178
Manitowash, Marvin 118
Mann Brothers 104, 105, 125
    Charles 104
Maple Associates, Inc. 11, 185
Markle, David 96
Mars 86
Martin, James (Shing) 43
Martinson, Ole 40
May Cornell 82
McAlvay, Mr. 10
McAndrews, Isaac 73
McBeath, Donald 128
McBlair, Capt. 53, 54
McCormick, Bette, Grayce, Janet, Justine, Leon, Margaret 163
    Don 93 163
    Douglas 93, 147, 163, 196
    James I 42, 85, 91, 92, 106, 158, 160, 163
    James II 163
    Mary 91, 147, 163
    Violet 163
McCreery, William B. 105, 176
McCullough, Dr. Hezekiah 53, 54
McDole, Rollie 106
McElwee, John & Lillian 125, 175
McFall, Cora 154, 191
McGregor, James 101
McIntosh, Edward 109
McKee, Dennis 106
McKinney, Rose 72
McNutt, J. O. 61
McPhillips, Joe 128, 137
McQueen, Orville 146, 148
McSawby, Jonas 71
Me-ka-te-bi-neshi 67
M. H. Stuart 111, 112
Michigan Dept. of Agriculture 17
    Dept. of Conservation 123, 129, 130
    Dept. of Natural Resources 28, 45, 97, 122, 128, 131, 135, 138-141, 145, 177, 181, 184
    Natural Features Inventory 202
    State Legislature 50, 51, 53
    State University 41, 139, 185
    Territory 49
Michigan, U.S.S. 53, 54
Michilimackinac, Province of 49
Middleton, Ed 44

Midland Company, The 177
Mielke, Gus 43
Milford, MI 138
Miller, Archie 74, 113, 147
Ivan 74, 149
Joshua 54
Susan 72
Milwaukee, WI 55, 79, 90, 92, 102, 104, 105, 112, 173
Minnesota 61
Minuet 79
Mirada Ranch 10-19, 64, 65, 125, 141, 150, 170, 171, 184
Miss Manistee 115, 168, 197
Mississippi State University 139
M & M Box Company 120
Monquagon 82
Moore, Frank L. 89
Moore, Mark 18, 139, 140
Moran, Bill 118
Morning Star 85
Morrow, Mr. & Mrs. Ed 111
Mt. Pleasant, MI 61, 157
Mt. Pleasant Indian School 157
Mull, Katie 29
Sarah 169
Susan 29, 181
Munger, Edwin 101
Munson, Linda 16
Murray, Jack 106, 107
Muskegon, MI 176

Nashville, TN 130
National Parks & Conservation Assoc. 181
Nauvoo, IL 50
Nebraska 139
Nelson, Augusta 91
Bruce 44, 113
Caroline 40
Charles 45
John 40, 125, 174, 175
Nels 42, 64, 91, 92, 93, 95, 125
Roy 44, 113
Netherlands 136
Antilles, West Indies 144
New England 174
New France 49
New York 39, 101
Newark, OH 149
Newaygo 50, 51
Newton, Archibald 55
Nickerson (vessel) 121
Nickerson, Bernice 168
Donaldine 167, 199
Eva 114, 116
Eve 116, 118, 119, 148
Evelyn 167
family & mill 25, 27, 74, 95, 115, 122, 125, 129, 136, 148-150, 166, 177, 178, 181;
list of employees 212, 213
Gregory 167
Janice 167
John 168, 199
Kathleen 168, 169, 194, 199, 200
Max I 114, 116, 129, 167, 168, 119
Max II 121, 168
Nickerson, Nancy 168, 199
Pamela & Patricia 167
Quentin 114-118, 129
Sterling I 74, 100, 114, 116, 118, 129, 130, 137, 148, 167, 168
Sterling II 114-117, 120, 121, 169
Sterling III 168
Nicolet, Jean 49
Niessink, Jim 20, 30, 128, 200
Noonan, Franklin 93
North Fox Island Enterprises 182, 184
Institute 182
Fur Farm 64
Subdivision 180
North Shore 115
Northport, MI 38-40, 42, 44, 45, 55, 62, 70, 73, 82, 85, 87-90, 93, 101, 109, 110, 113, 115, 116, 129, 137, 147, 153, 156, 158-160,163, 175, 189
Northport Point 175
Northwest Territory 49
Northwestern Michigan College 25
Norway 39, 62, 101, 102, 154

Oceanside, CA 149
Ohio 62, 95
Old Mission, MI 50, 89
Oleson, Benton 106
Oling, Capt. Jack 95
Oliver, Jeanette 71, 157
Joseph 36
Olsen, George 91
Olson, Andrew 101
Christian 39, 191
Ingra 39, 191
John 39, 192
Mary 39, 154, 191
Omena, MI, 55, 63, 69, 127, 159, 178
Onekama 26, 40
Ontario, Canada 63
Ontonagon, MI 113
Onward 42
Osborn, Chase & Stellanova 35
Pabo, Clara 70, 75, 158
Marceline 68, 69, 70, 158
William 68, 69, 70, 75, 158
Pacific Ocean 49
Packau, Josephine Susan 68
Palmer, Anna 39, 147, 155
Augusta 155
Eddie & Edwin 155, 191
Edward 155
Jeremiah 39, 155
Joe 39
Julia 39, 155, 191
Lincoln 155
Mary 39, 62, 155
Sarah, 155
Pappenaw, John & Minerva 55, 61, 67, 191
Paros Township 8, 52, 55, 59
Parr, Randy (Bean) 12
Patck, Gotlieb, 105
Patmos Township 8, 52, 55, 59, 173
Paul, Clifford 118

Peaine Township 50
Pence, Jim 137
Penhallow, William 177
Pentwater, MI 62, 107
Perew, Frank 77
Perrot, Nicholas 35
Peshaba, Ben 113
Peshawbestown, MI 73, 74, 113, 116, 149, 159
Petander, Gus 189
Peterson, John & Oscar 40
John Oscar 40, 103, 125
Petoskey, MI 11, 40, 184, 185
Phillips Flying Service 179
Pickard, Nancy 101
Nicholas 59, 101, 103, 105, 114, 115, 125
Pierces Island 8
Piggott, Cameron 18, 140, 185
Pine River, MI 51, 61
Plank, Alma 62, 64, 106, 113, 115, 116, 174-178
Cora, 62
Jeanette 160
John O. 61-64, 71, 90, 105, 106, 114, 115, 125, 129, 150, 159, 163, 164, 174-177
John II 105, 106, 160, 192
Plank's Grand Hotel 174
Planktown, OH 174
Plant & Moran, CPA's 185
Platt, James 82
Pope, Clifford 208
Porter House Hotel 160
Porter Ranch 129
Possing, Peter 104
Poule, Mary 79
Power Island 186
Powers, Jeffrey 14
Prairie Ronde, WI 37
Price, Bruce 113
Warren 44
Pridemore, Gwen 198
Pt. Betsie 95

Quebec 49

Racine, WI 55
Rambler 43
Ramsdell, S. 82
Ramsey, Joe 111
Raphael, Ambrose 71, 72, 75
Benjamin 72, 149, 158
brothers 63, 71, 86, 106, 147
Christine 70, 160
Hattie (Pewash) 72, 149, 158
Joseph I 71
Joseph II 72, 73, 158, 159, 189, 197
Mitchell 71, 72, 74
Peter 71-75, 149, 158
Raphael (Gagaishe) 71
Rose I 71, 72
Rose II 72, 73, 158
Rose III 72
Ratza, Leon 14, 18
Redding, CA 149
Reese, Gary 25, 27, 123, 202
Reichart, Jim 114
Reilly, Mark 149
Reno, Louis 131, 137
Retford, Elizabeth 39
Sarah & Thomas 38
Rice, Anna, Emma, Martha, Melissa & Sarah 37, 153, 155
Samuel 37, 60, 153, 155
Richelieu 49
Riley, Stanley 122, 136, 137, 181
Carole 137, 138, 144, 145, 169, 181, 200
Risdon, Orange 8, 37
Roe, Abigail 154
Catherine (Kate) 62, 67, 103, 104, 153-155, 174, 191
Charles 40, 85, 103, 104, 154
Elizabeth 39, 191
Florence 80, 154, 191
George I 39, 191
George II 39
Harriet 38, 61, 153, 191
Helen 154
Henry, (son of Rushand and Harriet) 38, 80, 153, 191
Henry (lightkeeper) 80, 154, 191
Henry (son on Robt. & Kate) 80, 153, 154
James I 154
James II & Harriet 200
Katherine 154
Laura 38, 153, 191
Mable 80, 154, 191
Marie 80, 191
Mary 154
Robert 62, 67, 80, 101, 103, 104, 113-115, 125, 149, 150, 153-155, 174, 191
Rushand 38, 61, 153, 191
Sarah, 149, 154
William 39, 191
Roen, John (Cap) 92, 114
Shipyard 92, 121
Roop, Betty, Glen II, Charlene, Sally 121
Glen I 120, 121
Roser, Carl 28
Ruchhoft, Robert 176
Ruhl, Harry 129

Sagitta Corp. 144
Sambo 44
Sample, Alexander 61, 101, 103
Samuel H. Foster 78
Sanchez, Luis 149
Sapelo Island, GA 93
Sault Ste. Marie, Canada 115
Scharf, William 24-26, 28, 210, 211
Schoolcraft, Henry 35
Schrader, Mr. 159
Scotland 38-41
Scot's Point, MI 39
Scott, James 62, 174, 191
Scovil, Alfred 61, 101
Sea Gull 37, 155
Sears dock 116
Selfridge Field, MI 110
Send, John 112
Seul Choix Point 165

Shelden, Alger 178, 180
Francis 25, 26, 127-129, 147, 177-180
Shimmell, Ivan 9
Shingleton, MI 73
Shocko, LeRoy 179
Shoor, Henry 179
Silver Star 43
Sleeping Bear National Park/Lakeshore 136, 181
Smith, Rev. George 37, 38, 54
Howard 111
Joseph 50, 53
Smiling Through 44
Smith, Capt. William 79
Snell, Mr. & Mrs. John 37, 153
Solon Township 178
Southbird (Shaw-we-ben-saey) Paynick & William 73, 75
Southfield, MI 138, 181, 185
Souvinouen, Myrna 115, 118, 119
Wayne 118
Spangle, Jay 189, 190
Spears, Lloyd 132, 137
Spencer, Jake 114
Star, The 44
St. Helena Island 55
St. Ignace, MI 49, 167
St. James, MI 52
St. Lawrence River 49, 174
St. Louis, MO 182
Staebler, Arthur 24, 208, 210, 211
Stafford, Charles 131, 137
Dorothy 159, 160
Frank 106
Mrs. Frank (Gertie) 106, 159, 162
Gertie 162
Wilbur 160, 162
Stallman, Andrew & Katie 107
Stanley, George 208
Stanwick, Louis 43
Stauffer, Kenneth 148, 149
Stebbins, Frederick 85, 87
Steimel, Howard 43
Nellie 106
Stella 43, 73
Stevens, Alva 175
Charles 112, 113, 175
George 128, 137
Joe 62
Thomas 97, 122, 123, 136-138, 144, 1445, 169, 181
Stibitz, John 88
Stocking, Kathleen 74
Pearce 27
Stoddard, Inspector 89
Stonewood Farms 14
Strain, Conrad 88
Strang, James J. 8, 21, 35-39, 41, 48-55, 59, 61, 67, 104, 153, 165, 173, 189
Strayer, L. J. 44
Stuart M. H. 111, 112
Sturgeon Bay, WI 92, 114, 120
Suarez, Rafael 175
Subnow, Catherine, Edell, John 38, 61, 153, 191
Sumac 89
Sunnyside 77, 78
Suttons Bay, MI 70, 73, 106, 109, 116, 170
Swanson, John 28
Sweden 40
Sweet, Beatrice & Howard 175, 192

Taenhoutentaron 49
Test, F. H. 24, 25, 202
Temple Emery 104
Texas 11
Thirtheenth Judicial District 55
Thomas Friant 102
Thomas Island 8
Thomas, Clayton 79, 179
Katherine 88
Paul, 58, 63, 64, 92, 106, 110, 111, 115, 125, 164
Stella 64
Thompson, Paul 25, 208
Thousand Islands 174
Thunder Bay 95
Tiffin, Ohio 105
Tilley, Charles 85
Timmer, Pete 93-96
Mrs. Pete 96
Tramp 115-117, 121, 122, 129, 197
Traverse Bay Transportation Co. 111, 112
Traverse City, MI 25, 38, 40, 42, 61, 105, 109-113, 122, 129, 147, 153, 177
Treaty of Ghent 49
Treaty of Paris 49
Troy ______ 55
Turner, Capt. Henry 82
Twin Brothers 37
Two Brothers 40, 44
Two Rivers, WI 104
Tyres, Alphonso 88

University of Chicago 24
University of Michigan 25
U. S. Army 148, 149
U. S. Coastguard 44, 90, 93, 94, 96, 120, 146-148, 163, 164
U. S. Grant 80
U. S. Lighthouse Service 80, 92, 93
U. S. Navy 190
Utah 50

Van Tyne, Josselyn 24, 208, 210, 211
Vannetter, Harriett 42
Jacob 42, 63, 91, 125
Llewellyn 91, 92, 161
Valentine 44
Van Raalte A. C. 176
Vega 86
Vega Alta, PR 149, 159
Vent, Myron 35
Victor Center 185
Corporate Park 185
Foundation 185
International Corp. 11, 18, 185
Vidosh, Denise 15, 18
Donn 17, 140
Vladi, Farhad 181
Voree, WI 50, 53

W. A. Gilcher 84, 85
Wagenschutz, Fred 28
Wakefield, Lawrence & Lucille 77
Walters, Paul 88
Walter, William & Susan 180, 181, 184
Wanegeshik, Elijah 74, 118
War of 1812 49
Warner, Clarence 81, 155
Elizabeth 81
George 1-83, 155
Lillian 81, 155
Sarah 81, 155
William, 155
Willis 81-83, 93, 198
Wau-goosh-e-min-iss 8, 35, 67
Waugoshance Peninsula 21
Wayne, MI 175
Webb, Dorothy 197
Wells-Higman Co. 109, 125
Wells, James 25
Wells, J. W. Co. 120
Wendall, Theodore 52
Wentworth, Alexander 53, 54, 55, 60, 61,125
West Germany 181
Whiskey Island 176, 177
Whiskey Point 40
White Swan 115
Whitecloud 104
Whitefish Point 77
Widerman (Weiderman, Wyderman) Christopher 39, 149, 155
Clara, Elizabeth, Elizabeth II, Elnora, Evaline, Gertrude, Grace, Jennie, Joseph 155
Julia 39, 155
William I 39, 125
William II 155
Wilder (Wilbur) 61, 101, 191
Wildwood Inn 174
Willard L. 159
Willard, Nelson 192
William H. Barnum 78
Williams, A. M. (Capt.) 86
Anna 39
Charles 190
Elizabeth 103, 121
family (unknown) 106
George 154, 190
Henry 154, 190
Jerry 39, 192
John 192
Joseph, 62, 155, 192
Mary 39, 62, 103, 155, 192
Otto 39, 62, 155, 192
Wilson, Douglas, Ella, Ethel, Mary II, William Edwin 160, 161
fishermen 44
Mary I 87, 160, 161
William P. 85, 87, 160, 161
Windridge 185
Winterstein, Scott 139, 140
Wisconsin 26, 45, 61, 62, 104, 114, 120, 195
Witchcraft 115
Wolfe, Larry 25, 202
Wood, Ray 128
Worrell, Glen 12
Wright, Thomas 85

Yannett, Silas 118
Yockey, Jano 183
Young, Brigham 50

Zapf Fruit Packaging Co. 71, 72, 94, 109-112, 125, 158
Charles 112
Zeller, Susan 61, 62, 174, 192

Lake Michigan Islands Series

Volume I
An Island In Grand Traverse Bay
ISBN 0-9625631-1-0

Details the story of the only Great Lakes island in Grand Traverse County, Michigan. Read of its history and natural features, its many owners throughout the years, including inventor Henry Ford, and its acquisition by the public. Includes bird and plant lists.

Hardcover, 107 pages, many color photos. $21.00 plus $1.26 Michigan sales tax.

Volume II
The Fox Islands, North and South
ISBN 0-9625631-4-5

The rich maritime and cultural histories of these islands includes lighthouse keepers, farmers, fishermen, children, Native Americans, deer hunters, lumberjacks, development issues and much more! Bird and plant lists are included.

Hardcover, 228 pages, 78 color photos. $29.95 plus $1.80 Michigan sales tax.

Watch for future volumes on other Lake Michigan Islands!

Order from your local book store or from the author:

Michigan Islands Research
412 South Shore Drive
Northport, Michigan 49670.

Inquire about updated information. Some photographs are available for purchase.

SCHOOLCRAFT
Good fishing ground
Big Bay de Noc
Lit Bay de Noc
Pte au Bay
Rocky Pt
Lit Summer I.
Pt. De Tour
Reefs
Summer I
Poverty I.
St Martins I
Pte au Barque
Bold rocky shore
Dangerous Shore
Squaw I.
Whiskey I.
Trout I.
High I.
Garden I.
Gull I.
Indian Reserve
Big Beaver I.
Cables Wharf
Light house
North Fox I.
or Paros I
South Fox I.
or Patmos I.
Patmos Isles
Louse I.
Light house
Great Manitou I
Manitou Isles
Manitou I.
Boardinghouse
Pier & Wharf
Lit Manitou I
Burtons Wharf
Light House
Cathead Pt.
North Port
Grand Traverse Bay
Sleeping Bear Pt.
LEELANAU